I0796676

Mamluks, Conquest & Culture

The Ghurid Empire & early Delhi Sultanate *c.*1150–1236

Mamluks, Conquest & Culture

The Ghurid Empire & early Delhi Sultanate c.1150–1236

Mark Kerr-Smiley

Unicorn

Published in 2025 by Unicorn,
an imprint of Unicorn Publishing Group
Charleston Studio
Meadow Business Centre
Lewes BN8 5RW
www.unicornpublishing.org

The author has asserted his moral right under the Copyright, Designs and Patents Act 1988 to be identified as the author of this work.

All rights reserved. No part of the contents of this book may be reproduced, stored in or introduced into a retrieval system, or transmitted, in any form or by any means (electronic, mechanical, photocopying, recording or otherwise), without the prior written permission of the copyright holder and the above publisher of this book.

Every effort has been made to trace copyright holders and to obtain their permission for the use of copyrighted material. The publisher apologises for any errors or omissions and would be grateful to be notified of any corrections that should be incorporated in future reprints or editions of this book.

ISBN 978-1-916846-76-0

10 9 8 7 6 5 4 3 2 1

Typeset by Matthew Wilson

Printed in Malta by Gutenberg

Contents

Acknowledgements ... *VII*
List of Plates ... *VIII*
Maps ... *X*
History of the Ghurids and their Ghulams in India: Timeline ... *XVI*
Glossary of Names and Terms ... *XXII*
Preface ... *XXIV*

Chapter One: *c.* 1146–1173 – The Rise of the Dynasty ... **1**
The Ghurid world: The geography of the eastern Iranian lands and northern India ... 2
Introduction to the Ghurids ... 3
The beginnings of Ghurid ascendancy ... 5
Coronation of the nephew ... 22

Chapter Two: 1175–1206 – Two Brothers ... **27**
Khurasan and India ... 28
Mu'izz al-Din as supreme sultan ... 52

Chapter Three: 1206–1236 – The Last Ghurids, their *Ghulams* and the Establishment of the Delhi Sultanate ... **87**
Qutb al-Din Aybak – 1206–1210: Independent ruler in India ... 88
Shams al-Din Iltutmish – 1210–1236: From mamluk's *mamluk* to sultan ... 97
ltutmish's *mamluks* ... 115

Chapter Four: The Ghurids and Their World ... **141**
Conclusion ... 148

Appendix I: Mamluks, *their Owners,* Iqta *and Origins* ... *150*
Appendix II: Military Logistics under the Ghurids and Early Delhi Sultanate ... *154*
Appendix III: Geneaological Lists and Regnal Dates ... *158*
Bibliography ... *162*
Index ... *166*

Acknowledgements

I am grateful to numerous individuals who have contributed to the preparation of this book. Peter Schröder, my friend and supervisor at University College London, for reading the early draft and kindly insisting that it was worthy of publication. The David collection in Copenhagen who generously granted me permission to use items from their collection as illustrations. James Verschoyle for designing and producing the excellent maps that serve to elucidate the evolution of the Ghurid Empire. I would like to thank my publisher, Unicorn, for taking on this project and their care and expertise in bringing it to fruition.

Above all, I am grateful to my family, especially my wife, Manuela, who has been subjected to the Ghurids for what must seem an eternity. She has read and commented incisively on numerous drafts of a complicated document in a language that is not her own. I thank my children Isabella, Frederick and Eloise for their endless assistance with syntax, improving the manuscript and deploying their invaluable I.T. skills. This book is dedicated to my wife and children.

London, January 2025

List of Plates

1. Qutb Minar a minaret and "victory tower" of the Qutb complex, Delhi's oldest fortified city, Lal Kot, India *(Alamy)*

2. Intricate detail of the Qutb Minar red sandstone tower (minaret), Delhi, India *(Alamy)*

3. Minaret of Jam, Ghor Province in Afghanistan. View of the Minaret of Jam from below showing detail of the geometric decoration. *(Jonathan Wilson / Alamy Stock Photo)*

4. Minaret of Jam and the Hari River in the Shahrak District, central Afghanistan's Ghor Province. The Minaret of Jam, along with its archaeological remains, was inscribed on the World Heritage List by the United Nations Educational, Scientific and Cultural Organization (UNESCO) in 2002. *(Saifurahman Safi/Xinhua/Alamy Live News)*

5. Iltutmish's tomb in Qutb Minar complex in Delhi (13th century). *(Sergii Rudiuk / Alamy Stock Photo)*

6. Copper and silver inlaid brass ewer, Herat *c.*1180–1200. The ewer's decoration features classical, figural and celestial imagery emphasised in silver. This includes lions, parakeets and signs of the zodiac accompanied by benedictory inscriptions in Arabic script. The object illustrates Herat's status as a major cultural hub and centre for the production of high quality metalwork. H: 40 cm. *(© The Trustees of the British Museum)*

7. Footed bronze dish with elephant in the centre, eastern Iran or Afghanistan, end of 12th–early 13th century. The elephant depicted in the central medallion makes it probable that the the dish was made under the Ghurids whose art shows the influence of Indian models. H: 9.8 cm; Diam: 31.8 cm. *(David Collection Inventory No. 43/1998, photographer Pernille Kemp)*

8. Earthenware bowl with incised decoration in a white slip and painted in green and manganese in a yellowish glaze (Bamiyan type), Afghanistan *c.*1200. H: 8.5 cm; Diam: 18 cm. *(David Collection Inventory No. 14/1989, photographer Pernille Kemp)*

9. Hexagonal table, poplar, covered in paper and coloured laquer and with incised decoration, Afghanistan 11th–12th century. H: 26 cm; Diam: 38 cm. *(David Collection Inventory No. 33/1997, photographer Pernille Kemp)*

10. Gold coin of Mu'izz al-Din as vassal of his brother Ghiyath al-Din, 597/ Dec 1200–Jan 1201, Ghazna mint. This 'bull's eye' type was modelled on contemporary Ayyubid coinage of Egypt. 26mm. *(David Collection Inventory No. C 480, photographer Pernille Kemp)*

11. Gold coin of Mu'izz al-Din, 600/1203–4, probably Ghazna mint. 35 mm. *(David Collection Inventory No. C 132, photographer Pernille Kemp)*

12. Greenish Limestone matrix for stamping leather, Afghanistan end of 12th–beginning of 13th century. The name of a Ghurid general is found in one of the matrices – he died *c.*1210 as governor of Herat. H: 33.5 cm; W: 18.5 cm. *(David Collection Inventory No. 4/2000, photographer Pernille Kemp)*

Maps

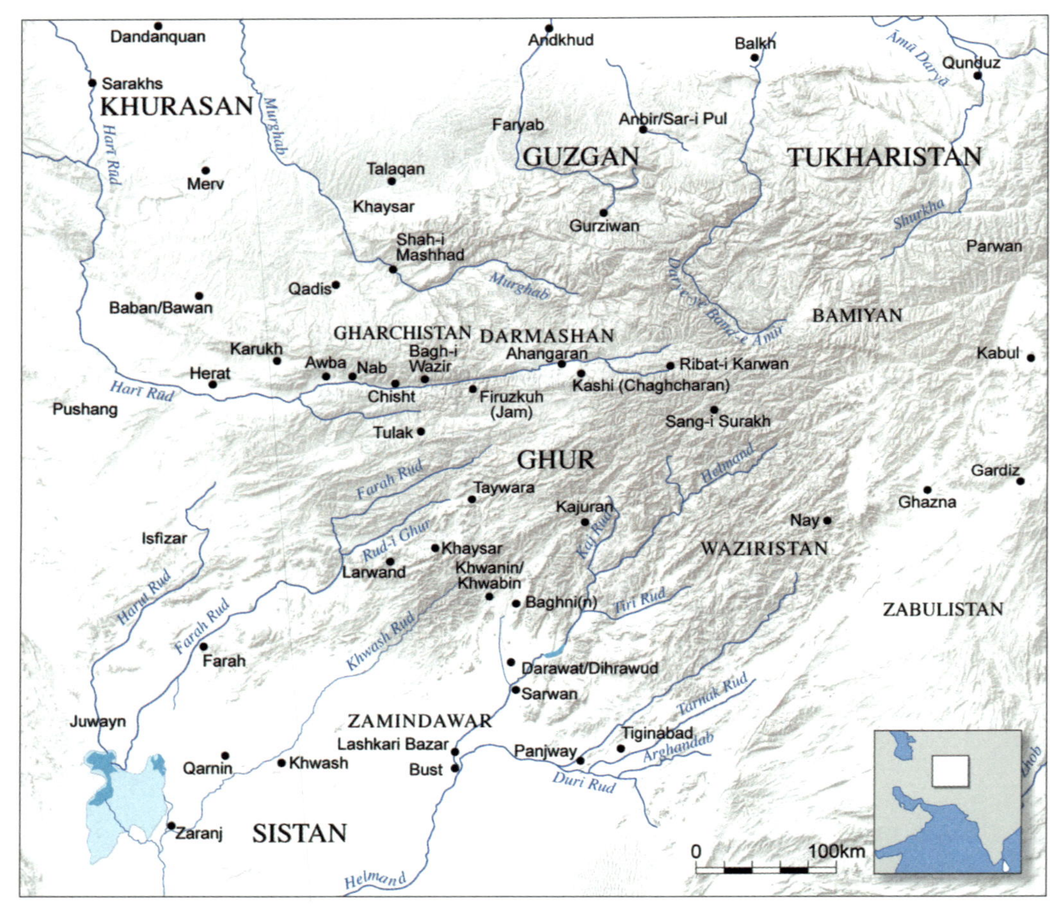

Map 1: The Ghurid Heartland

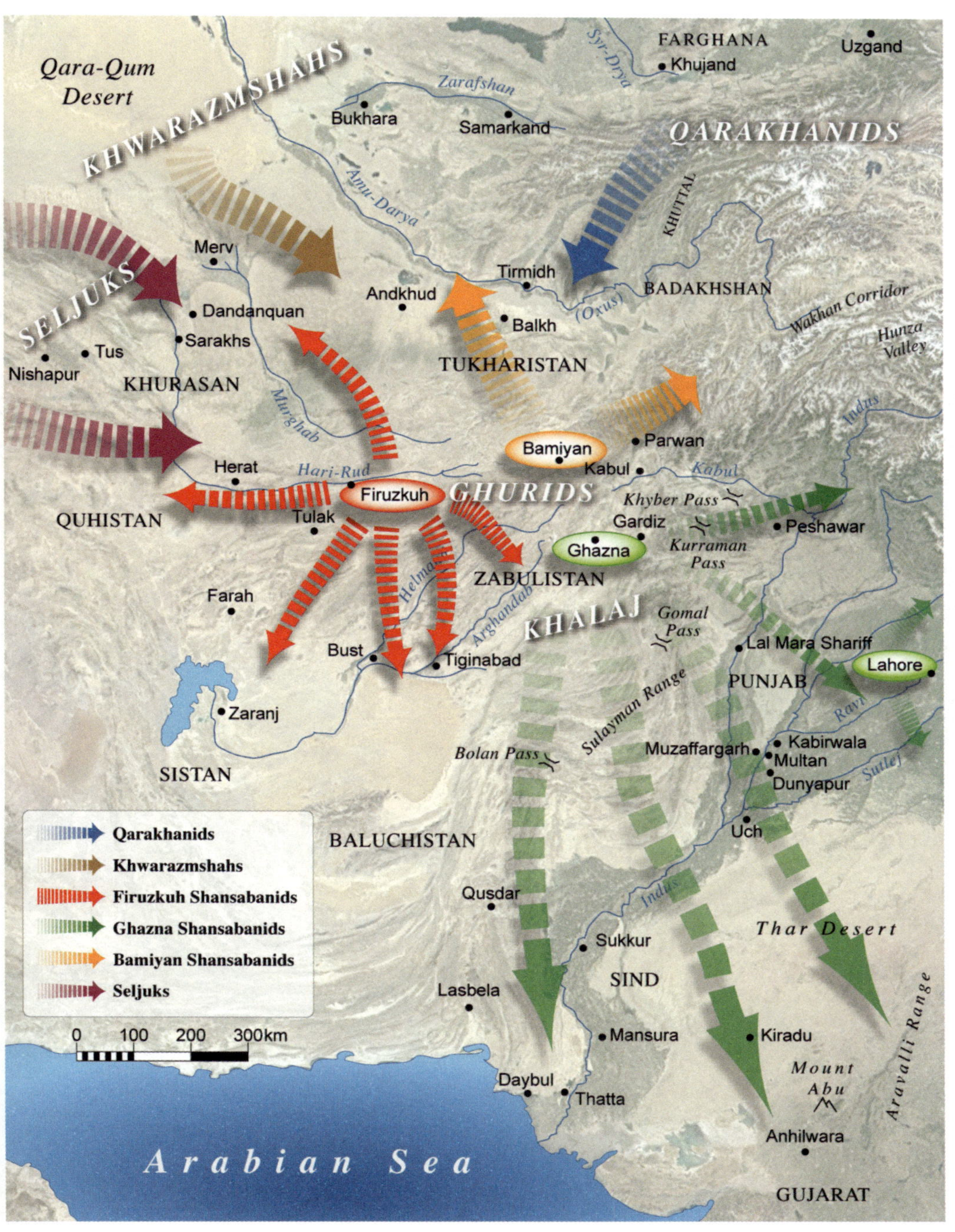

Map 2: The Ghurid Shansabanid expansion under the leadership of Ghiyath al-Din

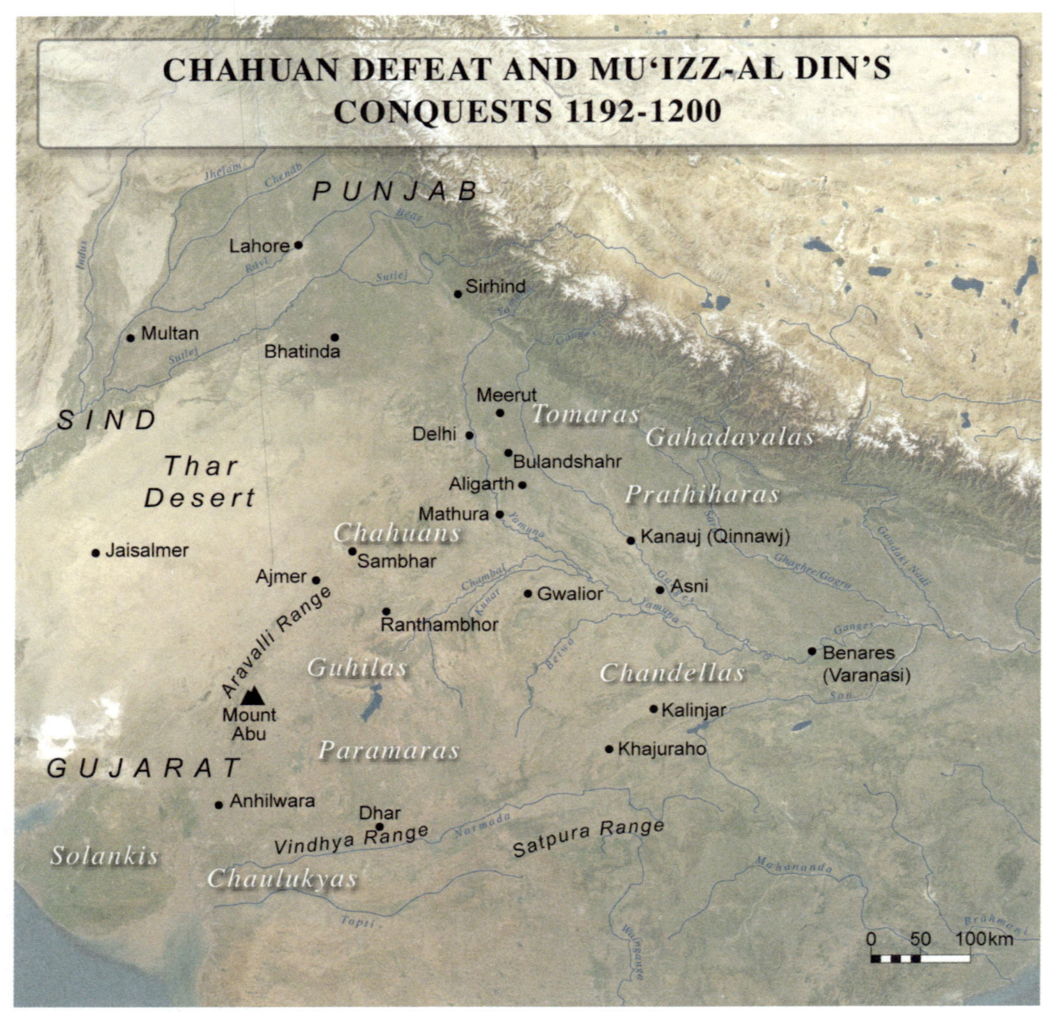

Map 3: The Chahuan defeat and Mu'izz al Din's conquests 1192–1200

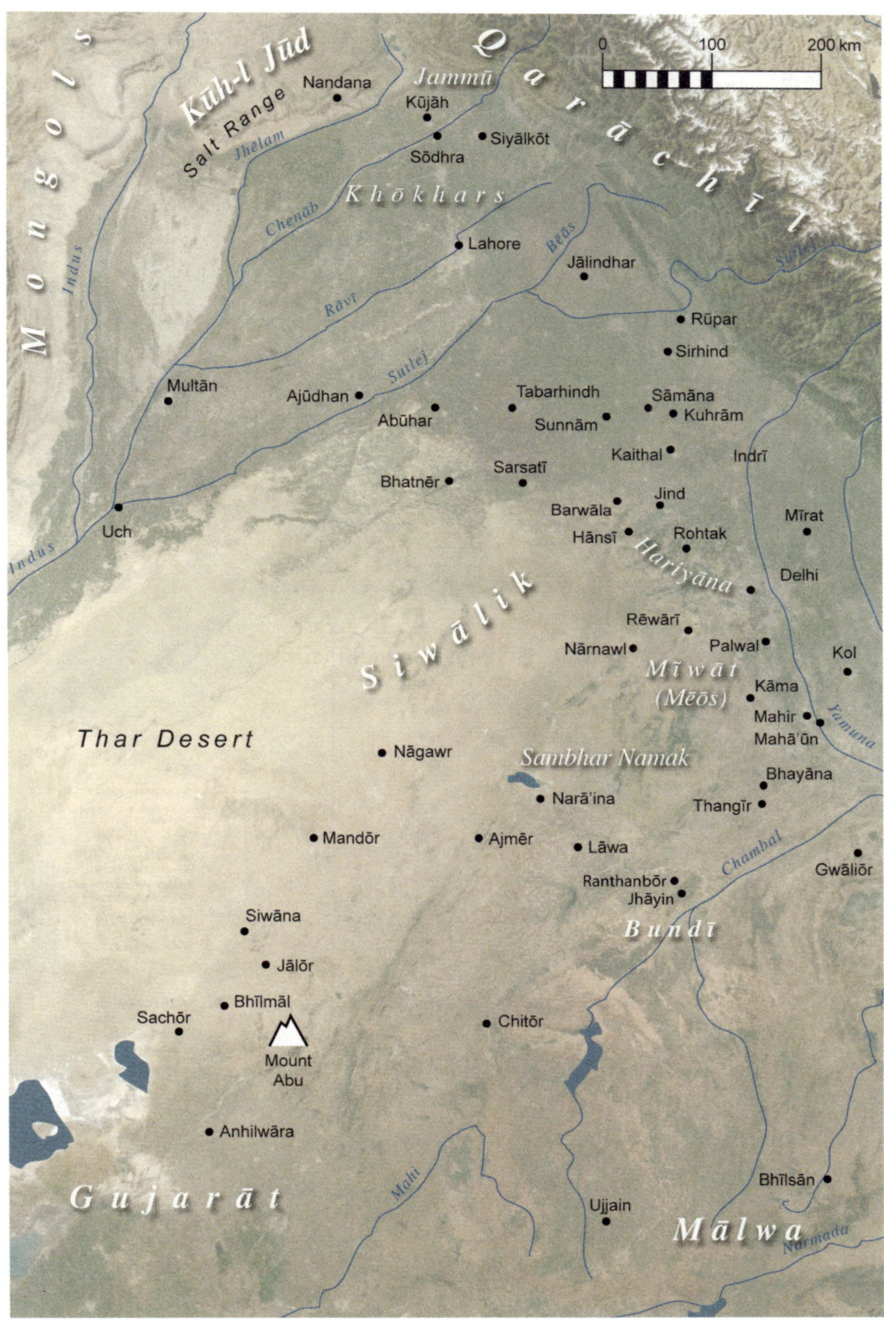

Map 4: North Eastern India the Upper Indus and The Five Rivers

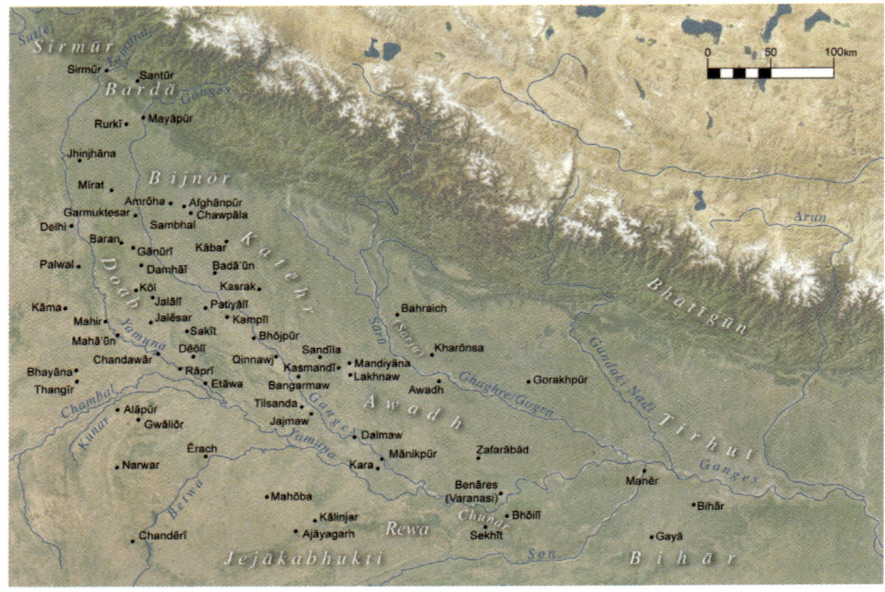

Map 5: Upper Ganges Plain

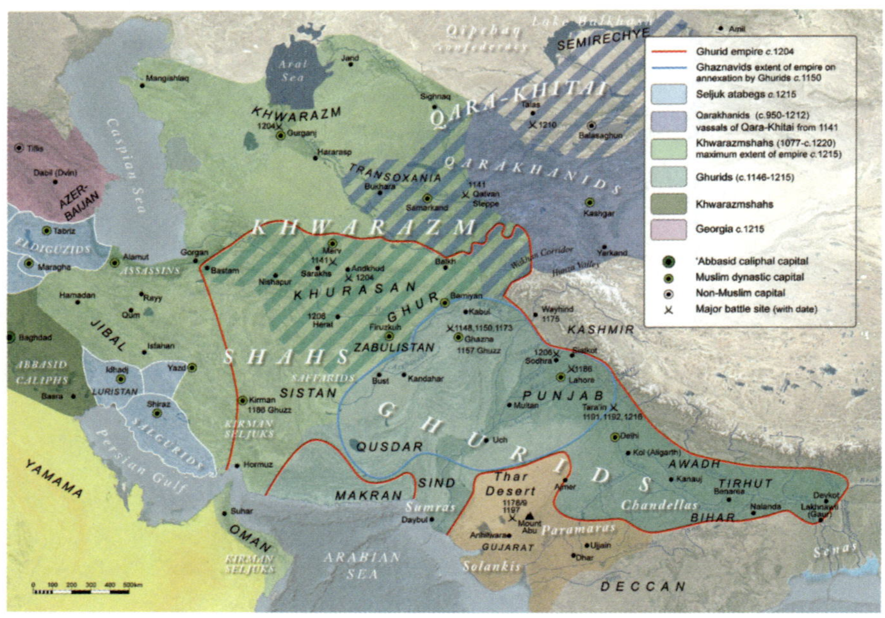

Map 6: Ghurid Empire and Eastern Iranian World *c.*1204

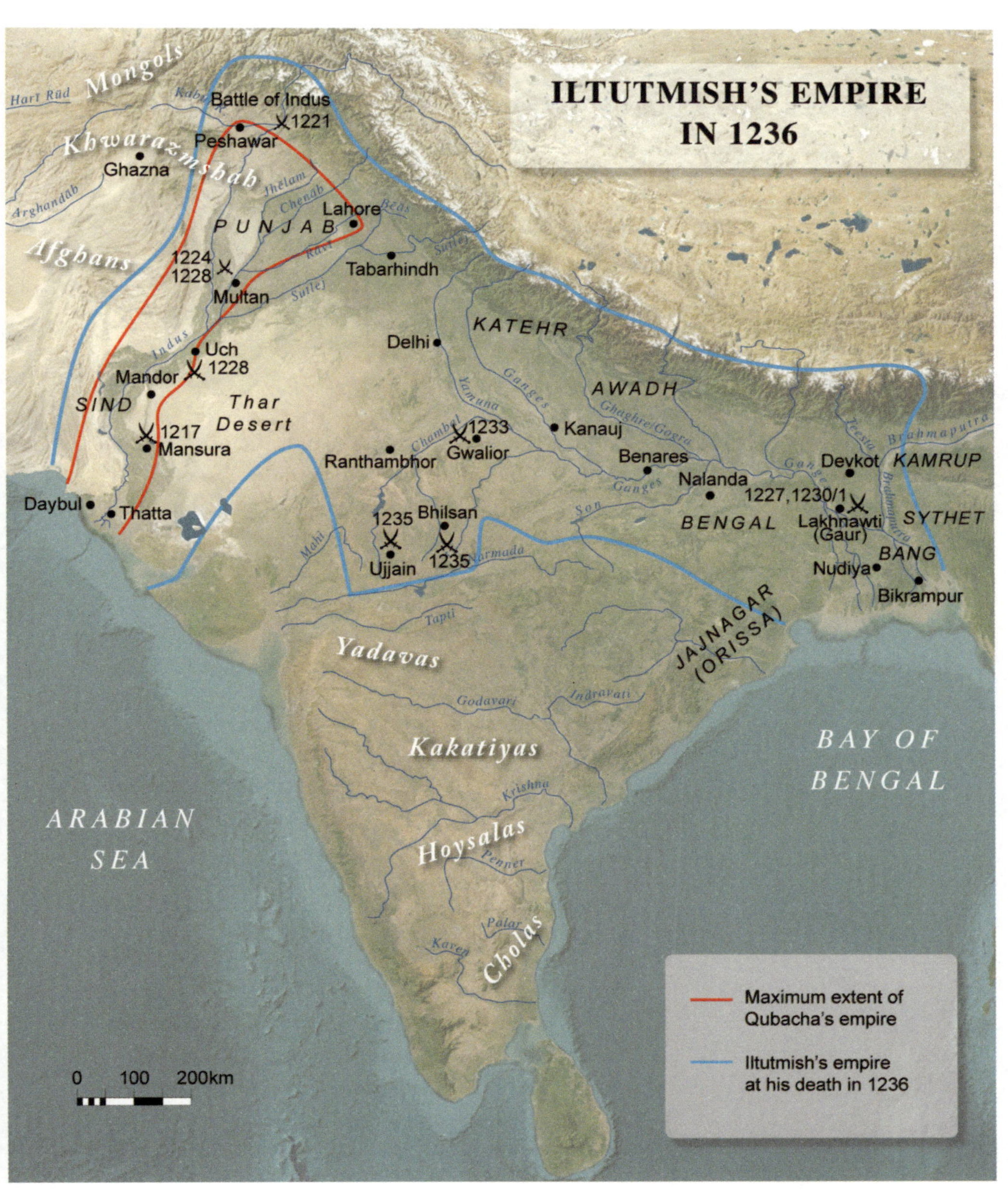

Map 7: Iltutmish's Empire in 1236

History of the Ghurids and their Ghulams in India: Timeline

The dates refer to the Islamic and Christian calendars.

AH	AD	Event
511?–52	1117–57	Reign of Ghaznavid sultan Bahram Shah, vassal of Seljuk sultan Sanjar.
543	1148	Barham Shah allegedly poisoned the Ghurid chieftain Qutb al-Din Muhammad b. Husain of Warshad, his son-in-law. This led to the Ghurids seeking revenge. Shansabani family primacy is established among the Ghurid factions. The Ghurids were primarily foot soldiers and begin to recruit/purchase free Turkish *mamluks/ghulams* particularly from among the Ghuzz and to a lesser extent Seljuks to compensate for their lack of cavalry.
543	Sept/Oct 1148	Ghazna is captured by Saif al-din Suri and his younger brothers Baha 'al-Din Sam of Sanga and 'Ala' al-Din Husain of Wajiristan. First major Ghurid success.
544	1149	Bahram Shah returns to Ghazna and defeats the Ghurids. Saif al-Din Suri and his vizier Majd al-Din Musawi are captured and crucified by Ghaznavids.
545–5	1150	'Ala' al-Din *jahan-suz* leads expedition to Ghazna to avenge his brother. Battle with the Ghaznavids at Tiginabad. Bahram Shah is defeated. A seven-day plundering of Ghazna follows. 'Ala al-Din Husain earns sobriquet of 'the world incendiary' *jahan-suz*.
547	1152	'Ala' al-Din *jahan-suz* defeated at Nab in Hari Rud valley by Seljuk sultan Sanjar and held prisoner for two years.

552?	1157–8	Death of sultan Bahram Shah, who is succeeded by his son Khusrau Shah (552–5/1157–60?) who, isolated in Ghazna with no possibility of Seljuk support, retreats to his Indian possessions in the Punjab.
552	1157–8	Capture by Ghuzz and death of Seljuk sultan Sanjar. Collapse of Seljuk Empire in Khurasan.
556	April 1161	Death of Ala al-Din *jahan-suz* succeeded by his son, Saif al-Din (1161–3).
555–82	1160–86	Khusrau Malik, last Ghaznavid sultan, succeeds his father in Lahore.
558–600	1163–1203	Ghiyath al-Din Muhammad succeeds his cousin Saif al-Din, and is proclaimed sultan.
569–600	1173–1203	Mu'izz al-Din Mahmud rules with elder brother as joint sultan. Sole ruler (1203–06).
569–70	1173–4	A band of Ghuzz who had seized Ghazna (*c.* 1157) are driven out by the Ghurid sultan, securing eastern Afghanistan and opening the way for Ghurid expansion into India. Ghiyath al-Din Muhammad appoints his brother as sultan in Ghazna under his supreme rule.
569	1173	Mu'izz al-Din drives Ghaznavids out of Zabulistan, obliging them to take refuge in Lahore.
569–601	1173–1204	Ghurid expansion westwards under Ghiyath al-Din against the Khwarzmshahs for control of Khurasan.
571	1175	Ghiyath al-Din seizes Herat from its Seljuk governor. Rulers of Sistan and Kerman acknowledge Ghurid suzerainity. Mu'izz al-Din captures Multan.
571–2	1175–6	Mu'izz al-Din invades India via Multan and the Thar Desert and is beaten by Chaulukya ruler Mularaja II of Nahrawala at Mount Abu, Gujerat.
575	1179–80	Mu'izz al-Din captures Peshawar.
577	1181–2	First Ghurid moves towards taking Lahore from Ghaznavids.

582	1186	Mu'izz al-Din, with the assistance of Vijaydeva son of Chakradeva, king of Jammu, captures Lahore. 'Ali Karmakh appointed governor.
582	1186	Ghurids under Mu'izz al-Din seize Punjab. Khusrau Malik and his son Bahram Shah sent to Ghiyath al-Din in Ghur and were never seen again.
586	1190	Ghurids defeat Khwarazmian ruler and his allies, the Qara-Khitai at Marv al-Rudh, annexing most of the Khwarazamshahs' territories in Khurasan.
587	119I	War with Khawarazmshahs Tekish and his brother Sultan Shah, supported by the Qarakhanids and their Qara-khitan overlords who invade Guzgan. Defeated by Ghiyath al-Din.
	1191	First battle of Tara'in. Mu'izz al-Din defeated by coalition of Indian rulers and is seriously wounded.
	1192	Second battle of Tara'in. Mu'izz al-Din defeats a major alliance of Hindu princes, kills Chauhan monarch Pritviraja III and establishes permanent Muslim presence at Indraprastha (Indrapat) near Delhi. This leads to Ghurid armies raiding into the Ganges Plain as far as eastern Bengal.
587–600	1193–1203	Mu'izz al-Din moves down from Ghazna to campaign in the cool season in India.
597	1200	Ghiyath al-Din and Mu'izz al-Din respond to succession of Khwarazamshah 'Ala- al-Din Muhammad b. Tekish by moving their armies westwards into Khurasan. Mu'izz al-Din sent on expedition to Ray. But he allows his troops to run amok and manages little further than Gurgan, earning rare admonishment from his brother. Taj al-Din Zangi appointed governor of Sarakhs, and another Ghurid, Nasir al-Din Muhammad Kharnak, appointed governor of Merv.
600	1203	Death of Ghiyath al-Din.

601	1204	Mu'izz al-Din invades Khwarazm. Suffers defeat by the Khwarazamshah's Qara-Khitan overlords at Andkhud – now Andkhoy.
601	1204	Ghurid sultan increasingly relies on his Turkish *mamluk* lieutenants in India – principally Qutb al-Din Aybak and his *ghulam* Shams al-Din Iltutmish.
601	1204	Mu'izz al-Din's defeat incentivises one of his lieutenants, Nasir al-Din Qubacha, to seize Multan. A more serious revolt occurs involving the Hindu Khokhars and the people of the Salt Range in the Punjab.
602	1206	Sultan Mu'izz al-Din is murdered probably by Isama'ilis from Khurasan, leaving no heir. His empire disintegrates and is split among Ghurid princes, his Turkish *ghulams* and the Khwarazmshah, 'Ala' al-Din Muhammad b.Tekish
601–02	1206	Sultan's senior *ghulam* Tajir al-Din Yildiz occupies Ghazna, ignoring the new Ghurid sultan Ghiyath al-Din Mahmud (601–02–609/1206–10).
601–02	1206	Aybak moves from Delhi to take up residence in Lahore, the former seat of the viceroy for Ghurid territories in India. He continues to maintain the *khutba* for the sultan Ghiyath al-Din Mahmud (1206–10) and issues coins in his name. He had been promoted to the status of viceroy 'from the gates of Peshawar to the furthest parts of India' a few weeks prior to Mu'izz al-Din's death.
605	1208–8–09	Aybak is presented by the caliph with a ceremonial parasol (*chatr*) with the style of sultan. His authority is recognised in Bengal after assassination of the Khalaj Muhammad b.Bakhtiar.
607	1210–11	Aybak dies in a polo accident. His former *ghulam* and son-in-law Shams al-Din Iltutmish is invited to Delhi and sets himself up as ruler and Delhi sultan.
607	1210–11	Aram Shah, a rival claimant and possibly another son-in-law of Aybak, marches from Lahore to Delhi and is defeated and killed by Iltutmish.

607	1210–11	In Bengal, 'Ali-yi Mardan, a former client of Aybak, entitles himself as Sultan 'Ala' al-Din.
607	1210–11	Nasir al-din Qubacha, a former *ghulam* of Mu'izz al-Din, consolidates himself at Multan. Assassination of Ghurid sultan Ghiyath al-Din Mahmud. Firuzkuh falls to Khwarazmshah.
609	1212–13	The increasing insanity and sanguinary behaviour of the ruler in Bengal, Ali yi Mardan, ends with his murder and the succession of Husam al-Din 'Iwad, a more balanced individual who takes the title of Sultan Ghiyath al-Din 'Iwad.
611	1214–16	The Khwarazmshah 'Ala' al-Din Muhammad overwhelms Ghurid princes and protégés alike.
612	January 1216	Taj al-Din Yildiz, late sultan Mu'izz al-Din's senior *ghulam,* is forced out of Ghazna by the Khwarazmshah and is subsequently defeated by Iltutmish near Tara'in, imprisoned at Bada'un and later put to death.
618–20	1221–3	Khwarazmian Empire is destroyed by advancing Mongols.
620	1223	Nasir al-Din Bakr b. Sari, one of a small number of the Ghurid dynasty to have survived, abandons Ghur to the Mongols, flees to India and becomes a *malik* of Iltutmish and later dies in Delhi.
622	1225	Ghiyath al-Din 'Iwad – possibly ruling with his son styled Mu'izz al-Din 'Ali-yi 'Iwad from (616/1219) – resists invasion of Bengal by Iltutmish.
623	1226	Ghur is finally overrun by the Mongols.
624	1227	Iltutmish's elder son and heir Nasir al-Din Mahmud, taking advantage of 'Iwad's' absence campaigning in Assam (Kamrup), seizes Lakhnawti, executing 'Iwad' on his return.

625	Early May 1228	Having weathered and been weakened by the Khwarazmshah Jal al-Din's attacks and Mongol predations, Qubacha is finally defeated and forced by Iltutmish to seek refuge on the island stronghold of Bhakkar on the Indus whence he throws himself into the river to avoid being taken alive.
626	Winter 1228–9	Nasir al-Din Mahmud, Iltutmish's son and viceroy in Bengal, dies.
626	February 1229	Embassy from Caliph al-Mustanir (623–40/1226–42) arrives in Delhi, bringing Iltutmish robes of honour and a diploma confirming his authority over all the territories he has conquered.
627	1229–30	Iltutmish's forces move against Khwarazamshah Jalal al-Din's legate in the northwest forcing him to flee to Iraq.
628	1230–01	Iltutmish invades Bengal overthrowing the usurper Ikhtiyar al-Din Dawlat Shah also known as Bilge Malik. Iltutmish is now the supreme Muslim ruler in India.
633	29 April 1236	Death of former Ghurid *mamluk* and later sultan Shams al-Din Iltutmish.
633–4	1236–66	Iltutmish's heirs are plagued by faction fighting among powerful *mamluks* often pursuing their own interests to the detriment of the ruler in Delhi.

Glossary of Names and Terms

al-sultan al-azam: the greatest sultan
al-sultan al-muazzam: the great sultan
amir: prince, ruler or military commander
amir-i-akhur: head/lord of the stables
amir-i-dad: military justiciar
amir-i-hajib: military chamberlain
amir-i-shikar: chief huntsman
chawgan: polo
dar: abode
dar al-harb: land of war/unbelievers
dar al-islam: Muslim world
dhimmi: non-Muslims protected under Islamic law
diwan: government ministry
royal attendant/carpet-spreader
farsang: approximately six kilometres
durbash: ceremonial baton
ghulam: military slave; Arabic equivalent of *mamluk*
habashi: Abyssinian
hajib: chamberlain
iqta: land grant on varied scale; could encompass an entire province or region
khasadar: falconer
khutba; sermon at Friday prayers mentioning the ruler's name, signifying his legitimacy to rule
Khwaja: lord or master
lak: one hundred thousand
madhhab: legal school; partic one of *hanafi, hanbali, maliki and shafi'i* of Sunni Islam
malik: prince, especially of royal house
malika: feminine
malik al-muazzam: king
mamluk: military slave; Persian terminology
muqta: holder of an *iqta*
na'ib: viceroy
naubat: band playing outside royal or princely residence as a mark of status
qadi al-quddat: grand *qadi* of the empire; a position occupied by Juzjani *qadi* meaning judge

qaghan: Turkic royal ruler's title
sar-i jandar, chief armour bearer *sayyid*: descendant of the Prophet Muhammad
shahnah: superintendent of rivers and vessels
sharabdari: head of liquor supply/store; not necessarily alchoholic
shihna: Mongol resident at the court of a subject ruler
sipah-salar: commander of the army *wazir*: chief minister or vizier
yaghantut: hunter of elephants
yuzban: keeper of the hunting leopards, that is, cheetahs

Glossary largely based on H.G. Raverty's translation of *Tabakat-i-Nasiri*; A.C.S. Peacock, *The Great Seljuk Empire* (Edinburgh, 2015); and p. Jackson, *The Delhi Sultanate: A Political and Military History* (Cambridge, 2003).

Preface

THIS BOOK HAS HAD A LONG GESTATION AND IS THE RESULT OF MY earliest interest in the eastern Iranian lands. My curiosity was sparked during my A levels through reading Claude Cahen's work on the Seljuk Turks within Setton and Baldwin's *History of the Crusades*, known to us consumers at the time as 'solid and boring' – which I hasten to add was not the case.[1] I subsequently bought volume 5 of the *Cambridge History of Iran*, which reinforced the interest.[2] At university, I enjoyed researching the Ummayad Caliphate, its ultimate decline and Abu Muslim's revolt in Khurasan. My PhD, an ongoing project, is on the Mediterranean policy of Ferdinand II of Aragon (1452–1516), husband of Queen Isabella I of Castile; this touches the western Islamic world, namely Ottoman incursions into the western Mediterranean and the relations of the 'Catholic monarchs' with the North African states and the Mamluk dynasty in Egypt in particular. More recently, my rediscovery of Clifford Bosworth's *The Later Ghaznavids: Splendour and Decay – The Dynasty in Afghanistan and Northern India 1040–1186* (Edinburgh, 1977) and *The Delhi Sultanate* by Peter Jackson prior to a visit to northern India drew my attention towards the Ghurids.[3,4]

The study is designed primarily to be a political and military history of the Ghurid world, that is, the eastern Iranian territories and northern India during the latter half of the twelfth century and the beginning of the thirteenth, a period of approximately eighty-five years (1150–1236). It is first and foremost a book of *évènements* but it tries to place the narrative in a wider context. The Ghurids were instrumental in spreading a Persian court culture, not just an Islamic one, into the Indian subcontinent. This was something they had inherited from the Ghaznavids. They in their turn had acquired it from the Iranian Samanid *amirs*. The Samanids were the first indigenous dynasty to rule in Iranian lands following the Arab invasions and collapse of the Sassanian dynasty in the early seventh century.

1 C. Cahen, 'The Turkish invasions: The Selchükids'. In: *A History of the Crusades. Vol. I: The First Hundred Years* (Eds K.M. Setton and M.W. Baldwin) (Philadelphia, 1969)

2 *The Cambridge History of Iran Vol 5: The Saljuk and Mongol Periods* (Ed. J.A. Boyle) (Cambridge, 1968)

3 C.E. Bosworth, *The Later Ghaznavids: Splendour and Decay* (Edinburgh, 1977)

4 P. Jackson, *The Delhi Sultanate: A Political and Military History* (Cambridge, 2003)

The Ghurids are sometimes described as an ephemeral dynasty, something one could say of many nomadic societies; Bosworth, for example, mentions the "Ghurid Interlude".[5] However, I believe they were more significant and exerted a far greater influence on northern India than being a mere interlude. Without the determined incursions of the Ghurids and their *ghulams* there would arguably not have been a permanent Muslim presence in India beyond the Punjab and small communities in Sindh, in what is now southeastern Pakistan, in the late twelfth century. *Ghulam* in Arabic and *mamluk* in Persian means 'slave'. The Ghurids bought Turkic slaves in the slave markets of the Central Asian steppes, Iran and modern Afganistan. Many of these Turkic slaves were expert horsemen, specialising in mounted archery and shock cavalry tactics. The Ghurid sultan Mu'izz al-Din created a succession structure that resulted in a number of *mamluks* establishing themselves as independent rulers by dint of their abilities. Among the most successful was Shams al-Din Iltutmish who established his own dynasty. Later in India this period would be known and studied as the 'slave dynasty'.

Ghurid rule gave rise to the foundation of the Delhi Sultanate, the first independent Muslim power in India, which led to the Muslim political domination of India until the arrival of the Europeans and most notably the British East India Company. It is true the Ghurids lost their western territories, including Balkh, Merv, Sarakhs, Nisa, Abivard, Tus, Nishapur and lands west towards the Caspian, within a few years of acquiring them. They were extinguished shortly afterwards – sultan Ghiyath al-Din Mahmud was forced to accept the Khwarazmshah 'Ala' al-Din Muhammad as his overlord by 604/1207–08. They faced pressure from more powerful and better resourced political entities – first, the Khwarazmshahs and their Qara-khitai overlords and ultimately the Mongols. However, in India they were the first Muslim invader to establish themselves with the intention to stay. This was unlike their predecessors the Ghaznavids 977/1186, a Turco-Iranian dynasty founded by Sebuktegin who limited themselves mainly to the northwestern Punjab. The Ghaznavids were content to continue the modus operandi of Mahmud, their greatest sultan, who had raided as far as the great temple of Shiva at Somnath in Gujerat. Bactrian camels that had been brought from northern Afganistan carried back hundreds of treasure chests laden with precious stones just from this one raid. The fabulous riches of India that came from this and other penetrative raids enabled the early Ghaznavids to fund their armies for campaigns of conquest in Central Asia and Iran. The later Ghaznavid sultans only campaigned irregularly into the upper Ganges plain against the Hindu rulers, supplementing their wealth with gold,

5 *CHI*. p. 166.

specie and gems, while acquiring recruits to bolster their armies, but never with the intention of establishing suzerainty and ruling northern India.

Of the great medieval Muslim rulers Mahmud of Ghazna, Alp Arslan, Malik Shah, Saladin and perhaps Baibars are well known. But the name of a man who rose from the rugged mountains of Afganistan and went on to lay the foundations of dominant Muslim rule in northern India is lost to obscurity. Sometime in 588/1163 Ghiyath al-Din Muhammad b. Sam established himself as the supreme ruler of the Shansabanids, a dynastic grouping, among petty chieftains in central Afghanistan. He hailed from the remote mountainous region forming part of a western strand of the Hindu Kush between Herat and Kabul – Ghur or Ghor as it is known today. From his capital in the fortress of Firuzkuh – which meant Turquoise Mountain – he was recognised as one of the great powers of the eastern Islamic world. He proceeded to create, within a forty-year reign 1163–1203, broadly contemporaneous to the Angevin Empire, a polity that at its height stretched from Bastam and Gurgan in the west, almost from the Caspian Sea to the shores of the Bay of Bengal. The area concerned encompassed most of Khurasan, Kuhistan, Sistan or Sind west of the Indus, the Punjab east of the Indus and the Gangetic plain as far as Gaur/Lakhnawti. Ghiyath al-Din's dynasty took its name from the place it sprang from – they would be known as the Ghurids. In time, the Ghurids and their *ghulams* raided into what has come to be known as Rajputana, to the cities of Ajmer, Anhilwara and Ujjain as far as River Narmada on the borders of the Deccan and as far east as the Brahmaputra and the jungles of Assam. Ultimately, two Ghurid *ghulams* of sultan Mu'izz al-Din, younger brother of Ghiyath al-Din, namely Aybak and his former *ghulam* and his former slave Shams al-Din Iltutmish, created the Ghurid successor state, the Delhi Sultanate.

The aim of this work is to study the Ghurid Empire in its territorial entirety highlighting their conquests in India as an integral part of their story as much as the eastern Iranian lands to the west of the Indus. The historic Ghurid polity in modern Afghanistan is often treated under Iranian studies and the Indian conquests of Mu'izz al-Din and his slave generals tend to be included as part of the emergence of the Delhi Sultanate and the history of the subcontinent. It is important to remember that the campaigns in the Indian subcontinent were sanctioned by the supreme Ghurid sultan Ghiyath al-Din, elder brother of Mu'izz al-Din, as part of an organised expansion from the core Ghurid territories, with the aim of permanent possession and occupation. The two brothers seem to have enjoyed an amicable and productive relationship, something that was rare in medieval society. It is also true that Mu'izz al-Din may have sought to conquer new territories where he held sole sway rather than as his brother's appointee. One of the differences of the two men was that Ghiyath al-Din appointed relatives or Ghurid *amirs* to rule and govern his conquests in the west whereas his younger brother chose to rule his conquests through his Turkish *mamluks.* These slave soldiers were completely reliant on their owner for preferment and were entirely at his disposal. They were recruited primarily from Turkic tribes beyond the Oxus for their military abilities and ruthlessness. In turn, the opportunities for advancement, for those with ability, were almost limitless – from the command of armies to the governorship of provinces and ultimately ruling in their own right. While the Indus itself forms a logical and physical geographical barrier it did not constitute a hindrance to the success of the emerging Ghurid state created by the *ghulams* and their conquests either under the initial personal leadership of sultan Mu'izz al-din himself or, as was to happen more frequently, through delegation to his paramount *mamluk* general Qutb-al-din Aybak or his own leading slave commander and son-in-law Shams-al-Din Iltutmish. The latter two became the first two Delhi sultans – ignoring Aram Shah's very brief attempt to take the Delhi throne – but they were first and foremost Ghurid servants in name and outlook. Even to some extent post manumission. Despite the collapse of the Ghurid dynasty in the west, in (1204), before the onslaught of the Khwarazmshahs and the Qara-Khitai, Aybak continued to acknowledge the last ruling Ghurid sultan, as his overlord until his own death in (1210). However, the death of Mu'izz al-Din (1206) had given rise to drawn out conflict between Aybak and other manumitted slaves for control of former lands held directly from or in the name of Mu'izz al-Din. In his turn Iltutmish, (1210–36) had to overcome these former Ghurid *mamluks* who had by this stage created their own substantial rival states: Sultan Nasir al-Din Qubacha in Multan, Sultan Taj al-Din Yildiz in Ghazna and later Lahore and the commander Muhammad b. Bakhtiyar Khalji's successors in Bengal.[6] Iltutmish's ultimate success in unifying the Ghurid conquests east of the Indus under his sole rule could be viewed as the final chapter of the Ghurid imperial project. He was the last Ghurid protégée to rule and attracted refugees to his court from their former lands west of the Indus. Delhi was to become the most important city in the eastern Islamic world – a place of refuge for those displaced by the Mongol onslaught. However, the dynasty he founded was his own, too much time had elapsed and the conquests by the Khwarzmshahs and subsequently the Mongols had put an end to any vestiges of Ghurid authority in Ghur and their original heartland.

6 Muhammad b. Bakhtiar was never a slave

PRIMARY SOURCES

This book has been written partly when there has been no direct access to libraries. The major source on the Ghurids, their times and empire, is Major H.G. Raverty's translation, first published in 1881, of the *Tabakat–i-Nasiri* by Maulana Minhaj-ud-Din Umar-i-Usman or al-Juznani as he is usually referred to, completed in Delhi in 658/1260. It was probably begun around 638/1240 and therefore describes events that would have occurred, for our purposes, up to ninety years prior to this date. This is not always an easy source to work with and there are gaps, particularly regarding early Ghurid incursions into the eastern Punjab and Gangetic plain. However, it is the most accessible. Raverty also mentions and acknowledges in the preface of volume I 'many rare and excellent works have been used; and some of them extensively drawn upon'.[7] However, the work has shortcomings regarding Indian affairs until Juzjani settled there in 623/1226.

The author hailed from the region of Guzgan and hence Juzjani. The exact location of this area is not certain, but it was probably one of the small districts in the northwest of Ghur, north of Herat. Raverty tells us that his ancestors on both sides had been noted as men of learning and religious scholars. Juzjani can be considered the official historian of the Ghurid dynasty. He could also claim Ghaznavid ancestry through the marriage of a daughter of sultan Ibrahim b. Masud to one of his forbears.[8] Following the Ghurid capture of Lahore in 582/1184Juzjani's father, Saraj-al-Din Muhammad, was appointed *qadi* and judge of the army stationed in Lahore. Juzjani was born in 589/1191 and his father later entered the service of Sultan Baha-al-Din, ruler of Bamiyan and Tukharistan, at which time Juzjani would have been three years old. He was born in a residence at Firuzkuh, the Ghurid summer capital. His mother was the foster sister of princess Mah.*malika,* the daughter of the sultan of Ghur, Ghiyath al-Din Muhammad. His youth was spent in the *haram* of her household. During the revolt of the Khwarazmshah, Sultan Tekish and his war with Al Nasir the Abbasid caliph emissaries were sent from Baghdad seeking assistance from the sultan in Ghur, and a return embassy was despatched to Baghdad that included Juzjani's father. Somewhere en route they were attacked, by bandits, and Saraj-al-Din Muhammad was killed. Juzjani was certainly well connected with the upper echelons of Ghurid society. He clearly felt a great affinity with and gratitude to

7 Maulana, Minhaj-ud-Din, Abu-'Umar-I-'Usman, *Tabaqat-I Nasiri* (Trans. H.G. Raverty) (Calcutta, 2010), vol. I, pp. XV–XVI

8 C.E. Bosworth *The Later Ghaznavids; Splendour and Decay. The Dynasty in Afghanistan and Northern India 1040–1186* (Edinburgh,1977), p. 113

the Ghurid sultans and his history reflects this. Consequently, these loyalties need to be considered when analysing the narrative. One of his cousins on his mother's side was Ziyad-al-Din Muhammad, who was given command of the fortress of Tabarindh when the sultan Mu'izz al-Din retired from India at the end of the campaigning season in 587/1189.

By 607/1210–11, Juzjani had reached the age of eighteen and was living in the Ghurid capital, Firuzkuh. He left in 611/1212–13, the year before the surrender of the city to the Khwarazmshah Jalal-al-Din. Two years later we find him in southern Afghanistan, at Zaranj, and there he remained. By this stage the former Ghurid territories up to and beyond the Indus as far as River Jhelum had fallen to the Khwarazmshah. The years 617–20/1220–24 saw him at the fortified town of Tulak in the Tulak district of modern Ghor, which he helped to defend against the Mongols. Chingiz Khan had crossed the Oxus in the spring of 1222 to attack the great cities of Khurasan, Samarkand, Bukhara, Balkh, Nishapur and Merv. By 623/1226 Juzjani had decided to leave for India and in 625/1227–8 he finally reached the territories of Sultan Nasir al-Din Qubacha, a former Ghurid *ghulam* in the Indus valley, at Uch. There he was made *qadi-yi lashgar* of the forces of his son 'Ala-al-Din, Bahram Shah. However, shortly after this event, Qubacha's rival, the sultan Iltutmish, arrived before Uch. At this point Juzjani switched camps. He was well received by the Delhi sultan Iltutmish and reached that city in Ramadan of 625/1227–28 where he spent the remainder of his life in the service of the Delhi Sultanate. He was 70 in 658/1260/61. The year of his death is unknown.

Other useful information concerning Ghurid affairs can be gleaned from Ibn al-Athir's *al-kamil fi'l-ta'rikh* written around 628/1231. This great chronicle is one of the pre-eminent sources for the medieval Islamic world and plots the course of Islamic history from the earliest times. The period that concerns us is covered in the following volumes: *The Chronicle of Ibn al-Athir for the Crusading Period from* al-Kamil fi'l-Ta'rikh. *Part 2, the years 541–589/1146–93: The age of Nur al-Din and Saladin* and *Part 3, the years 589–629/1193–1231: The Ayyubids after Saladin and the Mongol Menace*, translated by D.S. Richards.[9] In this general history, although written in Mosul, the author sought to cover the Islamic world in its widest perspective. The scope is perhaps more understandable if northern Syria is viewed as centrally located in an Islamic world imagined as a lateral construct stretching from Morocco/southern Spain to the Indus and beyond, and the lands bordering the Oxus. However, the eastern periphery was not necessarily the work's primary aim. It concentrates on the Crusaders and their states in the Levant and

9 *The Chronicle of Ibn al-Athir for the Crusading Period from* al-Kamil fi'l-Ta'rikh. Parts 2 and 3 translated by D.S. Richards (Oxford and New York, 2007 and 2008)

the Islamic responses to them. Even so, the sweep of the work is impressive given the difficulties that must have been faced by Ibn al-Athir 555–631/1160–1233 in reconciling accounts from disparate sources, chronicling Muslim military successes in distant eastern Islamic territories and beyond. The author himself came from an established family with close connections to the Zangid dynasty of Mosul 1127–1234, which for a time also ruled much of northern Syria.

SECONDARY SOURCES

Other works used for this research include Peter Jackson, *The Delhi Sultanate: A Political and Military History* (Cambridge, 2003); and his *The Mongols and the Islamic World: From Conquest to Conversion* (New Haven and London, 2017); H.C. Ray, *The Dynastic History of Northern India, Early Medieval Period,* foreword by L.D. Barnett, first published 1931–6 (New Delhi, 2017, 2 vols); and David C. Thomas's *The Ebb and Flow of the Ghurid Empire* (Sydney, 2018) – an archaeologically led study of the Ghurid heartland, focusing on their summer capital at Firuzkuh/Jam with its iconic minaret only rediscovered in 1957, and one of the most recent and relevant works.

CHAPTER ONE:
c. 1146–1173

THE RISE OF THE DYNASTY

The Ghurid world: The geography of the eastern Iranian lands and northern India

Before tracing the rise of the Ghurids and their road to domination in the eastern Iranian lands it might be helpful to give an idea of the extent of their world with its litany of possibly unfamiliar names. The Ghurids's geographical knowledge, despite the physical remoteness of Afghanistan and in particular Ghur itself, would have encompassed the Islamic territories east of the Abbasid caliphate situated in Baghdad. Recognition from this institution, despite being a shadow of its former self, during the Ghurid period was still important in securing dynastic legitimacy in the orthodox Islamic world. The eastern Iranian lands included Persian-speaking Khurasan, the Sassanian land of the sun, which also encompassed parts of modern Afghanistan and southern Central Asia. This region stretched west from the shores of the Caspian Sea and east to the Pamirs. They would have been familiar with River Oxus/Amu Darya and the land beyond as far as River Jaxartes/Syr Darya. The delta of the latter was the region of Khwarazm/ancient Chorasmia – and the name taken by the Khwarazmshahs their rivals for control of much of their surroundings. It formed a substantial desert oasis south of the Aral Sea. The area also included the great cities of Bukhara and Samarkand, capitals of ancient Sogdiana and, more recently, the Samanid Empire. The Ghurids were to campaign over and conquer large parts of these territories. To the south of Khurasan they would have known the Iranian provinces of Sistan and Kirman inland from the straits of Hormuz in the Persian Gulf. A Seljuk Sultanate ruled from Kirman and had conquered the coast of Oman and Fars but fell to the advancing Ghuzz in 581–2/1186)[10] They would have been familiar with the area of Makran, forming part of modern Baluchistan, a desert strip along the coast of modern Pakistan and southeastern Iran. This was the arid region across which Alexander the Great led his army, with disastrous consequences, on his return from India in 325–4 BC.[11]

They would also have been well aware of Central Asia beyond the Syr Darya, Transoxiana, through Islamic proselytising as well as the region being a source of slave soldiers who were recruited from these Turkish and Mongol speaking tribal heartlands. The Ghurids would also have had knowledge of the Qara-khitai

10 A.C.S. Peacock, *The Great Seljuk Empire* (Edinburgh, 2015), p. 121

11 R. Lane Fox, *Alexander the Great* (London, 1973), pp. 387–402

Khanate, ruled by a Buddhist dynasty over mainly Turkish-speaking Muslim subjects, including their rivals in the west, the Khwarazmshahs. Sultan Mu'izz al-Din was to suffer defeat at their hands at the battle of Andkhud in 1204.

Afghanistan formed the core of their world and once the Ghaznavids, who ruled from 977–1186, were in retreat the Ghurids rapidly conquered the regions of Guzgan, Tukharistan, Zamindawar and Zabulistan and other parts contiguous to Ghur.

Further to the south and east lay the Khyber, Gomal and Bolan passes into the Indus valley, the western Punjab and the former Ghaznavid territories around Multan, Lahore and Uch, together with the port of Daybul in the Indus Delta.[12] The latter ruled by the Sumra dynasty. Beyond the Indus lay the territories of not only small Hindu principalities but major dynasties, such as the Chauhans, Chaulukyas, the Ghadavala kingdom and the Chandellas. Further to the east, in Bengal, lay the lands of the Senas' successors to the once mighty Pala Empire, the last Buddhist dynasty to rule in India. The Ghurids would have become aware of some of these states due to recent Ghaznavid excursions into the upper Ganges valley and from their own contacts with Hindu subject rulers during their campaigns around Lahore.

Introduction to the Ghurids

This brief synopsis of the Ghurid's world at the middle of the twelfth century provides little actual information on the Ghurids and Ghur itself prior to this. The reason is that not much is known until the advent of the Ghaznavid dynasty. Even then it is only with the emergence of the Ghurids as challengers to Ghaznavid hegemony in eastern Afghanistan that we begin to learn anything concrete. A tenth-century chronicler refers to Ghur as the largest pagan enclave in the Islamic territories.[13] Then the area was known chiefly as a source of slaves.[14]

Prior to the arrival of Islam in the seventh and eighth centuries the area of modern Afghanistan and Pakistan would have felt the cultural influences of the

12 Daybul can be spelled in a number of ways; Debal, Daibul or Dēwal. Daybul is used for consistency.

13 D.C. Thomas, *The Ebb and Flow of the Ghurid Empire* (Sydney, 2018), p. 19. Thomas refers to Al-Istrakhi writing *c.* 350/951.

14 C.E. Bosworth, 'The Political and Dynastic History of the Iranian World (A.D. 1000–1217)'. In: *Cambridge History of Iran Vol 5* (Cambridge, 1968), p. 160

Gandharan civilisation. This was located in the fertile upper Indus valley and its tributaries around Peshawar. Ghur would have formed part of what has come to be termed greater Gandhara, which also encompassed the ancient regions of Udyana. Udyana included the Swat valley and Bactria to the northwest. The great wealth of Buddhist sculpture, monasteries and archaeological sites in the region would have required very substantial patronage. With the decline of Gandhara itself, the area west of the Khyber Pass in modern Afghanistan saw great building activity from the fifth to the eighth centuries when the giant Buddhas of Bamiyan were constructed.[15] The great Buddhist tradition ended in the eighth century or ninth with the arrival of Islam and the conversion of the ruling classes to the new religion. The conclusion is that until the attempts at conversion by Mahmud of Ghazna and his son Mas'ud the people inhabiting Ghur would, due to its inaccessibility, have continued their adherence to Buddhism in some form. This would have remained the case and the inhabitants of the remote valleys would have strenuously resisted incursions into their mountain strongholds and it is unlikely that Islam made any meaningful progress in these areas before the mid-twelfthcentury. For the ruling powers outside the environs of Ghur from the Sassanians, through the Saffarids, to the Samanids, Seljuks and Ghaznavids, the area remained, for the Islamic dynasties at least, *dar al- kufr* – land of the infidel. For our period it initially formed a buffer state between the Great Seljuk and Ghaznavid Empires, both being formed by dynasties of Persianised Turks. The tribesmen themselves were renowned for their banditry and the area as a source of slaves, arms, armour and fierce dogs of a specific local breed.[16] Ghurid society would have been largely nomadic[17] – the tribesmen moving to the high pastures, with their flocks and livestock, in summer and the valleys and plains in the winter, while other members of the Ghurid polity would have been more urban and sedentary. The supreme sultan and court used Firuzkuh as a summer capital and stronghold on the upper Hari-Rud. The court would then move to Bust Lashkari Bazar, a fertile frontier district, on the edge of the mountains, between Firuzkuh and Bust for the winter.[18]

15 K.A. Behrendt, *The Art of Gandhara in the Metropolitan Museum of Art* (New York, 2007), pp. 3–5

16 C.E. Bosworth, *CHI*, vol. 5, p. 158

17 D.C. Thomas (2018), p. 21 mentions that in the 1950s the nomadic population of Afghanistan numbered *c.* 2 million, that is, 17 per cent of the population. It is likely this figure had not changed since medieval times. If one were to include parts of eastern Khurasan the figure would have been substantial.

18 Thomas (2018), p. 19

Regarding the ethnicity of the Ghurids themselves there is some disagreement. However, the consensus seems to be that they were of Iranian stock, indigenous Tajiks who probably spoke a pre-Persian language or Persian dialect. The Ghaznavid Empire contained a significant Persian population and was culturally and linguistically Persian. However, the language spoken in Ghur was sufficiently different that the Ghaznavids under Sultan Mas'ud I required interpreters in their early dealings with them.[19]

THE BEGINNINGS OF GHURID ASCENDANCY

The expeditions of the Ghaznavid sultans Mahmud r. 388–421/998–1030 and his son Ma'sud I r. 421–32/1030–41 in the early eleventh century had served to establish the beginnings of Islam in Ghur. At the same time, they also initiated support for Abu 'Ali b. Muhammad r. 420s/1030s of the Shansabani family of Ahangaran on the upper Hari Rud, as their lead vassal among the petty chieftains of Ghur.[20] This, no doubt, assisted the Shansabanis in their struggle for primacy among their rivals. For the remainder of the eleventh century relations between Ghur and the Ghaznavid sultans depended on the willingness or ability of the latter to intervene in the region. Ghur remained divided until the early twelfth century and the influence of the Shansabani principality over the rest of Ghur is difficult to gauge. Juzjani regularly exaggerates the influence of the Shansabanis, and the region is likely to have remained fragmented politically.[21]

Juzjani clearly states in his chapter on the 'Shansabaniah Dynasty of Ghur':

> *[T]he sultans of the Shansabi have been divided into four groups: I…, of which Sultans Firuz-koh was the seat of government; II,the dynasty of the Sultans of Bamian, who were a branch of this great tree of sovereignty; III., … the dynasty of the Sultans of Ghaznin, which was the capital of Sultan Mu'izz-ud-Din … and*

19 Ibid., p. 8

20 Ibid., p. 52. Thomas states that Ahangaran means 'the ironworker', a reference to the mineral wealth of Ghur and its ability to produce weapons and armour for which it was renowned.

21 Bosworth (1977), p. 69

> *his own particular slaves ... ; and IV., the dynasty of the Sultans of Hindustan, the sovereignty of which monarchy passed to them...*[22]

This state of affairs gives an idea of the structure of the Ghurid state under the supreme rule of Sultan Giyath-al-din in Firuzkuh/Jam. The slaves referred to in reference to Mu'izz al-Din are his *mamluks*, who were to carve out their own states. The most notable of these *mamluks* was Iltutmish. However, at Ghiyath al-Din's accession the primacy of the Firuzkuh branch was not a given. At this juncture the rulers of Bamiyan, due to their wealth and geographical location, were in a stronger position. Nevertheless, before reaching this point in time it is necessary to dicsuss how the Ghurids, rather surprisingly, managed to attain this position given the historical scale and prestige of the surrounding Seljuk and Ghaznavid Empires.

By the beginning of the twelfth century the region of Ghur had been subject to both Ghaznavid and Seljuk spheres of influence. However, due to its inaccessibility, the Ghurid rulers were, in the main, left to their own devices.

On the accession of Izz-al-Din Husayn as *amir* of Ghur in 493/1100, Ghurid allegiance to the Ghaznavids, which had prevailed in the previous two generations, was to change. In 501/1107–08 the Seljuk sultan Sanjar led an expedition into Ghur. What precipitated this move is unknown. However, it is more than likely that Ghurid banditry and incursions into and harassment of Seljuk territory had reached unacceptable levels. Sanjar captured Husayn and from this point Ghaznavid influence into the affairs of Ghur declined.[23] Juzjani tells us that every year Husayn despatched to the court of Sultan Sanjar

> *armour, coats of mail and other equipments and war material ... there is also a remarkably fine breed of dogs in Ghur so powerful ... that everyone is a match for a lion. A number of this breed of dogs with valuable collars ... Malik Izz-ud-Din Husain was in the habit of sending to the sultan Sanjar's presence.*[24]

Juzjani also makes the point, 'Malik 'Izz-ud-din was wont to keep on good terms and friendship with the sultans of Ghaznin.'[25] This was, if nothing else, expedient behaviour on the part of the Ghurid ruler. However, following the death of Sultan Mas'ud III 508/1115 the Ghaznavids came to feel the increasing

22 Juzjani, Minhaj- ud-Din, *Tabaqat-i-Nasiri* (Trans. H.G. Raverty) (Calcutta, 2010), vol. I, p. 310

23 *CHI*, vol. 5, p. 157

24 *TN*, tr. Raverty, vol. I, p. 337

25 Ibid., p. 337

pressure of the Seljuks. A succession struggle had erupted in Ghazna between the brothers Malik Arslan, sometimes referred to as Arslan Shah r. 509–11/1116–17 and Bahram Shah r. 511–52/1117–57.[26] Bahram Shah fled to Sanjar's court in Khurasan, which in turn precipitated the intervention of Sanjar in the dispute. Significantly, Sanjar's sister who was married to Mas'ud III was treated badly by Malik Arslan, even though she was probably his own mother. He then compounded this insult by imprisoning one of Sanjar's emissaries.[27] The Seljuk army prevailed in battle with Malik Arslan's forces on a plain outside Ghazna at the ground used for formal reviews of the Ghaznavid army. One of the Seljuk commanders, Taj-ad-Din Abu l-Fadl, neutralised the threat from the Ghaznavid elephant corps by personally demonstrating how to rip open the soft unarmoured underbelly of the animals with a dagger. The right wing of the Seljuk army defeated the corresponding Ghaznavid force opposite and resistance collapsed. What lay ahead of the victorious Seljuk army was the dazzling city of Ghazna. At the height of Ghaznavid power, particularly under Mahmud, his court had accquired legendary splendour. The riches amassed from his Indian raids and successes in the west were still on display in his palace long after his death and continued to form an integral part of the coveted Ghaznavid treasury. The Ghaznavid court had become a place of patronage for art, literature and science attracting the finest minds. Some of the most illustrious names in Persian poetry and astronomy had embellished Ghazna and included Ferdowsi, Farrukhi and Al-Biruni. It was in Ghazna that Ferdowsi's imagination took flight while writing parts of the Shahnameh – the greatest and one of the most philosophically profound of Persian poems. The Shahnameh would for centuries serve as a guide to kingship and the moral responsibilities that accompanied it, particularly justice and honour. The city had become a centre of culture and learning with one of the largest libraries in the Muslim world attracting scholars from Baghdad and Central Asia. Abundant almond, fig and apricot orchards surrounded the city and as in Samarkand, mulberry trees lined the main streets. These exotic fruits had become one of the chief exports of the region and thanks to Ghaznavid encouragement of trade they could be found in India and the markets of Baghdad. While the Ghaznavid Empire had shrunk in territory and influence, Ghazna as a city with its fabled riches was now within the grasp of the Seljuik sultan. When the Seljuk army entered plunder began almost immediately and continued unabated for days. The significant visible wealth on offer forced Sultan Sanjar to intervene and execute a number of his soldiery who had run

26 C.E. Bosworth (1977), p. 90

27 *CHI*, vol. 5, p. 158. See also *TN*, vol. I, tr. Raverty, p. 108.

amok and begun an orgy of destruction in the city.[28] Ghazna had never been taken since the arrival of Sebuktegin in the late ninth century and the spoils available were significant. This event was to presage the plundering of the city by the Ghurid sultan 'Ala' al-Din Hussein *jahan-suz* thirty-five years later.

Bahram Shah was subsequently installed on the throne and forced to pay an annual tribute of 250,000 dinars. The *khutba* in favour of the caliph Al-Mustazhir, the supreme Seljuk sultan Muhammad Tapar – until his death in 512/1118, Sanjar who became supreme Seljuk sultan at this juncture and fourthly Bahram Shah was to be announced at Friday midday prayers in the mosques. This emphasised Seljuk sovereignty and legitimacy to rule over the Ghaznavid territories. *Malik* Arslan managed to escape to Lahore from where, on Sanjar's departure with his army, he tried once more to regain the throne. He managed to reoccupy Ghazna but left within a month, realising that with only the forces he had recruited from the Ghaznavid Indian provinces he would have been unable to resist the might of the Seljuk army. He sought refuge possibly in the mountains of the province of Paktika and was later captured by a Seljuk commander.

Malik Arslan was purchased from him by Bahram Shah who had him strangled 512/September/October 1118.[29] His brother's recent actions had proved that he remained a significant threat. Bahram Shah would also have been concerned that if he allowed his brother to be taken captive to Sanjar in Khurasan, he might be used as a pawn in any future disputes that could arise between himself and the Seljuks.

He was to reign for forty years r. 511– 52/1117?–57 as a Seljuk vassal apart from a brief hiatus in 529–30/1135–6 when he renounced his allegiance. This short episode may have been precipitated by the erosion of Ghaznavid resources due to the annual tribute payable to Sanjar. This was despite the wealth accruing to the Ghaznavid exchequer from Bahram Shah's campaigns in northern India. The approach of the Seljuk army towards Ghazna in the winter of 530/1136 was enough to concentrate Bahram Shah's mind and he fled to his Indian provinces. He duly returned to Ghazna again as a Seljuk tributary later the same year.[30]

Notwithstanding the stability engendered by the lengthy reign of Bahram Shah Ghaznavid power was in decline and its territory was much reduced. The area now consisted, at most, of present-day eastern Afghanistan, the western Punjab, Sind and Baluchistan. The reign marked the final chapter of a dynasty

28 C.E. Bosworth (1977), pp. 96–7

29 Ibid., p. 98

30 Ibid., p 101. Bosworth mentions the battle of the Qatwan steppe in Transoxiana 536/1141 against the Qara-Khitai where troops from Ghur, Ghazna and Mandaran fought with Sanjar – further proof that the Ghurids and Ghaznavids were very much Seljuk vassals at this stage.

that had once been the dominant power of the eastern Islamic lands. The decline of the Ghaznavids paved the way for a dynamic new dynasty to emerge from the mountains of central Afghanistan. This new house had, under the rule of Husayn I b. Hasan, Abu'l-Muluk, Izz al-Din 493–540/1100–1146 of the Shansabani family, achieved primacy in Ghur in the first part of the twelfth century. They had begun to expand from the limitations of their mountain homeland into the more culturally sophisticated and economically advanced Persianate worlds of the Ghaznavids, Seljuks and Khwarazmshahs. The Ghurids now constituted a serious threat to Bahram Shah. In 542/1147 the Ghurids, under Suri b.Husayn I Sayf al-Din, *Malik al Jibal*, self-styled lord of the mountains r. 540–44/1146–9, had shown their ambition by seeking to involve themselves in the affairs of the city of Herat whose governor had rebelled against their mutual overlord Sultan Sanjar.[31] Herat was a culturally dynamic and wealthy city and a far cry from the towns and fortified places of Ghur. It is said to have had 12,000 shops, 6,000 bathhouses and 444,000 households.[32] While these figures must be exaggerated it was still a city of considerable importance. Milan and Venice, probably the largest contemporary Western European cities, had estimated populations of 125,000 each and Paris in the region of 50,000.[33]

In order for the Ghurids to consolidate any expansion outside their own territories they would have required access to more substantial manpower and military skills than were available from within Ghur itself. The Ghaznavids had recruited large numbers of Turkish military slaves, and free agents from among the Central Asian nomads and the Ghurids would do the same. These *ghulams* or *mamluks* came to form the core of these imperial armies. The rulers of Ghur amassed armies of these Turkish *ghulams* from Central Asia to provide heavy cavalry and horse archers to supplement their Khurasani troops and their Ghuri soldiers, who were, in the main, recognised as infantry from the mountains and not as horsemen. These Central Asian *ghulams* were renowned for their fighting abilities and for their rigorous adherence to Sunni orthodoxy. As a result of their *ghulam* heavy armies, the Ghurid conquerors are described by contemporary Indian chroniclers in Sanskrit as *turushka* or Turks and referred to as such by the Indian rulers they fought against.

It is worth remembering that the Seljuks arrived as an Islamised Turkic group and established themselves in Khurasan before moving into Iran and Iraq. However, it was the establishment of the Qara-Khitan Empire *c.* 483–614/

31 *CHI*, vol. 5, p. 160

32 Richard M. Eaton, *India in the Persianate Age 1000–1765* (London, 2019), p. 40 note 34

33 C. McEvedy, *The New Penguin Atlas of Medieval History* (London, 1992), p. 76

c. 1124–1218, known in China as the western Liao, that brought significant changes to the lands beyond River Oxus. The dynasty was founded by Yelu Dashi/ Emperor Dezong r. 1124–43. He led remnants of the Liao dynasty westwards, following the conquest of northern China and the establishment of the Jin dynasty of Jurchen descent. This migration was to have a notable effect on the stability and structure of the eastern Iranian world. It ultimately dislodged large numbers of nomads from Transoxiana, notably unconverted Ghuzz Turkmen, who flooded into Khurasan. They were to capture the Seljuk sultan Sanjar who had come to the aid of his Qarakhanid vassals and would subsequently sweep Seljuk power away.[34] This collapse created a political void into which the Ghurids and the Qara-Khitan *Gur-Khan*'s vassals, the Khwarazmshahs, were to flow.[35]

Given the potential areas of conflict, it was only a matter of time before Ghurid–Ghaznavid relations reached a nadir. Despite the Ghaznavid sultan Bahram Shah's attempts to impose his dynasty's historic overlordship on the Ghurid territories the Shansabanids had become a force to be reckoned with. They were now well on their way to becoming the most powerful political entity in the eastern Iranian lands on this frontier of the Islamic world. The Ghurids seem to have spent the first part of the twelfth century consolidating their power and fortifying the territory of Ghur. Throughout this period, the Ghurids bolstered their traditionally infantry-heavy armies with mercenary cavalry and Turkish *mamluks*.[36] These bold and strategic activities served to further consolidate their own position in Ghur and can be viewed as a reaction to the perceived threat from the Ghaznavids to their independence.[37] The denouement came when Qutb al-Din Muhammad b.Hussein the Ghurid, ruler of Firuzkuh, the fortress city he was in the process of constructing, having fallen out with his brothers for reasons unknown, retired to the court of Bahram Shah in Ghazna.[38] Qutub al-Din Muhammad was the latter's son-in-law so the choice

34 P. Jackson, *The Mongols and the Islamic World: From Conquest to Conversion* (New Haven and London, 2017), p. 54

35 Ibid., pp. 56–7

36 D.C. Thomas (2018), chap 4. Specifically, p. 106 fig. 4.1 and table 4.1; p. 111 fig. 4.7; p. 112 fig. 4.8. These tables relate to fortified structures. On p. 144: 'The extant data suggest that the Ghurid heartland appears to have been demilitarised after the Ghaznawid campaigns in the early 11th Century. As Ghaznawid influence over the region waned, the Ghurids took the opportunity to re-establish and expand their fortified sites, building a secure base from which to raid, and eventually overthrow their more powerful neighbour.'

37 Thomas (2018), p. 80

38 *TN*, vol. I, tr. Raverty, p. 339 note 7 gives a description of the territorial division among and districts of the various Shansabani chiefs/brothers – described as mighty monarchs by Juzjani

of destination was not as unusual as it might first appear.[39] The incident also highlights the continuing instability of Ghurid society at the time and the lack of any supreme sultan to exercise control over disparate elements. However, it is also possible that Bahram Shah may have invited Qutb al-Din Muhammad to try to cement relationships between the two families to counterbalance the power of Sultan Sanjar, who obviously posed a potential threat to the security of the Ghaznavid sultan.[40] After a short stay in Ghazna, for reasons that are not entirely clear, Bahram Shah had his Ghurid visitor poisoned. Ibn-al-Athir says that it was believed that Qutb al-Din Muhammad and his brother Saif al-Din Suri, who had accompanied him, and had managed to escape back to Ghur, had been using their residence in Ghazna as an opportunity to reconnoitre the city prior to launching an attack.[41,42] Juzjani states that 'on this account, enmity and hatred arose between the Mahmudi family and the family of Shansabi'.[43] It was from this point that the two dynasties embarked on a journey of irreconcilable conflict that was to lead to the extinction of the Ghaznavids.

What followed as a consequence was an increase in attacks on each other's territory with the Ghurids thirsting for revenge on behalf of their murdered brother. Saif al-Din Suri together with his brothers Baha' al-Din Sam of Sanga and 'Ala' al-Din Husain of Waziristan marched on

Ghazna defeating Bahram Shah and capturing the city. However, Bahram Shah managed to escape and fled first to a place called Kurram in the North West Frontier province of modern Pakistan and from there on to his Indian territories.[44] This was the first important military success for the Ghurids. Following this conquest, Saif al-Din Suri remained in Ghazna and took the title of sultan while appointing his brother Baha al-Din Sam as ruler of Ghur at Firuzkuh. The other younger brothers, together with the major portion of the Ghurid army, returned to their territories, leaving Suri in Ghazna with only his household troops. At around this time Baha-al-Din Sam died suddenly – he was the father of the two greatest Ghurid sultans Ghiyath al-Din and Mu'izz al-Din. Consequently, 'Ala' al-Din assumed the throne of Ghur.[45] Due to the small numbers of retainers at

39 Ibid., p. 340

40 Ibid., p. 347

41 C.E. Bosworth (1977), p. 113 and note 6 p. 181

42 *al-Kamil fi'l-Ta'rikh*, part 2, tr. Richards, p. 25

43 *TN*, vol. I, p. 340. The Mahmudi family being the Ghaznavids.

44 Bosworth (1977), p. 114 and note 7 p. 181. See also *TN*, vol. I, p. 439.

45 *TN*, vol. I, p. 348 note 2. Raverty 'died of inflammation of the brain' … (phrensy, according to some, a tumour or smallpox according to others).

his disposal, Sultan Suri was forced to rely on existing Ghaznavid officials and the garrison that had been captured when the city fell, not only in the city itself but throughout the Ghazna territory. He chose a local *sayyid,* Majd al-Din Musawi, as his vizier – a decision his new vizier would come to regret. But the mood in Ghazna was still, unsurprisingly, given the length of Ghaznavid tenure in the city, in favour of Bahram Shah and it seems no number of gifts and favours could change this.

As the deep snows set in and winter 543/1148/9 began in earnest, communication between Ghur and Ghazna became practically impossible. Driving blizzards and howling winds forced the sultan and citizens indoors. Suri was effectively trapped in the city. It was as difficult for him to retreat to Ghur as it was for him to receive reinforcements from there. In the meantime, the poor strategic situation that the Ghurid ruler now found himself in had not gone unnoticed by the populace. One night a horseman covering his face with his turban tail and braving the weather rode out in stealth. He manouvered his steed through knee-deep snow, navigating the deserted curling ravines and narrow mountain passes. The rider carried a letter to Bahram Shah. In it was written 'throughout the entire city and parts around, only a small number of persons have remained with Sultan Suri of the forces of Ghur, the whole of the remainder are servants of the Mahmudi dynasty'.[46] Bahram Shah for his part had not been idle and had been gathering an army in the Ghaznavid Indian territories of the upper Punjab. With this force under the command of the *Salar* Ali b'. Hussein. B. Alawi, the governor of the Ghaznavid territories in India, he marched via Kabul to Ghazna.[47]

Juzjani talks of a night attack, and that Suri was taken by surprise and forced to flee with his modest household hoping to reach the safety of Ghur.[48] Given the lack of support from the populace in Ghazna and the inclement weather, it is easy to see how Suri was caught unawares by Bahram Shah's approach.[49] Along with his vizier the *sayyid* Majd ad-Din they took the road to Ghur. The small force was not to get far before they were overtaken by Bahram Shah's cavalry who had been despatched in pursuit of the fugitives. They were cornered at a place called Sang-i-Surakh – perforated rock or stone. Raverty suggests it is the name of a pass north, north, west of the road from Ghazna and Kabul into

46 *TN*, vol. I, tr. Raverty, p. 440

47 C.E. Bosworth (1977), p. 114

48 *TN*, vol. I, p. 440

49 Ibid., p. 348 note 2: 'Bahram returned from Hind with a numerous army and several elephants ... Suri came out with 300 Ghuris and 1000 Ghuzz Turks ... but the Ghuzz deserted to Bahram.' This was not a unique event and illustrates the unreliability of tribal *ghulams*.

Ghur.[50] Suri and his companions fought off their pursuers as long as they could but the weight of numbers forced them to dismount to fight on foot halfway up the mountain where horses could not easily follow. The result was predictable and, with their quivers empty, the survivors were taken prisoner.[51] When Suri and his vizier reached the gates of the city of Ghazna they were placed on camels according to Juzjani and the less salubrious transport of an emaciated bullock or asses by others.[52] Exposed to abuse and humiliation from the populace, they were led through the city until they reached the Pul-i-Tak, the city's one arched bridge where they were crucified and their bodies then hanged above the river.[53] Suri's head was later sent to Bahram Shah's overlord, the Seljuk sultan Sanjar in Ray. Juzjani, as the Ghurid relation and propagandist, bemoans the injustice and barbarous and cruel end of Sultan Suri. Raverty wryly notes that this sort of conduct is of course condoned if it is done by Ghurids to others and provides a list of examples of Ghurid brutality, untrustworthiness and general poor behaviour.[54]

When the news of his brother's horrific death and the insults and slurs he had been subjected to reached 'Ala' al-Din, he decided to unleash an assault on Ghazna, which transformed the Ghaznavid imperial capital to a blackened husk. The narrative, timescale and sequence of these events now becomes challenging. Raverty notes that 'of all the persons mentioned in Oriental history, greater discrepancy occurs with 'Ala'-al-Din, *Jahan-suz's* name and proceedings, probably, than regarding any other man.'[55] However, the main point to bear in mind is that 'Ala'-al-Din's vengeance, for the deaths of his brothers, Sultan Suri and the Malik al-Jibal, would reasonably have been swift. Professor Bosworth provides the most logical interpretation of the timeframe and reconciles Raverty's essentially accurate conclusion with his own deliberations on Juzjani and other sources, including Ibn al-Athir. The date for the attack on Ghazna should be placed at the end of 544 or beginning of 545/1150.[56,57] Sultan 'Ala' al-Din had ascended the Ghurid throne following the sudden death of his brother Baha

50 Ibid., p. 441 note 7

51 Bosworth (1977), p. 114. Mentions that Bahram Shah and his sons, Sama' ad-Daula Mas'ud, Mu'izz ad-Daula Khusrau and Mu'in ad-Daula Shahanshah, were all present and gives the date of the battle as 2 Muharram 542/12 May 1149. Juzjaini provides a list of Bahram Shah's sons; see *TN*, vol. I, p. 111.

52 *TN*, vol. I, p. 441 note 9

53 *al-Kamil fi'l –Ta'rikh*, part 2, tr. Richards, p. 25

54 *TN*, vol. I,tr. Raverty, p. 445 and note 2

55 Ibid., p. 347 note 2

56 Bosworth (1977), pp. 115–16

57 *TN*, vol. I, p. 347 note 2

al-Din Sam who had been preparing to march against Ghazna. 'Ala' al-Din continued these preparations recruiting soldiers from the Ghurid heartlands and Gharjistan an area northeast of Herat. 'Ala' al-Din had marched as far as Zamindawar when Bahram Shah's envoys reached him. They delivered a message from their sultan, 'return again to Ghur and in thy ancestral possession remain in quietness, for thou will not be able to resist my forces for I bring elephants'.[58] Bosworth mentions two hundred of these animals.[59] The days of the Ghaznavids being able to threaten the Ghurids into returning to their homeland and passivity were firmly in the past. The composition of Bahram Shah's army also included contingents from his Indian princely vassals later described by and attributed to 'Ala' al-Din in verse: 'The support of my foe although they were all Rae's and Ranahs, I reduced, with my mace to atoms, both the Rae's and Ranah's head(s).'[60] In response to the envoys, 'Ala' al-Din replied, 'if thou bringest elephants, I will bring the Kharmil; but God knows … thou has put my brothers to death and I have not slain any person belonging to thee…'[61]

With that, the envoys returned, and the armies were readied for battle at or near a place called Tiginabad, most likely a place close to Kandahar.[62] 'Ala' al-Din called for his two champions, Kharmil-i-Sam Husain and Kharmil-i-Sam Banji, and explained that they were each tasked with bringing down an elephant. They kissed the ground before the sultan and returned to their positions. The battle consisted of three separate engagements and began with the elephants of Bahram Shah mounting a charge. Meanwhile, the two Ghurid *pahlawan* had dismounted, tied up the skirts of their mail coats, to give them more mobility, and prepared to meet the elephants. They each chose an animal and moving beneath them proceeded to slash at the unarmoured belly with their daggers disembowelling them. Kharmil-i-Sam Banji remained under his elephant, which collapsed on top of him, killing them both. Kharmil-i-Sam Husain managed to immobilise his target and escaped to remount his horse. 'Ala' al-Din had ordered that a crimson satin surcoat be produced to cover his armour to hide any blood should he be seriously wounded. This was to disguise any adverse situation that might arise and affect the morale of his troops. The second phase involved the Ghurid infantry and their historic mode of fighting. The Ghurids, due, in part,

58 Ibid., p. 350

59 C.E. Bosworth (1977), p. 116

60 *TN*, vol. I, p. 357

61 Ibid., p. 350

62 Bosworth (1977), p. 149

to the mountainous terrain of their homeland, had evolved an effective method of fighting on foot. By taking and folding the hide of a buffalo or bullock and then stuffing this, probably with straw or hay, they could use it to form a screen, and, by placing this on their shoulders, cover themselves from head to toe. This defence formed, in close order, an impenetrable barrier, and due to the filling, was impervious to arrows and other projectiles. Juzjani states 'and when they close their ranks, they appear like unto a wall and no missile or arms can take any effect on it, on account of the quantity of cotton with which it is stuffed'.[63] This was the *karwah*. Raverty goes on to explain that the hide defences could also be manoeuvred and used in front of advancing troops as protection from arrows.[64]

The next move came from Daulat Shah, one of Bahram Shah's sons, who, with a troop of cavalry supported by a single elephant, charged the Ghurid infantry. As only a single elephant is mentioned in the text it could be that the plan was to use the force of the charging elephant to break up the *karwahs*.[65] In response, the Ghurid sultan ordered his infantry to open their defences and allow the Ghaznavid prince and his division to pass through. Having done this, they promptly closed ranks, leaving the enemy unit enveloped. Daulat Shah, the horsemen and the elephant, pressed from every side, were slaughtered. Having witnessed the destruction of Daulat's contingent Bahram Shah's army broke and fled. 'Ala' al-Din pursued Bahram Shah to a nearby place called Josh-i-Ab-i-Garm – the jet of hot water, where the latter turned to face his pursuer. Here, the Ghaznavids were defeated for a second time and fled to the walls of Ghazna itself, with the Ghurids still in hot pursuit. With the remnants of his Indian army, the garrison of his capital city and a substantial levy of local infantry Bahram Shah prepared to fight 'Ala' al-Din for the third time.[66] A further conclusive defeat forced Bahram Shah to abandon his capital and flee to his Indian possessions.

There now followed the terrible ordeal of the city of Ghazna, which earned 'Ala'-al-Din Husayn his sobriquet of *jahan-suz* – 'world incendiary'. This was vandalism and destruction on an unprecedented scale and Juzjani, despite his Ghurid allegiances, conveys the ensuing brutality in his description of the week-long assault of Ghazna.

63 *TN*, vol. I, tr. Raverty, p. 352. Juzjani mentions cotton but as Raverty says in his footnote hay or straw were probably more likely materials due to cost.

64 Ibid., p. 352 and note 2. It seems the *karwah* could be used by an individual and when deployed as a unit provided similar protection to that offered to Roman legionaries by their *testudo*. See also *CHI*, vol. IV, chapter 7 'Iran under the Buyids', pp. 251–2 – the role of Dailamite infantry and their use of large shields to advance in close formation.

65 Ibid., p. 353

66 Ibid.

> *that during these seven days, the air from the blackness of the smoke continued as black as night; and those nights from flames raging in the burning city, were lighted up as light of day. During these seven days likewise rapine, plunder, and, massacre were carried out with the utmost pertinacity vindictiveness. All men that were found were killed and the women and children were made captive.*[67]

The revenge meted out on the city by 'Ala'-al-Din for the deaths of his brothers at the hands of the Ghaznavids was of brutal and extensive proportions; an estimated 60,000 souls perished.[68] The Ghurid sultan was not just content with the destruction of the city and the slaughter and captivity of its citizens; he wanted to eradicate any evidence of the Ghaznavids, even the dead. The tombs of the sultans, with the exception of Mahmud, Ma'sud and Ibrahim, were broken into and the bonesexhumed and burned. Much of the splendour of the city, its *madrasas,* mosques and palaces, were destroyed forever. A city enlarged and embellished by a dynasty for almost two centuries with riches and spoils garnered from their campaigns into the Indian subcontinent and the West lay in ruins. Ghazna was also renowned as a literary capital from the days of the earliest sultans where scholarship was encouraged and great libraries had flourished. These collections had come to the city from conquests in Khurasan, Khwarazm and further afield in western Iran, sometimes with the scholars who had collected and nurtured them. Arguably the greatest loss was that of Ibn Sina – the Avicenna of western medieval scholarship – acquired with the capture of Isfahan in 425/1034.[69] This great centre of eastern Isalmic culture for more than one hundred and fifty years would never recover its former glory. Babur, the founder of the Mughal Empire, travelling through Ghazna in 910/1504–5, could not understand how such an unimpressive place could once have been the renowned capital of a great power.[70]

During this destruction 'Ala' al-din had been 'carousing within the palaces of the sultans of Ghaznin', presumably not the ones who were being torched.[71] He had ordered that the tombs of his brothers, Sultan Suri and the Qutb al-Din Muhammad, were to be opened and plans made to bear the two corpses back to Ghur while he prepared to place the army in mourning. On the eighth night

67 Ibid.

68 C.E. Bosworth (1977), p. 117

69 Ibid., p. 117 and note 20 p. 182

70 Ibid., p. 131

71 *TN*, vol. I, tr. Raverty, p. 354

'Ala' al-Din was still full of vigour celebrating his victory amidst the increasingly desolate city. He produced eulogistic verses to himself and directed his minstrels to sing them: 'The world knoweth that I of the universe am king … For their own sakes I have granted them their lives, that the granting of their lives may of mine be the bond.'[72] It is unlikely that the surviving Ghaznavid population would have recognised this benevolence after the slaughter of almost all their fellow citizens. Having spent a further seven days in mourning, the coffins of his brothers placed on biers and borne back to Ghur where they were interred among their ancestors. On the return journey the Ghurid army passed through the city of Bust where palaces, madrasas, mosques and other buildings with Ghaznavid connections were torched and similar retribution was delivered throughout Ghaznavid territory on their route to Ghur.[73] The army also brought with them a large number of prisoners from Ghazna, among them *sayyids* who had been particularly involved in the deaths of the two Ghurid leaders.[74] 'Ala' al-Din was not finished with his mission of retribution. Prior to his departure from Ghazna a chorus of female entertainers, who had sung satirical songs, had been suffocated in a *hammam* for their involvement in the executions and those *sayyids* most closely connected with the deaths of Suri and his vizier had been thrown off the tops of the nearest peaks.[75] The site of the execution itself was erased.[76] The remainder of the unfortunate citizenry destined to be taken to Ghur had been forced to fill bags of earth, which were placed on their backs. When these prisoners arrived at the incomplete city of Firuzkuh they were killed, and their blood was mixed with the earth from Ghazna to form mortar for towers.[77] 'Ala' al-Din had avenged his brothers.

'Ala' al-Din's treatment of Ghazna, Bust and Lashkari Bazar, the Ghaznavid winter capital, should not be considered as normal behaviour hence the sobriquet *jahan-suz* and his reputation in the eastern Islamic world at the time. The destruction and brutality were a result of a bloody feud between Ghurid and Ghaznavid rulers. As a rule, nomadic and urban societies were prepared

72 Ibid.

73 Ibid., p. 355. Raverty mentions the whole district of Zamindawar. Juzjani says, '[O]n reaching the city of Bust he entirely destroyed the palaces and other edifices of the Mamudi dynasty, the like of which were not found in the regions of the world.'

74 *Sayyid* meaning lord or master and used as an honorific recognising descent from the prophet Muhammad

75 *al-Kamil fi'l-Ta'rikh*, part 2, tr. Richards, p. 47. *Sayyids* were those recognised as descendants of Hasan ibn Ali and Husayn Ibn Ali, sons of Muhammad's daughter Fatima.

76 C.E. Bosworth (1977), p. 117

77 *TN*, vol. I, tr. Raverty, p. 356. Juzjani says just *Sayyids* but more likely others were deported to work on the uncompleted city. Bosworth also specifically mentions Alids.

to coexist in a more pragmatic manner. However, there were exceptions, most notably the activities of the Ghuzz in Khurasan in the mid-twelfth century and those of the Mongols in the early thirteenth.[78]

'Ala' al-Din now celebrated and enjoyed his victory in the secure confines of Firuzkuh. He had proved emphatically that he was no longer just the inconsequential ruler of a remote, peripheral and unknown region. He and his Ghurid cohorts had become the ascendant power in the eastern Islamic lands. The Ghaznavids had been thoroughly defeated and driven again from their ancestral capital, and their light was waning. This success encouraged the Ghurid leader to assume the title of sultan and with it the ceremonial parasol or *chatr* as a sign of his authority.[79] Despite this confidence the 'Ala'-al-Din remained wary of his adversaries. He did not take up residence in Ghazna, perhaps unsurprising given the destruction he had wrought there. Nor did he appoint a close family member to rule in the city as was to later become normal Ghurid practice; ultimately, the supreme Ghurid sultan would rule from Firuzkuh with lower ranking rulers in Bamiyan and Ghazna. Instead, he appointed a Turkish *ghulam* as governor. He may have felt that there was still the possibility of another Ghaznavid resurgence; after all they had raised a significant army from their Indian possessions before, and given time, might do so again. The fate of his brother Sultan Saif al-Din Suri remained a warning, too. He may also have felt that it was expedient to remain in the mountain fastness of Ghur to await the reaction of the Seljuk sultan Sanjar who was more than capable of responding to the unseating of his Ghaznavid subordinate. 'Ala' al-Din's insecurity did not just manifest itself in reaction to external threats. There was also a move closer to home against members of his own family. He took the opportunity to imprison his two nephews Ghiyath al-Din and Mu'izz al-Din in a fortress in Waziristan. Juzjani makes the point that 'an allowance was fixed for their support'.[80] However munificent these actions of their uncle were portrayed this was a suboptimal situation for the two young Ghurid princes to find themselves in and they could be disposed of on a whim.

Even if he harboured initial reservations 'Ala'-al-Din soon began to overtly express his independence in his exchanges with the Seljuk sultan. He cancelled the annual tribute the Ghurid rulers were bound to provide to Sanjar in his capacity as

78 D.C. Thomas (2018), p. 24

79 C.E. Bosworth (1977), p. 118 and note 22. Bosworth tells us that he was following Seljuk practice. Ibn al-Athir describes the title more precisely in the form of *as-Sultan al-Mu'azzam* and the use of the *chatr* or ceremonial parasol.

80 *TN*, vol. I, p. 357. Raverty also comments in note 9 that the location was a fortress that had been used as a prison by the Ghaznavid sultans. The location also illustrates how far Ghurid control now extended over the former Ghaznavid territories.

overlord of the rulers of Ghazna. He then sought to take advantage of the disloyalty of a former Seljuk official, Ali Chatri, and set out with the aim of taking the city of Herat.[81] Sanjar, who had recently received the head of Saif al-Din Suri, 'Ala' al-Din's executed brother, would have had few qualms about distributing swift retribution to another troublesome Ghurid, as paramount ruler of both the Ghaznavids and the Ghurids. He quickly gathered a large army and marched for Ghur. The two forces met near the town of Nab between Firuzkuh and Herat in the Hari Rud valley in 547/1152. The battlefield was an extensive plain named Sih-goshah-i-Nab. The day before the battle the Ghurid sultan had managed to flood the area in the rear of his forces, turning it into a morass. This was probably done to discourage anyone from fleeing during the engagement. However, his plans were undone when 6,000 Ghuzz nomads decided to swap sides, and join their Turk, Ghuzz and Khalaj brethren serving in the Seljukid army, bringing about 'Ala' al-Din's swift defeat.[82] This event not only highlights the potential unreliability of multi-ethnic armies but also the modest number of troops typically assembled on the battlefield at the time.[83] 'Ala' al-Din and his nephew Muhammad Shams al-Din, son of his elder brother Fakhr al-Din Mas'ud, the ruler of Bamiyan, were taken prisoner along with Ali Chatri who was put to death on the spot. The nephew seems to have fallen into the hands of Barankash, the *sipah- salar* of the Seljuk force. A ransom of 50,000 dinars was demanded for the Ghurid prince. This was raised in Bamiyan and paid to Barankash and Muhammad Shams al-Din was set free.[84] 'Ala' al-Din seems to have remained a captive for two years until a considerable sum in ransom had been raised and paid over to the Seljuk sultan.[85]

In the meantime, Bahram Shah returned to Ghazna following news of 'Ala' al-Din's defeat and capture at Nab. What resistance he met when he arrived, if any, we do not know. He seems to have died in early 552/1157 having reigned for around forty years, the second longest of the Ghaznavid dynasty. He was succeeded by his son, Khusrau Shah. 'Ala' al-Din, for his part, having returned to Ghur following his release discovered that moves had been made by various interested parties to replace him on the throne of Firuzkuh. The most notable candidate was his great nephew *Malik* Nasir al-Din Husayn whose support base centred on the inhabitants of the region of Kashi. Upon 'Ala' al-Din's approach,

81 *TN*, vol. I, tr. Raverty, p. 358 note 3. Ali Chatri held Herat on behalf of Sanjar and seems to have become disaffected with his overlord for reasons unknown.

82 Ibid., p. 359

83 D.C. Thomas (2018), p. 81

84 *TN*, vol. I, p. 358 note 3. This also gives an idea of the wealth at the disposal of the Bamiyan rulers.

85 C.E. Bosworth (1977), p. 119

the usurper is said to have been smothered by four of his concubines, each holding the corner of a pillow, in a plot concocted by 'Ala' al-Din loyalists.[86] The Ghurid polity was as unstable as ever and 'Ala' al-din spent much of the remainder of his reign securing his rule and re-establishing Shansabani primacy. The territory of Kashi with its numerous fortified villages, more than a thousand according to Juzjani, was a particularly recalcitrant area and gives an idea of the heavy militarisation of Ghur.[87] Having brought the mountainous regions of Ghur under his control 'Ala'-al-Din spent the rest of his rule conquering Bamiyan, Tukharistan and the districts of Zamindawar, Jarum and Bust. In eastern Khurasan he seized the fortress of Tulak in the mountains near Herat. Consolidating his control and the various conquests consumed six years.[88]

If matters were testing for the Ghurid sultan during this time the situation of his erstwhile suzerain the Seljuk sultan Sanjar was incomparably worse. During the years 547–52/1152–7 the Great Seljuk Empire in both the east and west began to disintegrate. In Khurasan and the Seljuk eastern territories the invasion and uprisings of Ghuzz tribesmen displaced from Transoxiana by the Qara-Khitai, combined with Seljuk inability to manage the incursions of these nomads, led to outright revolt. Sanjar was defeated and captured while coming to the aid of the city of Balkh with his army. The Ghuzz then moved on and sacked Merv with Sanjar in tow as their prisoner, which he was to remain for three years. During this time, he was often caged to further humiliate and dishonour him, while the nomads continued to ravage Khurasan.[89] Merv was a major Central Asian culturally Iranian city of great antiquity. Omar Khayyam the great polymath who achieved breakthroughs in the understanding of modern cubic theories had spent considerable time studying and writing there. A place renowned for its magnificent libraries and calm learning was now subjected to bloodletting and chaos by marauding Turkic tribesmen. Sanjar was finally released but died shortly afterwards in 552/April 1157. He was buried in the beautiful dun coloured mausoleum with its turquoise dome gleaming under the Khurasan sun that he had constructed for himself and that stands in Merv to this day.[90]

86 *TN*, vol. I, tr. Raverty, p. 365

87 Ibid., p. 362

88 Ibid., p. 362. 'Ala' al-Din was released in 550/1154 and died in 556/1161.

89 Sanjar's captivity brings to mind Tamerlane's treatment of the Ottoman sultan Bayezid I following the battle of Ankara in 1402 and Marlowe's references to this episode in his *Tamburlaine*

90 Peacock (2015), pp. 107–9 and the poem by Sanjar's court poet Anwari, 'The Tears of Khurasan'. 'O morning breeze if you pass by Samarqand, Bring the letter of the people of Khurasan to the [Qarakhanid] Khagan; A letter whose bodily grief and affliction of soul, A letter whose end is heartbreak and sorrow…'

For 'Ala' al-Din and the Ghurids their defeat and discomfiture of the Ghaznavids to the south and east and the collapse of Seljuk power in Khurasan to the west served to create a power vacuum – a situation that was to prove ripe for exploitation by the rulers of the mountain fastness of Ghur. 'Ala' al-Din continued to apply pressure on Khusrau Shah in the form of renewed Ghurid attacks and demands for territory. There is some indication that Khusrau Shah may have decided or been forced by renewed Ghurid incursions, and their control of Zamindawar, Bust and southeastern Afghanistan, to retreat to his possessions in the Punjab. Perhaps he hoped to return to Ghazna at a more opportune time – now that he was unable to call on a Seljuk overlord for assistance.[91] He died in 555/July 1160 and was succeeded by his son Khusrau Malik.[92]

In the meantime, 'Ala' al-Din continued to consolidate his position on the throne of Ghur. One interesting footnote to the end of his reign, according to and frowned upon by Juzjani, is his accommodation of Shi'i missionaries; 'he treated them with great reverence', and welcomed them after they had been despatched by the Nizari Isma'ilis (perhaps better known as the Assassins) from their stronghold of Alamut in the mountains of northern Iran.[93] Given *Jahan-suz*'s vicious treatment of the Alids associated with the deaths of his brothers in Ghazna, it seems a strange *volte face* to the Sunni orthodoxy espoused by the Ghurid rulers. Perhaps there was an element of flattery involved or a genuine reverence for Ali, the Prophet's cousin and son-in-law whom the Shi'i revered, and all Muslims respected. On the other side, perhaps the geographical inaccessibility of Ghur attracted the ruler of Alamut, Muhamad ibn Kiya Buzurg-Ummid r. 531–55/1138–62, and its historic instability persuaded him that the region was ripe for proselytising and conversion. Any Isma'ili religious ascendancy was not to last long. 'Ala' al-Din died in (556/1161) and he was succeeded as sultan by his son Saif al- Din Muhammad r. 556–8/1161–3. The new ruler put the emissaries from Alamut to the sword along with their followers and orthodoxy was restored. He also ordered the release of his two cousins, Ghiyath al-Din and Mu'izz al-Din, who had been imprisoned by his father in the fortress of Waziristan, and who were destined to oversee the apogee of Ghurid fortunes. Juzjani goes on to call the young Ghurid sultan Saif al-Din 'a youthful monarch of excellent disposition'. The following events prove that he was anything but.[94] One day the sultan was in his pavilion practising archery with his *amirs, maliks*

91 Bosworth (1977), p. 122

92 Ibid., p. 123

93 *TN*, vol. I, tr. Raverty, p. 363

94 *TN*, vol. I, tr. Raverty, pp. 366–7

of Ghur and other members of his household. The *Sipah-Salar* – commander of the army – War-Mesh, a powerful representative of the rival Shisani family, was wearing bejewelled gauntlets.[95] These had been given to him by the previous sultan, the current ruler's father, from his personal treasury. Given their origin Saif al-Din decided that they were his property. He ordered War-Mesh to run and collect his arrow from the butt. The *Sipah-Salar* duly turned and ran to retrieve the sultan's arrow, at which point his lord and master fitted a broad steel-headed arrow in the shape of a shovel to his bow and drew it to its maximum. He released the arrow, which hit the unfortunate *amir* and passed straight through him, flights and all, killing him instantly. This incident would not have helped Ghurid internal political stability. A fractious environment fuelled by the requirement for vengeance characterised twelfth-century Ghur. Having consolidated his control of the Ghurid territories Saif al-Din set out on a campaign against the Ghuzz. He had reached Marv al-Rudh on Murghab River in Gharchistan and later joined battle with the nomads beyond the town of Dajzak. During the engagement the Ghurid champion Abu-I-Abbas, brother of War-Mesh, came up behind the sultan and thrust his spear into his side, unhorsing him, saying as he did so 'men are not killed with their faces to the butt, as thou didst kill my brother, otherwise they {themselves} get killed in a place such as this'.[96] The Ghurid troops were subsequently defeated and abandoned the field, leaving the mortally wounded sultan behind. He was ultimately dispatched by a Ghuzz tribesman in the process of cutting off the ruler's rich garments with a knife.

Coronation of the Nephew

Ghiyath al-Din (558–99/1163–1203), who was to prove himself the most able and successful Ghurid ruler, was elected by the Ghurid *amirs* and *maliks* and the army as sultan. He would take his minor dynasty to pre-eminence in the Islamic east. On his release from prison, he had taken up residence at the court in Firuzkuh and had accompanied his cousin on the campaign against the Ghuzz to the north of Murghab River. He seems, at this juncture, to have had very little in the way of retainers and resources at his disposal, and relied heavily on

95 Given that they were practising archery, more likely they were bracelets or possibly cuffs of gold studded with jewels

96 Ibid., p. 367

the goodwill of individuals who had served his late father Baha al-Din Sam and the benevolence of his mother, the daughter of Malik Badr-al-din Kidani, and her Shansabani relations.[97] Despite his election to the throne by the army in the field, there was always the chance in Ghurid society that a rival would contest a succession – either through declaring dynastic seniority or simply because they thought they could. In this case Ghiyath al-Din's uncle, Fakhr al-Din (r.540–58/1145–63), the ruler of the Bamiyan branch of the Shansabanids, threw his hat into the ring. Shortly after Ghiyath al-Din's succession his brother Mu'izz al-Din, who had taken residence at their uncle's court in Bamiyan, joined his brother at Firuzkuh and was installed as *Sar-i-Jandar* – chief armour bearer. He was also given charge of the district of Istiah and Kajuran, a small area in a range of hills between Herat and Ghazna.

As opposition to Ghiyath al-Din's election to the throne of Firuzkuh grew so internal Shansabanid rivalries came to the fore. Furthermore, latent disputes with the Shisani resurfaced. Unsurprisingly, some of the opposition had gathered around the influential and powerful *Sipah-Salar* Abu-l-Abbas. The brothers resolved to deal with this problem. As we have seen, revenge and vendettas loomed large in the fractious environment of Ghur. They decided to summon Abu-l-Abbas to an audience, having taken the decision to have him assassinated and delegated a Turkish *ghulam* to carry out the deed. The Ghurid *amir* duly appeared before the sultan to do homage and Mu'izz al-Din acknowledged him by raising his hand to his headdress in greeting. This was the signal to the executioner to strike. Giyath al-Din in the meantime had engaged Abu-l-Abbas in conversation. The *ghulam* promptly beheaded the *amir*.[98] Having rid themselves of one rival the problem of their uncle remained. Fakhr al-Din had not been idle in his plans to acquire the throne of Firuzkuh and had sought assistance from Qumach, the ruler of Balkh, and Yildiz, the governor of Herat, both appointees of the last Seljuk sultan Sanjar. The arrangement seems to have been that Fakhr al-Din would retain all the captured Ghurid territories and the other two rulers would be given a free rein in any conquests of territory in Khurasan. The forces of Bamiyan, Balkh and Herat now converged on Firuzkuh. Fakhr al-Din and his army set out first followed by the troops from Balkh, which took a route through upper Gharchistan and up the valley of the Murghab River. Yildiz for his part followed the Hari Rud, hoping to defeat Ghiyath al-Din's army himself and reach Firuzkuh first. The two forces meet at Ragh-i-Zar, a plain between Herat and Firuzkuh. The battle began when two Ghurid *amirs* presented themselves, dismounted, and bowing before

97 Ibid.

98 *TN*, vol. I, tr. Raverty, p. 371. Raverty uses this incident as another example of Ghurid perfidy.

the sultan, said 'we two your servants will disperse the army of Herat'.[99] This incident seems to have shades of the Kharmils and the elephants in the battle with Bahram Shah at Tiginabad. The two Ghurid champions remounted and charged towards the ranks of the Herati army demanding they point out Yildiz. 'We seek Yal-duz,' they cried. His troops indicated to where the governor was sitting under his canopy and, 'like hungry lions and rampant elephants', they attacked, striking him with their swords and unhorsing him. With this show of bravado the opposing army took flight and the brothers turned their attention to the other two armies. They despatched a force of several thousand horses, according to Juzjani, who surprised Qumach's troops, beheaded Qumach and returned with his standard and head. Ghiyath al-Din had the head placed in a bag and entrusted to a horseman with the instruction to bring it to their uncle Fakhr al-Din.[100] With this unsubtle gesture clarifying his likely fate should he continue in his rebellion, Fakhr al-Din retired to Bamiyan having probably decided that it was not worth risking everything for the sake of a throne that at this juncture was not as attractive as the position he currently held. He died shortly afterwards and was succeeded in Bamiyan by his son Shams al-Din 558–588/1163–92. In the meantime, Ghiyath al-Din secured his position in Ghur. Another of Sanjar's former *ghulams*, Baha al-Din Tughril, installed himself in Herat, which for the moment remained outside the Ghurid orbit.

The Ghurid sultan now began to assert his authority in the outlying areas of Afghanistan, including Garchistan, Guzganan, Zamindawar and Badghis.[101] Ghazna itself had fallen into the hands of a band of Ghuzz tribesmen in 552/1157. Until the capture of the cities of Ghazna and Herat and the area around Balkh, any Ghurid expansion southeast towards India or west into Khurasan and north into Transoxiana was not viable. The Ghuzz revolt, which had begun in Balkh in 546/1152 and permanently destroyed Seljuk rule in Khurasan, left a political vacuum that was fought over by Khwarazmians, Ghurids, the Qara-khitai and the Ghuzz. However, the Ghuzz, despite their successes, were unable to consolidate their position and establish an enduring territorial entity. This was partly due to their lack of political sophistication and in particular not having a ruling family, unlike the Seljuks. A royal dynasty could act as a focus for loyalty among the essentially nomadic Turkmen and was an institution around which a nascent state might coalesce.[102] Ultimately, a former *mamluk* of Sanjar's

99 Ibid., p. 372

100 Ibid., p. 373

101 Ibid., p. 374

102 Peacock (2015), pp. 122–3

Mu'ayyid al-Din Ai Aba d.569/1174drove the Ghuzz from the main towns in Khurasan. These actions served to scatter various Ghuzz bands eastwards, one of which set themselves up in Ghazna.[103,104] When exactly they established themselves there is difficult to discern. According to Professor Bosworth it was early in Khusrau Malik's reign r. 555–82/1160/86 and the duration of their occupation was between twelve years according to Juzjani and fifteen as stated by Ibn al-Athir.[105] It became increasingly clear that for the Ghurids to expand towards the Ghaznavid Indian territories and beyond they needed to capture Ghazna. This they accomplished in 569/1173–4. Sultan Ghiyath al-Din and his brother Mu'izz al-Din prepared to invest the city with a large army drawn from various Ghurid territories.[106] Juzjani states that the Ghuzz '*Amirs*' were now unable to take on the Ghurids in the field, illustrating the strength of the forces now at the disposal of the Ghurid sultan. However, the Ghurid army initially suffered a setback in their attempts to take Ghazna, due to the strength of various protective fortifications erected by the Ghuzz. Ghiyath al-Din seems to have left the engagement presumably to gather reinforcements, which must have been stationed nearby. The Ghuzz in the meantime managed to capture the Ghurid royal standard and returned within the walls of Ghazna pursued by the left and right wings of the Ghurid army who assumed that the standard was still in Ghurid hands. The sultan returned, and the balance now tipped in favour of the Ghurid assailants. The Ghuzz were slaughtered and the city fell to Ghiyath al-Din who, subsequently, placed his brother on the throne of Ghazna and raised him to the title of sultan.[107] Herat also fell temporarily to the Ghurids in 569/70–1174/5 and two years later Fushanj, modern Zinda Jan on Hari River, now part of the modern city of Herat. Following the acquisition of the last two places the *maliks* of Nimruz, Sistan and Kirman submitted to Ghiyath al-Din.[108] These areas were to prove crucial to the Ghurid sultan as it ensured him of support and nominal

103 C.E. Bosworth (1977), p. 124

104 *CHI*, vol. 5, pp. 155–7

105 Bosworth (1977), p. 125

106 *al-Kamil fi'l-Ta'rikh*, part 2, tr. Richards, p. 49. Ibn al-Athir mentions a mighty army, 'which force contained sorts of Ghur, Khalaj and Khurasanians'. The Khalaj originated from the area of Bust and Zamindawar.

107 *TN*, vol. I, tr. Raverty, pp. 376–7. See also p. 449 notes 8 and 9. Bosworth (1977), p. 125 states that it was in the following year 570/1174–5, after Mu'izz al-Din's capture of Gardez, a strategic fortress in the Suleiman Mountains east of Ghazna and south of Kabul, that he was appointed sultan in Ghazna under Ghiyath al-Din's supreme overlordship. Today the city is the capital of the modern Paktia province of Afghanistan.

108 Ibid., p. 378

control of areas to the south and west as far as the Arabian Sea and the straits of Hormuz. The *amir* of Sistan Taj al-Din Harb b. Muhammad sent troops in a number of instances to serve in Ghurid armies, and the Ghuzz *maliks* in Kirman sent envoys to Firuzkuh.[109] No less important were the addition of territories to the north of Ghur: Talaqan, Andkhud, Faryab and Marv-al-Rudh. Here, the *khutba* in the mosques was read in the name of Ghiyath al-Din and his name now adorned the coinage.[110] The latter districts were dependent on the cities of Herat and Balkh and consolidated Ghurid control of lands to the north of their heartland while simultaneously facilitating access to Khurasan and Transoxiana. The routes to the north and west had been brought into the Ghurid sphere of influence by the Shansabanid rulers in Bamiyan. Earlier Fakhr al-Din had extended his rule as far as the Amu Darya and east to Badakhshan, whose mines were famous, in the ancient world as a source of Lapiz Lazuli, and Shagnan. His son Shams al-Din, with the encouragement of Ghiyath al-Din, added the whole of Tukharistan, the city of Balkh and the provinces of Chaghaniyan and Waksh.[111]

These territorial additions not only provided increased grazing territory and mineral wealth but also put the Ghurid dynasty in a strong position to intervene west into Khurasan, south into the Punjab and then India and north and east into Transoxiana. The latter region also provided the opportunity to take advantage of the trade routes of Central Asia, via Samarkand and Kashgar, emanating ultimately from the southern Song Empire in China.[112] The Ghurids were now poised under the leadership of Ghiyath al-Din to break out of Ghur and establish hegemony across eastern Iranian lands and northern India.

109 *CHI*, vol. 5, p. 163, p. 174. The last Seljuk ruler of Kirman, Muhammad Shah 579–82/1183–6, such was the upheaval caused by Ghuzz incursions into the region, abandoned any hope of its recovery. He ultimately took up service with the Ghurid sultan. See also Peacock (2015), pp. 121–2, the Kirman Seljuk ruler's surrender to the Ghuzz.

110 *TN*, vol. I, tr. Raverty, p. 378

111 *TN*, vol. I, p. 426

112 D.C. Thomas (2018), p. 82

CHAPTER TWO:
1175–1206

Two Brothers

KHURASAN AND INDIA

The Shansabanid-led Ghurid enterprise had shown, in the main, remarkable unity of purpose in the pursuit of their aims to expand the Ghurid polity. This common understanding among the Shansabanid elite was to persist for the duration of Ghurid hegemony and was vital to their military successes. Ghiyath al-Din seems to have been fully aware of this dynamic, and this pragmatic attitude is clearly shown by his dealings with his brother, Mu'izz al-Din, and his cousins, rulers of the Ghurid dynasty in Bamiyan. The Ghurid Empire was to reach its apogee in the years 558–600/1163–1204. This period encompassed the reigns of Ghiyath al-Din in Ghur and his brother Mu'izz al-Din in Ghazna. Their friendship and partnership were rare examples of fraternal cooperation in the medieval period. The agreed spheres of interest were due to geographical necessity as much as anything and made sense in the dual aspects of the empire. The conquest of lands in Khurasan were best approached from Ghur and the continuation of Ghaznavid raids into the Indian subcontinent best served from Ghazna and Lahore. However, the Ghurid emphasis was now on conquest and acquiring territory rather than raiding in the *ghazi* tradition of their Ghaznavid predecessors.

The Ghurid territorial ascendancy in Khurasan was to be challenged by the Khwarazmshahs, which led to skirmishing and, on occasion, serious fighting. During the reign of Ghiyath al-Din the Ghurids seem to have had the upper hand in these exchanges. The way to India, down the Kabul River valley through the Khyber Pass to Peshawar, was still barred by the remains of the Ghaznavid state in the Punjab ruled by Sultan Khusrau Malik from Lahore.

Mu'izz al-Din's initial attempts to campaign in the northern Indian subcontinent did not meet undiluted success. His first effort involved skirting Ghaznavid possessions and taking the Gomal Pass to the territories along the middle and lower Indus in the hope of finding an alternative route to the Gangetic plain. In 571/1175/6, Mu'izz al-Din had captured Multan and Uch, putting a large number of Isma'ilis to the sword in the process. This action seems to be consistent with the promulgation of Ghurid Sunni orthodoxy.[113] In a similar vein it is also suggested that he later attacked the Islamised Sumra rulers of Daybul, a port in the Indus Delta, who may have been Isama'ili sympathisers

113 *TN*, vol. I, tr. Raverty, p. 449. This community had been established following the Arab conquests of Sind in the early eighth century.

in 578/1182/3.[114,115] In 574/1178, the Ghurid ruler then made the disastrous decision to march his army across the Thar Desert via lower Sind. He was confronted at Mount Abu in Gujerat by the Rae Mularaja II, a prince of the western Chaulukya kingdom.[116] Whatever his precise status, the 'young in years' Bhim Diw, as Juzjani calls the Hindu ruler, led a large and fresh army with numerous elephants.[117] The invaders were soundly defeated, and the weary and starving remnants faced an arduous retreat to the safety of Ghurid territory.

Mu'izz al-Din realised that for the Ghurid enterprise to prosper in its Indian ambitions the rump of the Ghaznavid Empire in the Punjab centred on Lahore needed to be eliminated. This was easier said than done, the Ghaznavids having already shown in their attempts to retake Ghazna that they were able to raise substantial forces from their residual territories. Following the Ghurid capture of Ghazna Mu'izz al-Din had, almost immediately, pushed on through the hilly Afghan/Punjab borderlands hoping to capture the remaining Ghaznavid territories. Khusrau Malik responded by bringing up an army to dispute the Indus crossings, and Mu'izz al-Din was forced to think again.[118] In 575/1179–80 Mu'izz al-Din succeeded in capturing Peshawar, at the southern end of the Khyber Pass, an important stopping point on the way from the Afghan highlands to the upper Indus and the Ghaznavid garrison/administrative city of Lahore.[119] Khusrau Malik seems to have felt there was now little he could do to halt the Ghurid advance. In what seems a rather forlorn attempt to appease Mu'izz al-Din he despatched 'a renowned elephant and the finest Khusrau Malik possessed' accompanied by a son.[120] This time the Ghurid sultan was persuaded to withdraw, but the respite and reconciliation was to be only temporary. The following year Mu'izz al-Din's attention was diverted towards the Sumra rulers in the Indus Delta, and he launched an expedition against them.

114 Jackson (2003), p. 8

115 *TN*, vol. I, p. 452. 'The following year, 578 H, the Sultan led an army towards Diwal [or Dibal] and possessed himself of the whole of the territory [lying] on the sea-coast and acquired much wealth, and returned.'

116 C.E. Bosworth (1977), p. 128 and note 66 p. 185. The note states Bhima was a younger brother of Mularaja and succeeded him in 1178. However, it seems the ruler during the battle was Mularaja who must have died shortly afterwards. Perhaps of wounds received during the engagement?

117 *TN*, vol. I, p. 452

118 Bosworth (1977), p. 129

119 *al-Kamil fi'l-Ta'rikh*, part 2, tr. Richards, p. 49

120 *TN*, vol I., tr. Raverty, p. 115

It was not until 581/1185–6 that he again led his army towards Lahore. This time he was able to count on the support of Chakradeva, the rajah of Jammu, who had no love for the Ghaznavids. The dispute between them had arisen from the expansion of Ghaznavid territories, in the early years of Khusrau Malik's reign, up to the northern Punjab and the beginnings of Kashmir. In this endeavour the Ghaznavids had received support from Khokhar tribesmen who lived in these uplands and who were only too happy to renounce their allegiance to the ruler of Jammu.[121] Having ravaged the area around Lahore Mu'izz al-Din retired towards his own territories. But not before, on the advice of Chakradeva, restoring and garrisoning the fortress of Sialkot situated between two tributaries of the upper Indus on the fringes of Kashmir.[122] This fortress was in the heart of Khokhar territory and would be a useful bastion in the future control of the region. He left a son, Husain, of the Kharmil family – possibly a relation of one of the Ghurid *maliks*/champions mentioned above. Khusrau Malik gathered his forces and with the support of the Khokhars besieged Sialkot. Chakradeva's support for Mu'izz al-Din ensured that Khusrau Shah was unable to take the fortress. At this point the rajah who according to Juzjani was nearly eighty died and was succeeded by his son Vijayadeva. The following year Mu'izz al-Din crossed the Indus at the Nilab ferry. He was received there by Vijaydiva's *mian-ji* – emissary – and later on the banks of River Jhelum was joined by the rajah's son, Naransingh Diw, with a substantial force. The new rajah was presented to the Ghurid sultan by the garrison commander of Sialkot, Husain-i-Kharmil. The combined forces of Ghur and Jammu then proceeded to and captured Lahore.[123] Mu'izz al-Din appointed Ali Karmakh, his former governor in Multan, as his representative there. The rajah's son and his emissary were given honorary robes and entrusted with the fortress of Sialkot.

Juzjani seems to skirt around the details of how the city was actually captured. According to Ibn al-Athir, Mu'izz al-Din promised Khusrau Malik *aman,* a term denoting safe conduct for himself and his immediate family. He would be able to retain his wealth, and a marriage alliance would be arranged between the Ghaznavid sultan's son and one of Mu'izz al-Din's daughters and *iqtas* provided to support him. For this Khusrau Malik was required to surrender Lahore and recognise the supreme Ghurid sultan Giyath al-Din in the *khutba.* He initially refused, but there was no escaping the threat of the besieging army and the waning of his own influence in the city itself. Fearing betrayal he sent the *qadi*

121 *TN*, vol. I, p. 453 note 2

122 Ibid. p. 453 note 4

123 Ibid. p. 454 note 4

and *katib* of Lahore to negotiate the terms of a surrender. With this accomplished Khusrau Malik was allowed to remain in the city and given respect in accordance with his status. However, this period of security was not to last, and an emissary arrived from Firuzkuh demanding that Mu'izz al-Din bring Khusrau Malik and his son to Ghiyath al-Din.[124] Unsurprisingly, Khusrau Malik was reluctant to go as his bond of *aman* was with Mu'izz al-Din and not his elder brother with whom it had no validity as regards personal protection and security.[125] As Raverty comments on Mu'izz al-Din's behaviour 'having deceitfully enveigled this amiable monarch into his power, broke his promises and sent him and his family into Ghur[126] There is a rather sad quote of a verse in Arabic, said to have been uttered by Khusrau Malik to the son of the *katib* of Peshawar as he passed though that city, where Ghaznavid support still remained strong, 'for it is not like the old times in the encampments but chains have been placed around our necks'.[127] Khusrau Malik and his son were never brought before Ghiyath al-Din but, according to Ibn al-Athir, they were imprisoned in one of the numerous Ghurid fortresses and never seen again.[128,129] Juzjani provides us with a few further details. He states that Khusrau Malik was imprisoned in the castle of Balarwan in Gharjistan and his son Bahram Shah – who was probably the son given up as a hostage to Mu'izz al-Din in 577/1181–2 – in the fortress of Safrud in Ghur itself. They were, he says, both put to death five years later in 587/1191.[130] Ghiyath al-Din and Mu'izz al-Din may have decided that the two surviving Ghaznavids posed a potential threat should they ever be freed and could then potentially be used as pawns to destabilise the Ghurid hegemony. Hence the decision to kill them. The Ghurids had finally triumphed over the Ghaznavids after forty years of conflict and were now in a position to pursue their ambitions into the Indian subcontinent and west into Khurasan.

In Iran and the areas to the west of the Ghurid territories, following the demise of the Seljuks and the expulsion of the Ghuzz, or at least the roving bands who had not taken up a more sedentary existence, the territory fell to the Khwarazmshahs who were to fight with the Ghurids for control of Khurasan.

124 *al-Kamil f'il-Ta'rikh*, part 2, tr. Richards, p. 50

125 C.E. Bosworth (1977), p. 130

126 *TN*, vol. I, p. 379 note 6

127 Bosworth (1977), p. 131 and note 70 p. 185

128 Ibid., p. 131

129 *al-Kamil fi'l-Ta'rikh*, part 2, p. 51

130 *TN*, vol. I, tr. Raverty, p. 379 and p. 456

The Khwarazmshahs and the Qarakhanids of Bukhara and Samarkand were both vassals of the Qara-Khitai, a semi-nomadic sinicised dynasty of Manchurian origin, with a Buddhist ruling clan. In 567/1172 the Khwarazmshah Il–Arslan died fighting a Qara-Khitai invasion prompted by his late payment of tribute owed to his overlord the *Gur-Khan*. This in turn led to a disputed succession between his eldest son Tekish and Sultan Shah his younger brother. The Qara-khitai displayed an evenhandedness in the matter and chose Tekish. They were more interested in stability and prompt payment of taxes than in dynastic struggles among their vassals. The younger brother, Sultan Shah, ultimately sought refuge at the Ghurid court in Firuzkuh.[131]

The Ghurids had become a major power and were recognised as such beyond the boundaries of their core territories. They had become particularly strong supporters of Sunni orthodoxy. In the late 1190s under Ghiyath al-Din the Ghurid elite abandoned the literalist *karramiyya* school, which the dynasty had followed since their conversion to Islam and was now well entrenched and popular among the Ghurid population in general.[132] At this juncture they decided to pursue the more intellectual and prestigious *shafi'i* law school.[133] This change of direction was to cause problems in the Ghurid heartlands and destabilised a number of other significant urban centres within the Ghurid dominions.[134] Why did they implement this change? Probably to curry favour with and to seek legitimacy from the Abbasid caliphs who, at this time, were becoming more heavily involved in eastern Islamic diplomacy and politics. The caliphs in their turn were keen to encourage Ghurid ambitions in Khurasan as a counter-balance to the power of the Khwarazmshahs. Ghiyath al-Din exchanged numerous ambassadors with Baghdad. The sultan also sought admission to one of the *futuwwa* chivalric orders as championed by the caliph al-Nasir 575–622/1180–1225 in his efforts to restore the political and religious influence of the caliphate.[135]

The presence of Sultan Shah at Firuzkuh was not to last long. Ghiyath al-Din refused him military assistance in his dispute with Tekish. However, any idea that there was an agreement between Tekish and the Ghurid supreme sultan

131 *CHI*, vol. 5, pp. 188–9

132 *al-Kamil fi'l-Ta'rikh*, part 3, tr. Richards, pp. 46–7 and p. 46 note 9

133 *CHI*, vol. 5, p. 162

134 Thomas (2018), p. 322

135 *CHI*, vol. 5, p. 163, p. 168

is most unlikely, despite Juzjani's claims of a treaty.[136] Sultan Shah eventually succeeded in securing support from the Qara-khitai and occupied Merv.[137] From there he assembled an army and proceeded to ravage the Ghurid frontier regions and in particular the district of Baghdis northwest of Herat on the border of modern Turkmenistan. In 586/1190 Ghiyath al-Din summoned his brother from Ghazna, his cousin *malik* Shams al-Din from Bamiyan and the *amir* Taj al-Din-i-Harab, ruler of Sistan. Their combined forces then set out to confront the army of Sultan Shah who marched out from Merv to meet them. After six months of skirmishing and harassment between the protagonists along the banks of Murghab River Mu'izz al-Din ordered a ferry to be established.[138] With this in place the Ghurid army crossed over and comprehensively defeated the forces of Sultan Shah.[139] His death the following year (588/9–1192) removed a dynastic threat from his brother Tekish enabling him to consolidate his position inKhwarazm.[140]

Among the casualties on the Khwarzamian side was Tughril, the former *ghulam* of Sultan Sanjar and ruler of Herat, whose head was brought to Ghiyath al-Din by soldiers of the Bamiyan contingent. Tughril had previously ruled in Herat for seventeen years having lost the city to the Ghurids for a short time around 569/1174. On the approach of the Ghurid armies he had thrown in his lot with Sultan Shah and paid the consequences, as Herat now passed into the Ghurid realms. For his contribution the ruler of Bamiyan, Shams al-Din, was raised to the position of sultan by Ghiyath al-Din.[141] Alongside the title and obvious *kudos* the position came with a black canopy of state as an outward sign of the increased status of the individual. This event can be viewed as another example of Ghiyath al-Din using the promotion as an opportunity to cement Shansabani family unity.[142] The appointment must also have served to give the

136 *TN*, vol. I, p. 243 and see note 9 where he states that 'a treaty with sultans of Ghur is out of the question…' A clash between the two major powers of the eastern Islamic world did not take long to materialise.

137 Ibid., p. 378

138 *TN*, vol. I, tr. Raverty, p. 248 and p. 515. During one of the forays Qutb al-Din Aybak, a *mamluk* of Mu'izz al-Din's and his *Amir-i-Akhur* – master of horse – and later Delhi sultan, was captured by Sultan Shah's troops and later freed following the defeat of Sultan Shah.

139 *al-Kamil fi'l Ta'rikh*, part 2, tr. Richards, p. 382

140 *TN*, vol. I, pp. 248–9 and *CHI*, vol. 5, pp. 190–01

141 Ibid., p. 379

142 Ibid., p. 427

Bamiyan rulers an added legitimacy and impetus to continue Ghurid expansion across the Oxus and into Central Asia.

The Ghurids had now reached the point where they were to fulfil their territorial ambitions. The Bamiyan rulers would be charged with extending Ghurid rule into Central Asia and with fighting the Qara-khitai for their territories either side of the Amu Darya. Mu'izz al-Din, the Sultan-i- Ghazi, as Juzjani sometimes likes to describe him, was to be assigned the task of conquering upper India and the Gangetic plain. These operations could now be initiated from Ghazna and the newly acquired forward base in Lahore. All expeditions took place under the auspices of and instruction from Ghiyath al-Din, the supreme sultan, who took it upon himself to mastermind Ghurid expansion westwards into Iran, taking on the Khwarazmshahs in the process.

Sultan Shams al-Din, formerly *malik,* who ruled Bamiyan from 558–88/1163–92 immediately set out to expand and establish Ghurid power east and north westwards from his seat. These initial conquests where in Tucharistan, ancient Bactria, with the aim of dislodging the Qara-khitai south of the Oxus and pushing them out of territory they held to the north of the river. In 594/1198 Baha al-Din, who had succeeded his father as sultan of Bamiyan, occupied Balkh following the death of its governor, a Turk named Azyeh, who had been paying an annual tribute to the Qara-Khitai. The *khutba* was now made in the name of Ghiyath al-Din, and Balkh became part of Islamic territory.[143] By 1204, the zenith of Ghurid power, Baha al-Din, had greatly expanded Ghurid territories in the east, as far as the boundaries of Kashmir, up to Termez and Balkh in the west and the limits of Kashgar in western Xinjiang. According to Juzjaini the *khutba* was read in these regions in the name of Baha al-Din.[144]

The year 595/1198 also saw the outbreak of general hostilities in Khurasan. If not initially triggered by the fall of Balkh, they were most certainly brought about by Ghurid incursions into Qara-khitan subject territories and by instabilities in the region in general. In 590/1194 the last Seljuk sultan in the west, Toghril b. Arslan, died. The ensuing collapse of Seljuk authority in the west enabled the Khwarazmshahs to extend their territories to the edge of Iraq, pressuring the lands of the caliphate in Baghdad. The caliph al-Nasir sent an embassy to Firuzkuh seeking help from Ghiyath al-Din. The Ghurid sultan responded by threatening to attack Tekish who in turn sought help from his Qara-Khitai overlords. Tekish argued that if the Qara-Khitai did not respond they would lose not only more of

143 *al-Kamil fi'l-Tarikh*, part 3, p. 35

144 *TN*, vol. I, tr. Raverty, p. 431. It is more likely that the name of the supreme sultan was read ahead of Baha al-Din's (d.1206).

their territories, like Balkh, but also his own. The Qara-Khitai sent a large army into Guzgan, the area of what is now part of northern Afghanistan threatening Ghurid-controlled territories and demanding that the Ghurid rulers of Bamiyan pay tribute for Balkh.[145] This force was under command of a man known as Tayanku.[146] When news of the enormous approaching army reached Ghiyath al-Din he immediately summoned Mu'izz al-Din who had been campaigning with the bulk of the Ghurid forces in India. To make matters worse Ghiyath al-Din had been incapacitated with gout or rheumatism and was unable to ride.[147] In the meantime Tekish had marched to Tus with the intention of besieging Herat. As soon as the army of the Qara-Khitai had crossed the Oxus they plundered Ghurid territories around Talaqan, the capital of the modern Takhar province in northeastern Afghanistan, killing and enslaving the population. Initially, it seems that Ghiyath al-Din did not have sufficient forces to confront the invaders. Local Ghurid emirs, Muhammad ibn Kharnak a fief holder in Talaqan, al Husain ibn Kharmil who held the citadel of Kurzaban and *amir* Kharwash with the troops at their disposal marched against the invaders.[148] They decided upon a night attack. Under cover of darkness they hoped their lack of numbers would not put them at such a disadvantage. Initially, the Ghurids achieved some success. However, once daybreak occurred, the Qara-Khitai realised they were fighting a reduced force and not the main Ghurid army under Mu'izz al-Din.[149] With their backs to the Oxus the Qara-Khitai consolidated their position and counter-attacked, resulting in great slaughter on both sides, which continued for most of the day. Slowly reinforcements arrived from the main Ghurid army and the odds began to favour the Ghurids. Finally, the Qara-Khitan force collapsed, those who still resisted were slain and many were drowned trying to escape across the river.

The Qara-Khitan *Gur-Khan* was livid at the destruction and loss of what must have been, perceived by the standards of the time, a substantial army. He demanded reparations from the Khwarazmshah: 'You have killed my men. I want 10,000 dinars for every man slain.'[150] According to Ibn al-Athir there

145 *CHI*, vol. 5, p. 164

146 *al-Kamil fi'l-Tarikh*, part 3, tr. Richards, p. 35. See also note 6. Referring to Juvaini, *History*, vol. I, p. 322 and note 14: Tayanagu probably means 'chamberlain' in old Turkish. 'It is probably a title here, rather than the name of a commander.'

147 Ibid., p. 35

148 Ibid., p. 36

149 Ibid. Ibn al-Athir states Giyath al-Din but it was more likely to be Mu'izz al-Din given his brother's affliction with gout or rheumatism.

150 Ibid., p. 36

were about 12,000 dead. Tekish now sought accommodation with Ghiyath al-Din and explained his situation with the Qara-Khitai. The Ghurid sultan for his part responded by ordering him to obey the caliph and restore Islamic territory captured by the Qara-Khitai. This is something that Tekish seems to have agreed to do.[151] The Khwarazmshah responded to the *Gur-Khan* in his own fashion.

> *Your army's sole intention was to recover Balkh. They did not come to my aid, nor did I meet with them, nor did I order them to cross over. If I had done that, I would produce the money demanded of me, but since you have been unable to deal with the Ghurids, you have turned on me with this demand. I have made peace with the Ghurids and entered into their allegiance. I owe you no allegiance now.*[152]

This response had predictable results. The ruler of the Qara-Khitai despatched another substantial army against his ungrateful and uncooperative vassal and besieged him, in the Khwarazm oasis, presumably at his capital Gurganj. Ultimately, the Qara-Khitai were repulsed and Tekish then proceeded to take Bukhara. This episode confirmed the Ghurid sultans as the major power in the eastern Iranian lands and made Ghur the pivot from where these territories including Central Asia and parts of northern India could be controlled.

Tekish seems to have been true to his word and made peace with the caliph who sent both him and his son Qutb al-Din Muhammad robes of honour together with a missive confirming the territories the Khwarazmshahs held. It looks as though he spent the last year of his life in ill health, while dealing with internal dissent and campaigning against the *al-mulahida,* literally the deviators or Assassins as they are more usually known.[153] Tekish died on (20 Ramadan 596/14 July 1200) between Khwarazm and Nishapur. He had chosen to travel under the blistering summer sun across the deserts to Khurasan against the advice of his doctors and succumbed to a throat infection.[154] On hearing of his death Ghiyath al-Din, despite the enmity that had existed between them, ordered three days of ceremonial music to be played and held a service of condolence. A succession dispute among the heirs of the Khwarazmshah led Hindu Khan, Tekish's grandson, to seek help from Ghiyath al-Din who received him at Firuzkuh and promised support. Hindu Khan's uncle Khwarazmshah Muhammad b. Tekish r. 596–617/1200–1220 despatched an army into Khurasan under the Turk Jaqar who invested the city of Merv and in so

151 *al-Kamil fi'l -Ta'rikh*, part 3, tr. Richards, p. 36. Ibn al-Athir says the contrary but see note 11.

152 Ibid., p. 37

153 Ibid., p. 47

154 Ibid., p. 51

doing captured Hindu Khan's mother and children. He was ordered to send them to Khwarazm. Ghiyath al-Din wasted no time and despatched the emir Muhamad ibn Kharnak to threaten Jaqar and commanded him to make the *khutba* in the name of the Ghurid supreme sultan or leave the city. The Turk responded with threats of his own to the Ghurid *amir*. However, he also wrote secretly to ibn Kharnak saying that he sought to serve Ghiyath al-Din. Once he had read the letter Ghiyath al-Din realised that the Khwarazmshah Muhammad was in a weak position and saw this as a perfect opportunity to invade Khurasan and seize the territories of the Khwarazmshah.[155] The Ghurid sultan then sent a despatch to his brother Mu'izz al-Din ordering him to invade Khurasan in concert with him.

Following his conquest of Lahore and the remaining Ghaznavid territories in the Punjab, Mu'izz al-Din was able to take on the Ghaznavid Khusrau Malik's mantle as the champion of Islamic orthodoxy in the Indian subcontinent. However, the Ghurid sultan was faced with serious obstacles to his ambitions in the shape of several powerful Hindu dynasties. In a previous expedition he had been heavily defeated at Mount Abu in (574/1178) by an army of the mighty Chaulukya dynasty. However, the most formidable of these powers was the Chauhan (Chahamana) kingdom of Sakhambari (Sambhar) ruled by Prthviraja III – referred to as Rae Pittora by Juzjani and other Muslim chroniclers.[156] The Chauhan expansion and dominance of much of northwestern India was a relatively recent phenomenon 547–560/*c.* 1153–64, and covered a not dissimilar time frame to the rise of the Ghurids to paramountcy in Afghanistan.[157] The senior branch ruled from Ajmer and claimed primacy throughout the territory, encompassing an area north of the Vindhaya mountain ranges, as far as the foot-hills of the Himalayas. This included a large proportion of the territory between the Sutlej and Jamuna rivers. Chauhan cadet branches ruled at Nadol (Naddula) and Jalor (Javalipura).[158] Delhi itself and parts of modern Haryana were ruled by the Tomara princes as feudatories of the Chauhans. However, this Chauhan ascendancy had been forged in the face of fierce opposition from the Chaulukyas ruling from Anahilapataka (modern Patan) in Gujerat – who had already proved their mettle against Mu'izz al-Din at Mount Abu and still had expansionist designs on their former territories beyond Gujerat. To the east, in what is now part of modern Uttar Pradesh, the Chauhans came up against the Ghadavala kingdom of Varanasi and Kanyakubja as well as the

155 Ibid., p. 52

156 *TN*, vol. I. tr. Raverty, p. 460 note 3

157 H.C. Ray, *The Dynastic History of Northern India: Early Medieval Period, 2* vols (New Delhi, 2017). foreword by L.D. Barnett (Delhi, 2017), vol. II, p. 1,077

158 Ibid. *Genealogies*, vol. II, pp. 1,138–9

Chandella dynasty of Jeja-Bhukti – Bundelkhand, centred on the fortress city of Kalinjar. It seems that, for the last quarter of the twelfth century, the Chandellas were under increasing pressure from the Gahadvalas and were also forced to cede some of their western territories to the Chauhans. To the east of their realm, the Gahadvalas were expanding into Bihar. Here, they came into competition, with the Sena dynasty centred on western Bengal, for the residual territories of the recently extinguished Pala Empire.[159]

These states functioned to all appearances in an almost feudal system where the rulers/*rajas*-referred to as *rais* by the Muslim invaders received military service from lower ranking rulers/potentates described as *ranakas* or *thakuras* in return for estates. They, in their turn, donated parcels of land to their lower ranking commanders, the *rautas* or *nayakas,* the latter being the *ranas* and *rawats* of the Muslim chroniclers.[160] This system calls to mind the *iqta* system of the Islamic world that emerged in the fourth/tenth century under the Abbasid caliphate. These grants, originally to collect taxes-*iqta*- over a specific area, became increasingly militarised under the Buyids, Samanids and especially the Ghaznavids 373–582/977–1186.[161] The practice was to manifest itself in India in respect of grants of territory particularly to Iltutmish and his *ghulams.*[162] Mu'izz al-Din was prepared to try his luck again in India, following his disastrous earlier defeat, with an expedition into the eastern Punjab. Sometime in either 583/1187–8 or more likely 587/1191he captured the fortress of Tabarindh – possibly modern Bathinda.[163] According to Juzjaini he left a force of 1,200 Ghurid horsemen from Tulak with instructions to hold the place for eight months until his return.[164] This seems to infer that the fortress was to serve as a foothold in enemy territory while the sultan returned to Ghazna to raise a more substantial force over the summer in preparation for the following campaigning season. The Ghurids would come to rely mainly on cavalry from the steppes of Central Asia in the form of *mamluks* for these campaigns; their indigenous horse alone would not have been adequate.

159 Ibid. vols I and II. Chapters: VI (Senas), VIII (Gahadvallas), XI (Chandellas), XV (Chaulukyas), XVI (Chahmanas) and see also Jackson (2003), p. 9

160 *TN,* vol. II, p. 828. '…the whole army of Rae Nahar Diw, notwithstanding it was very numerous, well provided with arms and elephants, with choice horses and famous Rawats.' The latter were individual champions. See also Jackson (2003), p. 9.

161 *CHI,* vol. V, pp. 231–4. See also Peacock (2015), p. 79 and note 32 'The *iqta* had been the Buyid answer to the problem of paying the military in a period when specie was in short supply: in lieu of salary an amir would be granted the right to collect taxes over a given area.'

162 Jackson (2003), pp. 95–6

163 Ibid., p. 10

164 *TN,* vol. I, tr. Raverty p. 458

However, just as Mu'izz al-Din was preparing to depart for his own territories he was made aware that Prthviraja was close at hand at the head of a substantial army, consisting of elephants, infantry and cavalry. This force also contained the troops of the Tomara ruler Govindaraja of Delhi and 'the whole of the *ranas* of Hind…'[165] The battle took place at Tara'in – modern Taraori in Haryana. There can be no doubt that the Ghurid force was outnumbered by the Hindu troops. Fighting in the thick of battle the Ghurid sultan vigorously sought the elephant ridden by Govindaraja. This animal reportedly roamed along the front line of the Indian army, acting as a rather unruly mobile command post. Mu'izz al-Din in the melee managed to wound the Hindu prince with a javelin and knocked out two of his teeth in the process. In response Govindaraja hurled a short javelin, which 'inflicted a very severe wound'.[166] The Ghurid sultan, who was badly hurt, turned his horse away and sought to distance himself from the conflict. With his army disintegrating around him, Mu'izz al-Din slumped in the saddle from loss of blood, and was only saved by the quick thinking of a 'Khalj stripling', as Juzani describes him.[167] The Khalaj were a nomadic people from the regions of Bust and Khandahar in southern Afghanistan and provided tribal cavalry to the Ghurid sultans as they had to the Ghaznavids before them.[168] The Khalaj were probably a Turkicised group rather than ethnic Turks who later merged with the Afghans.[169] This youth jumped up behind Mu'izz al-Din, supported him in the saddle and guided him from the field. Ultimately, they reached the safety of Ghurid lines. The Ghurids were routed, and Mu'izz al-Din was lucky to come away with his life. Prthviraja and his forces invested and recaptured the fortress of Tabarindh. The Ghurid sultan retired to Lahore to recuperate and raise the substantial army that would be required to defeat the Chauhans and their subordinates. He was deeply unhappy with the performance of the Ghurid *amirs* and their troops whom he felt had failed him.[170] Determined and with a steely resolve to defeat Prthviraja, Mu'izz al-Din busied himself in Ghazna and the surrounding areas with the objective of raising an enormous fighting force. The following

165 *TN*, vol. I, p. 459

166 Ibid., p. 460

167 Ibid.

168 Jackson (2003), p. 11

169 Thomas (2018), p. 343

170 *al-Kamil fi'l-Ta'rikh*, part 2, tr. Richards, p. 405. Mu'izz al-Din is reported to have said to a Ghurid shayk, 'Understand that since this infidel defeated me I have not slept with my wife, nor have I put off my winding sheet. I am marching against my enemy and I rely on God, not on the Ghurid troops or anyone else…'

year (588/1192) Mu'izz al-Din left Ghazna with his army. Juzjani mentions a man who was part of this multitude, saying, 'I was in the army along with the Sultan-i-Ghazi and the number composing the army of Islam that year was one hundred and twenty thousand arrayed in defensive armour.'[171] Ibn al-Athir talks of 70,000 being just a part.[172] These numbers, while not to be taken at face value, do give an impression of the substantial size of the force that Mu'izz al-Din had assembled over the previous months. The sultan, when he reached Lahore, sent two emissaries to Prthviraja at Ajmer instructing him to accept Islam and acknowledge Ghurid overlordship. Unsurprisingly, the Indian king refused. He had just routed Mu'izz al-Din and was capable of fielding a massive army of his own. He set out to meet the invading force and the two armies clashed again near Tara'in. The Chauhan ruler advised his opponent to return to his own territory and promised not to pursue him there. The sultan replied with terms and stated that he was operating by command of his sovereign and brother Ghiyath al-Din and any agreement would have to be sanctioned by him.[173]

The Ghurid sultan had no intention of seeking sanction for peace from Ghiyath al-Din in Ghur, and had already begun his preparations for battle.[174] There is the possibility that Mu'izz al-Din attacked the Chauhan army while the Chauhan generals were under the illusion that a truce existed between the two opposing rulers. Mu'izz al-Din had left a portion of his army, including his war elephants, baggage, standards and paraphernalia of state, together with the centre of his army – almost certainly the heavy cavalry – some miles to the rear. He split his light cavalry of 10,000 mounted archers into four divisions, who were instructed to harass the enemy, from all sides, as they mobilised. They were to retire and feign flight as necessary. The remaining division of 12,000 men, of what we assume to have been the elite heavy mailed *mamluk* cavalry he held in reserve. According to Hasan Nizami the Ghurids attacked shortly after dawn – Raverty mentions 09:00 a.m.[175] The mounted archers gradually wore down the Chauhan army, which we are told amounted to 300,000 men – considerably more than the Ghurid force. This gigantic Indian army consisted of elephants, cavalry and infantry. As the day wore on the Chauhan army seems to

171 *TN*, vol. I, tr. Raverty, p. 466

172 *al-Kamil fi'l-Ta'rikh*, part 2, p. 406

173 *TN*, vol. I, tr. Raverty, p. 466 and note 1. Raverty refers to the contemporary historian Hasan Nizami who began his *Tajul-Ma'asirin*, with the second battle of Tara'in, in Delhi in (1205), the year before Mu'izz al-Din's assassination.

174 H.C.Ray (2017), vol. II, p. 1,090

175 *TN*, vol. I, p. 468 and note 2; p. 466 and note 1

have been compressed into an uncontrollable mass of horses, men and elephants, tormented by the arrows of the light cavalry. In the early afternoon the Ghurid sultan unleashed his heavy cavalry. In a tactic almost reminiscent of Crusader practice of the time, the concentrated mailed charge routed the Hindu army.[176] Prthviraja tried to escape by dismounting his elephant and fleeing on horseback. He was captured and later executed. Govindaraja was killed in the battle and his head was recognised by Mu'izz al-Din from his two broken teeth, a result of their meeting the previous year. The Muslims took much plunder from the defeated Indians, including fourteen elephants and more specifically the animal that Mu'izz al-Din had had his *contretemps* with in the first battle.[177]

The second battle of Tara'in was a convincing victory for the Ghurids and a battle of significant strategic consequence. It dismantled the power of the Chauhans, the dominant kingdom in northern India, facilitating the invasion of the subcontinent from territories to the northwest. Consequently, the Hindu potentates of the eastern Punjab acknowledged the primacy of Mu'izz al-Din and became his tributaries. The victory also facilitated the establishment of a permanent Muslim presence in the Ganges plain with the foundation of a garrison at Indraprastha not far from Delhi. Following the battle Mu'izz al-Din proceeded to Ajmer, the Chauhan capital, where he installed Prthviraja as a client ruler. This episode seems to have been brief and the Chauhan was ruler was executed shortly afterwards. Presumably, for an act of subterfuge or chicanery about which we know nothing, to be replaced by his son. Delhi was granted to the heir of Govindaraja as a subject ruler.[178] Elsewhere, the same practice applied with the installation of local princes as clients of the Ghurid sultan. Leaving his slave general Qutb al-Din Aybak as governor of the newly conquered territory based in the fortress at Ghuram, he returned home to Ghazna, by way of the hills of the northern Punjab. The victory at Tara'in in 588/1192 seems to have extended Ghurid sway in India to include the territory south of the high Himalayas between the rivers Sutlej and Ganges and possibly as far as the alpine regions and the foothills of Kashmir and south to the fortress city of Hansi in Haryana.[179]

176 Ibid. p. 468 and see also R.C. Smail, *Crusading Warfare 1097–1193* (Cambridge, 1976), pp. 113–15

177 *al-Kamil fi'l-Ta'rikh*, part 2, tr. Richards, p. 406

178 P. Jackson (2003), p. 10. See also Ray (2017), vol. II, pp. 1,090–93, 1094 and genealogies p. 1,138. There is a certain amount of confusion over who replaced who and when as rulers in Ajmer and Delhi. Ibn al-Athir says Prthviraja was taken to Ajmer whereas Juzjani states he was taken prisoner and 'despatched to hell' on the field.

179 *TN*, vol. I tr. Raverty, pp. 468–9 and note 4

For much of the following decade, Mu'izz al-Din spent the summer months in Ghazna and continued to raise cohorts of cavalry from the steppes to augment his forces in India. With the onset of the cooler season, he would return to take command of the campaigns in the *dar al-Harb*, the land of the infidel. In 590/1193 the Ghurids, under Mu'izz al-Din, came up against the Ghadavala ruler Jayachandra. They met in battle at Chandawar – modern Chandawal near Firozabad – on the banks of River Yamuna not far from Agra. The battle was hotly contested and the Hindu army constituted a very large force supported by elephants. There was great slaughter, and the Indian king was killed. His body was unrecognisable due to disfigurement from the wounds it had received. According to Ibn al-Athir only boys and women were taken prisoner; the men were killed, and ninety elephants were captured.[180] The Ghurids then proceeded to occupy Benares (Varanasi), having looted the treasury at Asi (Asni) and carried away 1,400 loads of treasure. Given that a camel can carry up to 400 kilos and a mule around 70 these are substantial values. The Ghurid sultan then returned to Ghazna.[181] However, the successful consolidation of Ghurid conquests in the eastern Punjab and beyond into the Ganges valley should mainly be credited to the *mamluk* general Aybak. Sallying forth from his base at Ghuram he had swiftly conquered the city and fortress of Meerut three months after the great battle at Tara'in and in 591/1194 that of Kol near Aligarh. Both were in the territory of the Ghadavalas who were unable to prevent him. In the same year, he acted decisively 'passing over hill and desert like a wild ass or an antelope' to prevent a Chauhan revival by defeating and executing Hiraj brother of Prthviraja who had designs on his nephews' throne in Ajmer. The ruler of Ajmer was rewarded for his loyalty and, in turn, as a token friendship, sent three, ingeniously cast, golden melons as part of his tribute 'for the service of the state'. Aybak then put a swift end to any further Chauhan ambitions by capturing Delhi and establishing the Ghurid centre of government there. Govindaraja's heir, 'the Rai had fled from Delhi had raised an army of idolatrous, turbulent, and rebellious tribes, the vapour of pride and conquest having entered his thoughtless brain. Kutb-ud-Din pursued him … and his head was severed from his body.'[182] In 593/1197 the *mamluk* general was campaigning against the Chaulukyas on the borders of Gujerat. The forces met near Mount Abu, the scene of Mu'izz al-Din's catastrophic encounter with

180 *al-Kamil fi'l Ta'rikh*, prt 3, tr. Richards, p. 13. See also *TN*, vol. I, p. 470 and note 2. Raverty tells of a series of engagements with the Ghadavala ruler and mentions between 600 and 640 elephants and a vast quantity of assorted spoils.

181 Ibid. and see Jackson (2003), p. 10 and *TN*, vol. I, p. 519 footnote

182 H.C.Ray (2017), vol. II, p. 1,092. Quoting Nizami.

the Chaulukyas in 574/1178. The Indian army was led by Bhimadeva II 1178–1241. The battle itself was a closely fought affair, lasting from dawn to midday, that left around 15,000 dead on the Indian side and provided 20,000 prisoners and treasure. Aybak had vanquished Bhimadeva II and had avenged his masters' earlier defeat. Again, we cannot be certain of the numbers involved but the implication is that losses among the Hindu army were heavy. Bhimadeva escaped abandoning twenty elephants in the process. Having eliminated this threat and stabilised the border with Gujerat, Aybak made his way back to Delhi via Ajmer. He was careful to divide the spoils accrued during this campaign. Jewels and the most attractive female and male prisoners were despatched in tribute to Ghiyath al-Din in Ghur and his master Mu'izz al-Din in Ghazna. Aybak made sure he included the *mamluks* in his generosity, as well as the less fortunate among the Muslim population in Delhi.[183] In 594/1197–8 it was the turn of Buda'un to be annexed and then Kanauj/Qinnawj 595/1199.[184] There now seems to have been a lull in Aybak's campaigning activities at least until 597/1200–1. It is more than possible that having effectively dealt with any immediate threats from the major Indian dynasties he now took the opportunity to establish a Ghurid administration and consolidate his hold on these, not inconsiderable, newly acquired lands. This, together with Mu'izz al-Din's absence, due to the demand from his brother to bring an army to invade Khurasan, being the other factor.

In 596/1200 the brothers turned their attention to Khurasan. The combined armies of Ghur and Ghazna, a large force that included ninety elephants, began their invasion. The Ghurid sultans swiftly conquered Merv, Sarakhs, Abiward and Nisa both in modern Turkmenistan and Tush and Nishapur. At Merv Ghiyath al-Din installed the late Khwarazmshah Tekish's grandson Hindu Khan as ruler, instructing him to treat its people well. At Sarakhs, where he had negotiated a handover to Ghurid authority, he appointed a cousin, the *amir* Zanki ibn Masud, to rule. In addition, he also included Nisa and Abiward as part of that fief. Having devastated the area surrounding Tus, the city surrendered on terms. The *amir* was given a robe of honour in return for his cooperation and sent to Herat.[185] The city of Nishapur chose to resist under Ali Shah, the governor and brother of the Khwarazmshah Ala al-Din Muhammad. Both Ghurid armies invested the city, captured and sacked it. When Ghiyath al-Din heard that the Ghurid troops had run amok, he ordered 'whoever plunders or harms any

183 *TN*, vol. I, tr. Raverty, p. 516 and footnote pp. 522–3

184 P. Jackson (2003), p. 12

185 *al-Kamil fil-Ta'rikh*, part 3, tr. Richards, p. 57

person, his blood may be shed with impunity'.[186] Order was swiftly restored and looted goods were returned to their owners. Ali Shah complained at the way he and his officials had been handled. His former nurse demanded 'is this how the sons of kings are treated!' and Ghiyath al-Din replied, 'No, but rather like this' and he took Ali Shah by the hand, giving him a seat on the throne by his side and peace of mind.[187] Ali Shah, the Khwarazmian *amirs* and the garrison of Nishapur were then despatched to Ghur.[188] It is plausible that the chivalry and magnaminity displayed by Ghiyath al-Din towards his defeated counterparts and their innocent subjects came from his reading of the *Shahnameh*. By this time the legendary poem by Ferdowsi had stirred the hearts of many Persian and Turkic rulers. Most had read it in parts at least, if not in entirety. At its core was the concept of 'Farr', the divine right to rule bestowed on kings – a fundamental pillar of kingship, which demanded that kings be just and wise and rule with compassion. Ferdowsi warned that a king who did not abide by these morals could lose 'Farr', resulting in a swift downfall. The Ghurids through these military successes acquired control, albeit of short duration, of Khurasan as far as Bastam and Gorgan only twenty miles from the Caspian Sea. Ghurid territories had now reached their largest extent west of the Indus. Ghiyath al-Din appointed his cousin and son-in-law, Diya al-Din Muhammad, as governor of Khurasan and having installed a Ghurid administration departed for Herat. Mu'izz al-Din, for his part, one imagines on instruction from his brother, continued his campaign into Quhistan, to consolidate Ghurid control in this area of Iran. The region lay roughly east of Yazd, north of Sistan, south of Khurasan and west of Herat. He seems to have been campaigning largely against Isma'ilis and at Gunabad he laid siege to the city with a large Isma'ili presence, having already killed or enslaved various populations in the area. The ruler of Quhistan sent an appeal to Ghiyath al-Din complaining that he had a treaty with him and asking why his brother was causing such destruction in his territories. Having captured Gunabad and expelled the Isma'ilis, Mu'izz al-Din seems to have continued plundering Isma'ili held fortresses presumably all in the name of Sunni orthodoxy. Shortly afterwards a messenger arrived from his brother and said, 'I have a command of the sultan Do not be furious if I act on it.' 'No [I will not]', he replied, so the other said, 'He says, "What are you doing with my subjects? Depart!"' 'I shall not depart,'

186 Ibid., p. 57

187 Ibid., p. 58. The Khwarazmshahs were in many respects a more illustrious dynasty than the upstart Ghurids.

188 *TN*, vol. I, p. 255. Raverty says Ghur. Ibn al-Athir states several Khwarazmian *amirs* were sent to Herat.

said Shihab al-Din. The messenger went on, 'Then I shall do what he ordered me', and he drew his sword and severed the guy ropes of Shihab al-Din's pavilion and said, 'Depart on the sultan's command.'[189] Unhappy, Mu'izz al-Din left with his army for his own territories in India. He did not tarry in Ghazna, angry at the humiliation caused to him by his brother. This is the only recorded instance we have of the brothers falling out; otherwise they seem to have had an exemplary relationship, acting in concert, with Mu'izz al-Din accepting his elder brothers' authority. So, what went wrong in this instance? Quite likely Mu'izz al-Din lost control of his troops at some juncture and rather than consolidating Ghurid authority in wider Quhistan, as he had been instructed to do, was diverted from his main task of trying to eradicate Isma'ilis. He sought to impose strict Sunni adherence in areas with significant Alid populations. The rulers of these districts had already acknowledged the supreme sultan in Ghur as their overlord and paid their dues to him. Perhaps Ghiyath al-Din was more pragmatic in matters of religion and his brother rather less so. Could Mu'izz al-Din's campaigning against unbelievers in the Indian subcontinent have made him less tolerant of deviators from Sunni orthodoxy, even Muslims?

On his return to the Ghurid Indian territories Mu'izz al-Din seems to have wasted little time in despatching his general Aybak to continue his campaigns, first towards the Chaulukya territories in the borderlands of Gujerat. The chronologies and descriptions of these campaigns, in the various sources, are difficult to follow and at times contradictory. According to Ibn al-Athir, sometime in 597/1200–01 the Ghurid general captured Nahrawala – a Muslim corruption of Anahilapataka – an ancient site near modern Patan in Gujerat. Aybak took this Chaulukya capital by storm after fierce fighting – the ruler, probably Bhimadeva II, fled to raise another army. The description of the engagement by Ibn al-Athir could well be a misinterpretation of previous events. The sixteenth-/seventeenth-century Persian chronicler Firishta states that the capture of Nahrawala took place following the second battle at Mount Abu in 593/1197, that is, not on the return of Mu'izz al-Din from his campaign in Khurasan.[190] Having won an outstanding victory and taken large numbers of prisoners and booty, would Aybak have then decided to attempt to fight his

189 *al-Kamil fi'l-Ta'rikh*, part 3, tr. Richards, pp. 58–9. Ibn al-Athir refers to Mu'izz al-Din as Shihab al-Din.

190 *TN*, vol. I, tr. Raverty, p. 522. See footnote regarding Firishta's comments on the second battle of Mount Abu and that the city was captured after the battle. Ibn al-Athir's description of the occupation and return of the city to Bhimdeva seems credible even if the chronology is debatable. The Ghurids would have been unable to furnish the city with a meaningful garrison and maintain it in hostile territory. They never conquered Gujerat.

way into a large city with all this baggage? Whatever the chronology, the scale of the defeat was comprehensive. The defeated rulers' departure to raise another army is a good example of the almost inexhaustible supplies of manpower that the major Indian rulers could mobilise. The Ghurids for their part, although in time they also used Indian soldiers, would always be restricted by the numerical limits placed on them by their ability to recruit *ghulams* from Central Asia. In the case of Nahrawala, Mu'izz al-Din was aware that, given its great size, unless he permanently occupied the city himself he would not have the troops to hold it. Ibn al-Athir describes it as 'one of the greatest in India and most populous'. The Ghurid sultan therefore made peace in return for tribute to be paid half in advance and the rest at another date and the city reverted to its existing ruler.[191] While this decision might look counterproductive it was necessarily pragmatic. The scale of the victory and the resulting stipulations can only have served to grind down Chaulukya resistance and dissuade them from interfering in Ghurid lands. No matter how many armies you are able to raise, constant heavy defeats and loss of specie, elephants and personnel must have a demoralising effect on both rulers and ruled. Mu'izz al-Din then took charge of the campaigning himself and led his forces towards the great fortress of Gwalior.

The first place to fall was Thangir, approximately sixty miles to the northeast of Gwalior, quite possibly in 597/1201. This fortress was made over to Baha-al-Din Toghril, one of Mu'izz al-Din's longstanding, senior and greatest *ghulams*. Juzjani describes him as 'a Malik of excellent disposition, scrupulously impartial … and adorned with humility'.[192] This location seems to have been too far from Gwalior for conducting operations against that fortress. Toghril proceeded to establish himself at Sultankot, now part of Bahayana in Madhya Pradesh. From here, he was able to despatch cavalry to raid the area surrounding Gwalior, up to the city walls. Using Sultankot, the Ghurids tried to take the fortress, but the place was too large to invest properly with the numbers of troops at their disposal. The ruler of Gwalior, Rae Mangal Diw of the Pratihara/Parihar dynasty, realised this. He sent presents to Mu'izz al-Din to mollify and buy him off, and this worked, for now.[193] At around this juncture, Mu'izz al-Din received a summons, from his brother, ordering him to return north to deal with a resurgent Khwarazmshah. The siege of Gwalior was left in the hands of his *mamluk* generals. Before departing, Mu'izz al-Din informed Toghril that

191 *al-Kamil fi'l-Ta'rikh*, part 3, tr. Richards, p. 60

192 *TN*, vol. I, tr. Raverty, p. 544

193 *TN*, vol. I, p. 546 and p. 619. See also Ray (2017), vol. II, p. 829 regarding identity of ruler of Gwalior.

should the fortress fall it would be given as a fief to him.[194] After being besieged in the city for about a year, the ruler of Gwalior sued for terms. Having sent emissaries with presents and offerings to Aybak, the fortress was delivered up to him in Mu'izz al-Din's absence. Unsurprisingly, this caused great enmity between the two Ghurid generals. However, due to their allegiance to their master, they probably would not have dared to engage in violence against each other while Mu'izz al-Din was alive. Again, the precise date of the fall of the Gwalior remains a mystery. Juzjani gives no indication. Peter Jackson states 1201 and Ibn al-Athir tells us that Mu'izz al-Din had reached Ghazna by Rajab, 28 March–26 April 1202, and there is no mention of the fall of the city/fortress.[195] In the meantime Aybak continued his campaigning eastwards into the territory of the Chandellas. He along with his *mamluk* Shams al-Din Iltutmish invested and captured the fortress capital of Kalinjar in April 1202. The Rae of Kalinjar, the Chandella ruler Paramardideva r. 560–99/1165–1203, had attempted to dispute the issue but had been forced to seek refuge in the fortress. The Ghurid forces acquired a great number of slaves, arms, horses, cattle, elephants and jewels in spoils. The temples were converted into mosques. Apparently, Paramiradideva died of natural causes shortly after the fall of the city and Aybak left a Ghurid governor in situ.[196] Aybak and his *ghulam* Iltutmish then proceeded to take Mahoba, a temple city in the Bundelkhand region. This city formed part of the principality of Kalpi and was probably no longer part of the Chandella dominions.[197] The Ghurid generals then returned to Delhi via Bada'un, which was also occupied.

Despite his recent setbacks against the Ghurid sultans, the Khwarazmshah 'Ala' al-Din Muhammad r. 596–617/1200–20 had realised that the withdrawal of the Ghurid armies from Khurasan and Mu'izz al-Din's absence campaigning in India, presented him with an opportunity. In this endeavour, he could also call upon the Qara-khitai to assist him in regaining his lost territories. His first move was to threaten Ghiyath al-Din's governor in Khurasan, 'Ala' al-Din al-Ghuri. It is interesting to note that Ghiyath al-Din always chose his close family or Ghurid princes as his representatives in conquered lands and appointed them to positions of authority whereas his brother always chose his *mamluks*. Mu'izz al-Din's logic seems to have been that his *mamluks* relied entirely on him for their preferment. There were no issues with family factions, so their loyalty to him

194 Ibid., p. 546 note 7. Unfortunately, we do not know when Toghril died. Juzjani says after the fall of Gwalior giving no detail.

195 P. Jackson (2003), p. 12 and *al-kamil fi'l-Ta'rikh*, part 3, p. 65

196 Ray (2017), vol. II, pp. 720–21. See also Raverty footnote p. 523.

197 Ibid., p. 722

was guaranteed. As long as he retained his authority he could rely on his *ghulams* – and this seems, by and large, to have been the case. Having captured Merv and ejected his nephew, Hindu-Khan, who fled to Firuzkuh, the Khwarazmshah proceeded to besiege Nishapur. Ghiyath al-Din now had to play for time as he was ailing and was too crippled with gout or rheumatism to campaign in person. After about two months of being besieged and with no hope of relief in sight 'Ala' al-Din was forced to seek terms, from the Khwarazmshah, for himself and his Ghurid garrison. An agreement was reached, the Ghurids were well treated and sent on their way. 'Ala'-al-din had been asked by the Khwarazmshah to act as an intermediary between himself and the two Ghurid sultans to try to make peace. Another senior Ghurid who was treated generously was *amir* al-Husayn Kharmil, and he was later to become an ally of the Khwarazmshah after the deaths of Ghiyath and Mu'izz al-Din.[198] The Kwarazmshah then moved on to Sarakhs where the ruling *amir* was Taj al-Din Zanki, a cousin of Giyath al-Din. The sultan Muhammad tried to persuade the Ghurid to relinquish the city on favourable terms but *amir* Zanki, due to his close relationship with the Ghurid sultans, was unwilling to give up the place, despite the friendly overtures. The Kwarazmshah departed, leaving some of his officers to continue with the siege. At this point, another Ghurid *amir,* Muhammad ibn Kharnak, set out from Talaquan with the intention of making a surprise attack on the besieging Khwarazmians. However, they seem to have received prior knowledge of his plans and abandoned the siege. The Ghurid garrison at Sarakhs joined the force of Muhammad ibn Kharnak and together they sought out the Khwarazmian army. At Marv al-Rud, the Ghurid *amirs* levied the land tax and did the same at other places in the neighbourhood.[199] The mention by Ibn al-Athir that they halted their march to collect taxes, when they were on an urgent campaign, begs the question: Were these dues actually outstanding or was it opportunistic money grabbing? The Ghurids seem to have had difficulty maintaining their authority in Khurasan due in part to the rapaciousness of their tax collectors. Mu'izz al-Din himself imposed taxes and seized properties in Tus, as well as taking grain for his troops that had already been allocated to the shrine of the Imam 'Ali al-Rida.[200] However, it is doubtful whether, in earlier times, Ghaznavid tax agents were greeted with much alacrity in Khurasan either.

The Khwarazmian army led by a maternal uncle of the sultan Muhammad was comprehensively defeated by the smaller Ghurid force under Ibn Kharnak

198 *al-Kamil fi'l-Ta'rikh,* part 3, tr. Richards, p. 64

199 Ibid., p. 64

200 *CHI,* vol. 5, p. 164

who, armed with his mace, struck down and killed the Khwarazmian standard bearer. This caused the Khwarzmian troops to lose heart and flee. According to the chronicler, the Ghurid force numbered 900 men and the Khwarzmian force 3,000. The latter were pursued for some distance, and many were killed.[201] At this point, the Khwarazmshah again sought peace from Ghiyath al-Din who responded by despatching, as his ambassador, the powerful *amir* al-Husayn ibn Muhammad al-Marghani. 'Ala' al-Din Muhammad promptly arrested this man on his arrival. Neither ruler seems to have been very serious about peace. Ghiyath al-Din was playing for time, waiting for the arrival of his brother with their Indian army. In the meantime, the Khwarazmshah moved to invest Herat having been encouraged that he might be able to take the city easily by subterfuge. He was relying on the treachery of two brothers who had once served his uncle the sultan Mahmud, before entering Ghurid employment following the death of Sultan Shah. Somehow, a Khwarzmian let slip to Muhammad al- Marghani, the imprisoned Ghurid emissary, what was afoot. He promptly wrote to the *amir* of Herat, Umar al-Marghani, who happened to be his brother, and the plotters were apprehended and thrown in prison along with their supporters. Shortly afterwards, Alp Ghazi, a nephew of the Ghurid sultan, arrived and established a camp about fifteen miles from Herat. From here, he was able to interdict supplies destined for the besieging army. They, in their turn, sent out a raiding party, which was met and destroyed by another Ghurid force, led by al-Husayn ibn Kharmil in the district of Talaqan – modern Taloqan – in northeastern Afghanistan. In the meantime, Ghiyath al-Din had marched with his forces to Herat. It would seem as though he felt compelled to leave Firuzkuh to offer support to the besieged city. However, despite the city's significance to Ghurid prestige and stability, Ghiyath al-Din realised that his presence in the field was all he could accomplish, as the troops he had at his disposal were too few to confront the Khwarazmshah. The situation again clearly illustrates the Ghurid manpower dilemma. They were unable to field two substantial armies in the Indian subcontinent and the Iranian lands to the west simultaneously. This was a minimum requirement if they were to effectively control the enormous territory over which they now held sway – particularly, with a resurgent Khwarazmshah. As Ibn al-Athir clearly states, 'his troops were too few, as most of them were with his brother in India or Ghazna'.[202]

However, although the Khwarazmshah spent forty days besieging Herat, he could not afford to do so indefinitely. Alp Ghazi's troops threatened his supply lines, he knew that Ghiyath al-Din was in the field, not far away, and that the

201 *al-Kamil fi'l -Ta'rikh*, part 3, p. 64

202 *al-Kamil fi'l- Ta'rikh*, part 3, tr. Richards, p. 65

Indian army of Mu'izz al-Din was on the march. In the end, news of the total loss of the raiding force to Talaqan made up his mind. He made peace with the Ghurid *amir* 'Umar al-Murghani and having paid some tribute departed the city. On his arrival in Ghazna, Mu'izz al-Din was swiftly apprised of the situation in Khurasan. He learned of the territorial losses sustained and wasted little time in seeking out the Khwarazmshah. Having marched to Balkh and then to Bamiyan he reached Merv where Sultan Muhammad had taken up residence. The two vanguards clashed, leaving large numbers of dead on both sides. At this juncture the Khwarazmshah evacuated Merv and retreated to the Khwarazmian heartland, opening the dykes and flooding the irrigation channels as he did so, to hinder any Ghurid pursuit. He killed the *amir* Sanjar ruler of Nishapur, as he passed through, due to suspected treachery.[203] Mu'izz al-Din for his part moved to the borders of Tus and Sarakhs southwest of Merv where he prepared to winter, with the intention of continuing the campaign in the spring.[204] While he was there, he learned of the death of his brother, Ghiyath al-Din, at Herat, this occurring sometime between 16 January and 14 February 1203. He promptly set out for Herat where condolences and mourning ceremonies were conducted during Rajab 599/16 March–14 April 1203. It was then that the death was publicly announced.[205]

During a reign of forty years 558–599/1163–1203 of comparative stability Ghiyath al-din had presided over an extraordinary achievement. Through sheer personality and ability, he had managed to control Shansabanid rivalries and create a vast empire with the cooperation of his younger brother. They had sprung from a line of petty princes in the mountain fastness of Ghur, the western extension of the Hindu Kush, and came to dominate the eastern Iranian lands and initiated the Muslim colonisation of India – from Bastam in the west, to Bengal in the east and from the straits of Hormuz through Khurasan north into Transoxiana to the borders of ancient Sogdiana and modern Tajikistan. Never again was a native dynasty from Afghanistan to have so much influence on the Islamic world. He was a successful general, although he rarely took the field himself. According to Ibn al-Athir, 'Never was his banner defeated … He was simply cunning and wily. He was generous and his creed was sound. He built mosques and madrasahs in Khurasan and caravanserais on the highways.'[206] The latter a proof of his encouragement of existing trade routes and that he appreciated the value and strategic position of Ghur in this context. He presided over a thriving court

203 Ibid., p. 66

204 *TN*, vol. I, tr. Raverty, p. 471

205 *al-Kamil fi'l- Ta'rikh*, part 3, p. 68

206 *al-Kamil fi'l-Tarikh*, part 3, tr. Richards, p. 66

culture where Alids were tolerated and poets and literary men were encouraged. Religious tolerance seems to have been a theme. The same could not perhaps be said of his younger brother, Mu'izz al-Din. The chronicler tells us Ghiyath al-Din made 'Korans with his own hand' and 'did not reveal partisanship for any school of law … but would say "Partisanship for law schools in a ruler is reprehensible". … He inclined towards the Shafi's without encouraging them at the expense of others.'[207] In his youth he had been, perhaps more typically for a Persianate Islamic ruler, keen on the convivial life and the chase. At Zamindawar, the winter capital, he laid out a substantial and magnificent garden; 'its glades were adorned with pine and juniper-trees and various sorts of shrubs and odiferous herbs; and the sultan had commanded, so that adjoining the wall of that garden a plain had been cleared corresponding in length and breadth with the garden itself'.[208] Every year a great hunt was organised and an area of hundreds of square miles around was encompassed by retainers and huntsmen and, over the period of a month, gradually the animals of all varieties were encircled and driven onto the plain. Ghiyath al-Din seems to have used these events, particularly in the early years of his reign, as an opportunity to cement relationships with his *maliks* and *mamluks.* These activities appear to have borne fruit with loyalties that endured during his lengthy reign. The sultan would appear from the pavilion, in the garden, where various entertainments ensued and his servants were given permission, one by one to mount up and hunt the game before him.[209] The event must have lasted days. We learn from Juzjani that, as he grew older, Ghiyath al-Din ceased to drink wine 'and devoted himself to rectitude and goodness', this seeming to have been the case by the time Sultan Shah had begun to harry Ghurid territories.[210] The motto on his signet bore the words 'for me God alone is sufficient'.[211] He was buried in a mausoleum attached to the Masijd-i Jami, the congregational mosque he had rebuilt and embellished in Herat. He was sixty-three years old when he died.

207 Ibid., p. 67

208 *TN*, vol. I. tr. Raverty, p. 386

209 Ibid.

210 Ibid., p. 387

211 Ibid., p. 390

MU'IZZ AL-DIN AS SUPREME SULTAN

Mu'izz al-Din was now the supreme Ghurid sultan and his responsibilities and the pressures that went with them illustrate the inherent difficulties and weaknesses of the Ghurid polity. He assumed the title Sultan *ul-A'zam*, that is, the greatest sultan that was previously held by his elder brother. Prior to this, he had been Sultan *ul-Mu'azzam*, that is, the great sultan.[212] His first task was to reallocate Shansabanid fiefs among family members. However, as Ibn al-Athir clearly states, whatever the reallocations and appointments, military and administrative, Mu'izz al-Din was the supreme ruler. Regarding Ghiyath al-Din's son, Mahmud, he writes, 'He kept him detached from all sovereign power and did not bestow on him nor any other member of his family the succession to his father.'[213] He then returned to Ghazna, rather than remaining at Firuzkuh, taking various Ghurid *maliks* and *amirs* with him to prepare for the forthcoming campaign against the Khwarazmshah. He may also have been keen to return to his own powerbase from where he could not only organise the expedition to the west, but also gauge, from Ghazna's better communication with Lahore, the situation in the Ghurid Indian territories. These lands had been conquered by Mu'izz al-Din's own endeavours and no other Shansabanid could lay claim to them.

While Aybak and his *mamluk* Iltutmish, together with other Turkish *ghulams*, had been consolidating Ghurid rule in the upper Ganges valley and contiguous regions, another Muslim warrior had been carrying Ghurid arms further afield into the Ganges Basin towards western Bengal. Muhammad b. Bakhtiyar was a Khalaj tribal headman from Garmsir in Helmand in southern Afghanistan. He had tried to join Mu'izz al-Din's forces in India and having been granted a small salary by the *diwan-i-ariz,* the muster master, in Ghazna he proceeded to Lahore. There, he failed to impress Aybak, and had moved on into India. His humble appearance may have had something to do with this. We are told his outward aspect was nothing particularly remarkable. However, he was endowed with great physical strength and was known for possessing very long arms. He was to prove himself to be brave, enterprising and fearless. He finally found satisfactory position with the *malik* Husam al-Din Ughul Bak or Oghulbeg, a *mamluk,* who was in possession of the large fief of Kol in the Doab between

212 Ibid., p. 472 and see note 6

213 *al-Kamil fi'l -Ta'rikh*, part 3 p. 68. Mahmud took the title Ghiyath al-Din on his father's death.

the confluence of the Ganges and Jumuna rivers[214] – apparently beyond the control of Aybak at that time. In his service, he campaigned into Awadh and was rewarded with a territory in Mirzapur in the southeast of modern Uttar Pradesh, immediately due west of the Karamnasa River. From here, he raided into the Hindu territories of Maner and Bihar.[215] These *razzias* across the river provided him with copious quantities of booty, including arms and horses. News of his successes filtered back into the Ghurid world. Even Aybak, who had treated him dismissively earlier, sent him a robe from Lahore honouring his achievements. Muhammad b. Bakhtiyar was soon raiding into Bihar. On one of these expeditions he reached a fortress and attacked it with 200 heavily armed and mailed horsemen, a fairly inconsequential force, one might think, given the extent of these conquests. No doubt, as news spread of these successes, more adventurers joined his ranks. Forcing the postern Muhammad b. Bakhtiyar and his band were able to take the fortress in 590/1193–4, acquiring great riches in the process. However, the fortress that had been captured turned out to be a Buddhist monastery, hence perhaps the ease with which it was taken. Practically all the monks were slaughtered. This place could well have been Nalanda, the great centre of learning and last stronghold of Buddhism in India. Juzjani doesn't specify the name of the location. The surviving monks deserted the site.

These raids into Bengal and the ensuing destruction hastened the decline of Buddhism in its last redoubt in Bihar and western Bengal. The religion was struggling from the loss of patronage following the disappearance of any vestiges of the once mighty Pala dynasty.[216] According to Ray, at the time of Mohammad b. Bakhtiyar's incursions, and one assumes a contributory factor to his success, the area had no major dynasty ruling it. The Gahadavalas had abandoned the region following the defeat of the Chauhans at the second battle of Tara'in in 588/1192. The Senas, who were the main beneficiaries of the decline of the Palas, ruled to the east and only occasionally raided westwards.[217] Muhammad b. Bakhtiyar's sorties must have finally destroyed any remnants of Pala authority.

214 *TN*, vol. I, tr. Raverty, p. 516 note 2 para 11. According to Juzjani Mu'izz al-Din had installed Ughul Bak as ruler of the fortress of Kol and its dependencies in (590/1193–4), following his victory at Chandawar. See also Jackson (2003), p. 26 note 13. Oghulbeg from Turkish *oghul* son, boy and *beg* prince ref (Clauson, *Etymological dictionary*).

215 Ibid., p. 550 and note 6. See also Ray (2017), vol. 1, p. 370 note 3. Muner is situated at the confluence of the rivers Son and Ganges.

216 Skelton, R., 'Bengal; The historical background'. In: *The Arts of Bengal: The Heritage of Bangladesh and Eastern India* (Eds Robert Skelton and Mark Francis) (London, 1979), pp. 19–20

217 Ray (2017), vol. 1, p. 371

Following his successful expedition, Muhammad b. Bakhtiyar presented himself to Aybak, who was now established in Delhi and was treated with great 'honour and distinction', so much so that he engendered feelings of jealousy among a number of Aybak's *amirs* at the viceregal court.[218] Matters came to a head and he was forced to prove himself in combat against an enraged elephant. This he did by striking the beast on the trunk with his mace, causing the animal to run away. This episode had the desired effect of reinforcing the Khalaj leader's reputation for bravery. He impressed Aybak to such an extent that he gave him a special robe, possibly an earlier gift from his master Mu'izz al-Din, from his own collection along with other presents. The *amirs* who had derided him and doubted his abilities were ordered to do the same. Muhammad b. Bakhtiyar departed to terrorise the populace as he continued his conquests through Lakhnawti and Bihar – western Bengal as far as the territories of the Sena kingdom. These included the Ganges/Bramaputra Delta as well as the district known as Bang – the eastern delta/part of modern Bangladesh – and areas of Kamrup – Assam. While he acknowledged the Ghurid sultan and was careful to deliver a proportion of the booty to Aybak he seems to have been largely left to his own devices. There are no reports of any reinforcements from the Ghurid heartland, and he must have relied on his own successes to attract men to his banner.

The Sena dynasty at this time was ruled by Lakshmana Sena r. 574–602/1185–1206. The depredations of Muhammad b. Bakhtiyar's raids had encouraged a retreat of the populace to the eastern parts of the Sena realm. The king continued to rule from his capital at Nudiya, modern Nabawip, in western Bengal and this was taken and sacked in 601/May 1205.[219] He was forced to flee to one of his other capitals at Bikrampur, south of modern Dhaka in Bangladesh. According to Juzjani, Muhammad b. Bakhtiyar arrived at the city with only eighteen accomplices on horseback, the rest of his force following later. He proceeded to the gates of the palace 'steadily and sedately … that the people imagined that his party were merchants with horses for sale'. He drew his sword when he reached the palace gates and mayhem ensued. The king managed to flee barefoot and escaped by boat downriver, leaving his wives, domestic servants, a large amount of plunder and a number of elephants, which were all captured.[220] The city apparently delivered untold wealth. Having sacked Nudiya Muhammad b. Bakhtiyar departed and established his own capital at Lakhnawti/Gaur, a former Sena capital in western Bengal just to the north of the Ganges. He ordered the *khutba* to be read in the

218 *TN*, vol. I, tr. Raverty, pp. 552–4

219 Jackson (2003), p. 10

220 *TN*, vol. I, p. 558

name of the Ghurid sultan in the newly conquered territories. These were extensive, comprising a large area of the Ganges basin and reaching as far as the western Ganges/Brahmaputra Delta. He issued gold coins in the name of the Ghurid sultan Mu'izz al-Din depicting a galloping horseman with a lance and bearing Arabic and Sanskrit legends. If nothing else, he was affirming his loyalty to the Ghurid dynasty. He dutifully continued to send tribute to Aybak as he and his *amirs* set about establishing Islam in the newly conquered lands.

Far to the west, Mu'izz al-Din had been continuing his fight with the resurgent Khwarazmshah 'Ala' al-Din Muhammad. Following his earlier departure from Tus to Herat and the subsequent fall out arising from his brother's death, the supreme sultan had retired to Ghazna. He had left as his governor in Merv the renowned Ghurid *amir* Muhammad ibn Kharnak, who seems to have spent much of his time confronting constant Khwarazmian sorties into Ghurid territory.[221] He had achieved some success, and on a night raid, had surprised and routed several Khwarazmian *amirs,* whose heads along with the survivors were sent to Herat. This city had become increasingly important to the Ghurid Sultanate, particularly in the latter years of Ghiyath al-Din's reign. Quite possibly due to its wealth, scale and strategic position in relation to Khwarazm and Iran, it was becoming a de facto western capital as Firuzkuh seems to have declined in importance – if for no other reason than its inaccessibility and seasonal limitations. These made it less suitable as a seat of government from which to manage the large area that the Ghurid sultans now controlled to the west. Mu'izz al-Din's preparations to invade Khwarazm were well advanced when Muhammad Shah sent an army under the Turk Barfur against Muhammad ibn Kharnak. The two forces clashed about fifteen miles from Merv, the only details known being that it was closely contested with significant losses to both sides. The Ghurids ultimately came off worse and retreated to Merv. According to Ibn al-Athir, Muhammad ibn Kharnak was left with ten horsemen, from which we should probably read *amirs* and *mamluks* and their surviving retainers. He was now without sufficient troops to hold the large city. After a siege of fifteen days, he was forced to sue for terms and having been promised that his life would be spared, he surrendered and was promptly killed.[222] Mu'izz al-Din was incensed and sent envoys to the Khwarazmshah, but no peace was agreed. The supreme sultan, as we have seen, before leaving for Ghazna, had allocated some of the Ghurid ancestral lands to close Shansabanid relations. He had appointed his nephew Alp-Ghazi as governor in Herat. To his nephew

221 *TN*, vol. I, p. 471 note 5. According to Raverty he would have been the second cousin of Ghiyath and Mu'izz al-Din.

222 *al-Kamil fi'l-Ta'rikh*, part 3, tr. Richards, p. 68

Sultan Ghiyath al-Din Mahmud he had allocated Bust and the districts of Farah and Isfizar, but this appointment carried no real administrative power. Another nephew, *malik* al-Haji 'Ala' al-Din Muhammad, and son-in-law of Ghiyath al-Din, received the Ghurid heartland of Ghur, the Garmsir and the throne at Firuzkuh. He was one of the rare Shansabanid princes who had previously campaigned in India with Mu'izz al-Din, and who saw fit to donate him two elephants. He was also appointed military commander of the Ghurid territories in Khurasan and oversaw all affairs of state in that region.[223] While Mu'izz al-Din must have trusted him, one wonders what sort of military force he could bring to bear without the assistance of his uncle.

In the spring of 601/1204, Shah Muhammad Khwarazmshah again put Herat under siege following unsuccessful peace talks with Mu'izz al-Din. The Ghurid sultan had left Ghazna and marched to Lahore, aiming to raid into India. We have no more detail of this campaign and by May of that year, he and his army were on their way back to Khurasan. The primary purpose was to reimpose Ghurid authority there, recover lost territories and avenge the death of Muhammad ibn Kharnak. The fighting raged throughout Khurasan. In one instance, a Ghurid prince, Al Husayn ibn Kharmil, as part of a ruse, offered to handover the elephants and treasury he held on behalf of Mu'izz al-Din. The Khwarazmshah promptly despatched 1,000 cavalry to take the surrender. In an astonishing turn of events the Ghurids under Al-Husayn and another Ghurid *amir* al-Husayn ibn Muhammad al-Marghani joined battle and destroyed the Khurasani force, killing them almost to a man. The Khwarazmshah was less than happy and regretted his naïve decision to send his troops in the first place. At this point, Alp Ghazi fell ill and died. The Ghurid governor, due to his illness, had earlier agreed to make a gesture acknowledging the Khwazamshah and agree peace terms to allow him to raise the siege and depart with honour from Herat. None the wiser the Kwarazmshah had lifted the siege, destroyed his siege engines and left to install himself at Sarakhs.[224]

Mu'izz al-Din by this stage (late spring 600/1204) had reached the borders of Khurasan with his Indian army and substantial forces gathered from the Ghurid territories west of the Indus, possibly as far as Sistan and Kirman. The plan seems to have been to bypass the Khwarazmshah in Khurasan, and strike directly at the heart of his empire in Khwarazm and the capital Gurganj. According to Ibn al-Athir, Mu'izz al-Din and his army reached a place called Maymand. If this is modern Meymand in Kirman province, then the Ghurid sultan had taken

223 Ibid., p. 68 and *TN*, vol. I, p. 472 and notes and p. 391

224 *al-Kamil fi'l-Ta'rikh*, part 3, tr. Richards, p. 72

his substantial army far to the west of Herat onto the Iranian plateau. From there he would have needed to turn northwest to approach Khwarazm. This would seem highly unlikely due to the aridity of the area and, in particular, the lack of accesible water, pertinent in the case of his elephants and horses. The Khwarazamshah sent a letter commanding, 'Return to me that I may bring you to battle otherwise I shall go to Herat and from there to Ghazna.'[225] In the meantime Muhammad Shah had moved northeast to camp outside Merv. Mu'izz al-Din replied, 'Perhaps you will be defeated as happened on the other occasion. No we shall meet at Khwarazm.'[226] Moving into Khurasan along River Oxus, Mu'izz al-Din was unwavering in his aim of destroying the centre of Khwarzmian power, once and for all: he had amassed a sizeable army capable of accomplishing this. He had moved northwestwards, from Ghazna, and joined the Oxus at Balkh. By taking this route he would have hoped to reach Khwarazm without engaging the Khwarazmian forces in Khurasan en route and also ensuring a fresh water supply for his horses, elephants and soldiers. Juzjani makes no mention of Maymand or the route that the invading army took on what was to be the last great Ghurid campaign in the west. Once the Khwarazmshah realised what was happening, he burned any supplies that could prove useful to Ghurid foragers, split his army and made for home.[227] It now became a race to see who would reach the Khwarazmian Oasis first. Muhammad Shah sought the fastest route across the desert from Merv and reached Gurganj first, to rally the forces of Khwarazm. He also sent emissaries to his overlord, the Gur-Khan of the Qara-Khitai, seeking help. The Khwarazmshah, having won the race, set about delaying the Ghurid arrival. Gurganj itself is situated on the south bank of the Amu Darya. The river was dammed, as it reached the Caspian, and a series of canals had been constructed in the delta, to irrigate a vast area of what was a highly prosperous trading centre and one of the great cities of Central Asia. The Khwarazmshah flooded the area surrounding the city and this delayed the Ghurid army. Due to the inundation and damage caused, it apparently took Mu'izz al-Din forty days to reach the Khwarazmian oasis.[228] The two armies finally clashed at a place called Qarasu or 'Black Water', a canal running from the Amu Darya to the east of Gurganj. A desperate struggle ensued and the waters of the canal turned red with blood. There were considerable casualties on both sides. Among the dead on the Ghurid side was the *malik* al-Husayn al-Marghani.

225 Ibid.

226 Ibid.

227 Ibid., p. 73

228 Ibid.

Mu'izz al-Din had ordered any Khwarazmian prisoners taken to be executed.[229] The numbers favoured the Ghurids. The Khwarazmshah apparently had at his diposal approximately 70,000 men on horse and foot. The Ghurid force, on the other hand, comprised of up to 140,000 men and included between 300 and 400 elephants.[230] Whatever the figures involved, we know Mu'izz al-Din had assembled a vast host planned over many months and all that can be said with any certainty is that they outnumbered the forces of the Khwarazmshah, by some margin. The urgent appeal by the Khwarazmshah to the Qara-Khitai refelects his inferior force. According to Juzjani, these hostilities raged for a number of days, around various water courses, culminating in the engagement at Qarasu. Raverty describes how Mu'izz al-Din was in the process of drawing up his elephants in battle formation, in preparation for the crossing of the canal, when he heard that the Khwarazmshah had arrived accompanied by the forces of Sultan Uthman of Samarkand and that the Qara-Khitai were in the field.[231] The arrival of the latter would have been the most concerning for the Ghurid sultan. He had failed to take the city in part because he lacked the necessary siege equipment.

The delay caused by the flooding had eroded his supplies and reduced the efficacy and cohesion of his army. He had failed to take Gurganj so the riches and supplies therein were not about to become available. His forces had received a mauling from the Khwarazmians and adding to his predicament he now faced a substantial and fresh steppe army somewhere to his rear. Mu'izz al-Din resolved to abandon any heavy equipment and materiel and retreat along River Oxus towards Balkh, closely followed by the Khwarazamshah. The beleagured Ghurid army turned and stood to face their Khwarazmian pursuers at Hazar-Asp, modern Hazorasp, at the head of the Amu Darya Delta in what is now Uzbekistan. In this engagement the right wing of the Ghurid army was destroyed and the captives taken included Ghurid *amirs*. The Khwarazmians then withdrew into their own territory with their prisoners and spoils, which included numerous elephants, to celebrate their victory and deliverance. However, for the Ghurids as they continued their retreat, matters were about to become incomparably worse. At this juncture, they were still a fighting force, although admittedly much reduced. On reaching Andkhud modern Andkhoy just to the south of River Oxus, they found their way barred by the forces of the Qara-Khitai led by Baniko of Taras. The Ghurids were trapped. Arriving late in the day the Ghurids, led by the commander of the vanguard *salar* Husain-i-Kharmil, drove off the Qara-Khitai who had appeared, but this was to be

229 Ibid., p. 73 and see note 1

230 *TN*, vol. I, tr. Raverty, p. 473 note 2 para 2

231 *TN*, vol. I, tr. Raverty p. 473 note 2 para 3

a brief respite. At this juncture, Juzjani puts an absurd statement in the mouth of the Mu'izz al-Din: 'for years past I have been seeking an encounter such as this…'[232] For anyone to seek a confrontation with the Qara-Kitai on the borders of their own territory would be considered unwise at the best of times; with the current state of the Ghurid army, it was tantamount to lunacy. Andkhud itself offered little protection and some of the Ghurid *maliks* and their ravaged retinues realised the hopelessness of the situation and made themselves scarce during the night. This included members of the Shansabanid elite, among ithem *malik* Izz-ud-Din Husain ibn Kharmil, lord of Talquan and later governor of Herat. The following morning, the Ghurid sultan drew up what remained of his force. This consisted of horsemen from the central division of the army, and his own personal retinue of *mamluks.* The reduced Ghurid force was now surrounded by the overwhelming might of the Qara-Khitai. Mu'izz al-Din sought to hold his ground and fight it out. As the perimeter shrank, the force was reduced to the sultan's household, another 100 horsemen or so, elephants, the *mamluks* and the remaining Ghurid elite. Despite remonstrations from his household urging that any resistance was futile and to retreat, Mu'izz al-Din remained unmoved. By this stage withdrawal was probably not an option. His soldiers sold their lives dearly and the sultan's silk canopy of state was riddled with arrows and resembled a porcupine.[233] In the end, one of Mu'izz al-Din's *mamluks* grabbed the sultan's bridle and the remaining Ghurids managed to fight their way into the small fortification at Andkhud. This place was swiftly invested by the Qara-Khitai and with its perimeter crumbling it seemed only a matter of time before Mu'izz al-Din would be captured. The situation was saved by the intervention of the ruler of Samarkand, Uthman. He, as a Muslim, did not wish to see the humiliation of a sultan of Islam, by infidels, and pleading with Mu'izz al-Din urged him to see sense. The Ghurid sultan was told to hand over his remaining elephants, treasury and materiel. Having accomplished this, and at great risk to himself, the ruler of Samarkand managed to negotiate with and persuade the leaders of the Qara-Khitai to give Mu'izz al-Din safe passage with his remaining troops and to return to his own territory.[234]

232 Ibid., p. 475

233 Ibid., p. 477. Regarding Husain ibn Kharmil's later activities in Herat see p. 257 note 2.

234 *TN*, vol. I, tr. Raverty, p. 478 note 6. Ibn al-Athir provides a different take on events. He says that Mu'izz al-Din split his army due to a shortage of water on the retreat and remained with the rearguard. As the Ghurid detachments emerged from the desert they were annihilated by the Qara-Khitai. When the Ghurid sultan appeared he was unaware of the situation. He managed to reach Andkhud that he defended for several days before the intervention of the ruler of Samarkand. The ensuing agreement was that the Qara-Khitai should not cross the Oxus into Ghurid territory and vice versa. See *al-Kamil fi'l-Ta'rikh*, part 3, p. 74.

According to Juzjani, on his return to Ghazna Mu'izz al-Din resolved to raise a force sufficient for a three-year campaign across the Oxus against the Qara-Khitai. Given his recent mauling at their hands and lucky escape one would have thought that an element of circumspection would have been more appropriate.[235] In any event, his defeat at the hands of the Khwarazmians and the Qara-Khitai had not gone unnoticed and various groups and individuals sought to take advantage of this setback to Ghurid hegemony. At this stage, a truce seems to have been agreed between Shah Muhammad and Mu'izz al-Din. It was not long before news from Khurasan reached him of issues with the Isma'ilis. This was in precisely the same area where his earlier dealings with that population had led to the falling out with his brother. He promptly despatched his nephew 'Ala' al-Din Muhammad, governor in the historic Ghurid lands, to deal with the problem. 'Ala' al-Din Muhammad, as instructed, duly marched into the region of Quhistan, in southern Khurasan, and was joined in this endeavour by the ruler of Zazan, modern Zozan, close to the Afghan border to the west of Herat, who in so doing abandoned his allegiance to the Khwarazmshah. He besieged various Isma'ili strongholds including Kakhk, which he took, killing all the men of fighting age and enslaving the children. This campaign was ongoing at the time of Mu'izz al-Din's death in 602/1206.[236] Elsewhere, in 601/March–April 1205, a Ghurid force that had been despatched to Merv was ambushed at Sarakhs by the Kwarazmshah's *amir* Jaqar and defeated.[237] Any pretence of a truce between the two sultans would seem to have been short lived.

From Mu'izz al-Din's perspective, the most pressing issue was a serious revolt by the Hindu Khokhars. This tribe inhabited the Salt Range in what is now the Pakistani Punjab. The mountains lie to the south of the Potohar plateau, to the north of River Jhelum and extend west towards the Indus. The Khokhars and other local tribes had paid tribute to the Ghurid sultan but on hearing of his defeat and rumours of his death they rebelled. In doing so, they blocked the road between Ghazna and Lahore hindering communication with the Ghurid Indian provinces. Mu'izz al-Din responded by first killing one of his *mamluks,* Aybak Bak, who had escaped from Andkhud. This individual had used the uncertainties caused by his master's rumoured death to takeover Multan. The sultan then ordered his governor in Lahore and Multan, Muhammad ibn Abi 'Ali, to send him the revenues he held for the years 601/1203–04. These would have included not only monies collected locally but probably those taxes and plunder accrued

235 *TN*, vol. I p. 481

236 *al-Kamil fi'l-Ta'rikh*, part 3, tr. Richards, p. 75 and note 5

237 Ibid., p. 87

from the now considerable Ghurid territories across the Indus. Mu'izz al-Din specifies that these revenues were required for the planned forthcoming and lengthy campaign against the Qara-Khitai. He seems to have been determined to defeat the forces of the Gur-Khan, to prevent them from intervening in the unfinished struggle with the Khwarazmshah for control of Khurasan and Khwarazm. Muhammad ibn Abi 'Ali responded to his master saying that the Khokhars had cut the road and had already plundered a caravan on that route. Consequently, he was unable to despatch the funds.

Mu'izz al-Din wasted little time and ordered Aybak, the commander of his Indian armies, who seems to have been in Lahore at this juncture, to threaten the Khokhars. Aybak duly despatched one of his *mamluks* to remonstrate with the rebellious tribesmen. They were having none of it. They told the envoy that Mu'izz al-Din was dead and that he was to inform Aybak that he should abandon Peshawar, Lahore and the surrounding territories. Then, they would be prepared to make peace. Mu'izz al-Din, on receipt of this news, promptly ordered Aybak back to Delhi to gather his forces and return to attack the Khokhars. We can see that following the defeat at Andkhud, the Ghurid sultan no longer had adequate forces locally to deal with, what was proving to be, a major insurrection. However, he was still set on preparing for war with the Qara-Khitai; it was almost as if he was not prepared to acknowledge the seriousness of the revolt in the Punjab. With this in mind, he left Peshawar and returned to Ghazna. On arrival, he told his *mamluks* and the Ghurid *amirs* to prepare for the forthcoming campaign beyond the Oxus. He ordered that the army be ready to depart on 602/22 May 1205.[238] Meanwhile, the Khokhars caused other local Indian potentates to rebel, jeopardising Ghurid control over a large swathe of the Punjab. The *amir* of Lahore wrote to Mu'izz al-Din urging him to come in person. The Khokhars had expelled locally appointed Ghurid officials and collected taxes using their own representatives. Furthermore, they were so confident that they told the *amir* in Lahore to abandon the region and hand over the elephants stabled under his control. The situation was patently serious, with Mu'izz al-Din's governor saying 'if Shihab al-Din i.e. Mu'izz al-Din does not come in person with his armies, the country will pass from his control'.[239] Given that the Khokhars had managed to amass a considerable army, the Ghurid sultan had to react fast. Mu'izz al-Din gave up on his planned campaign into Transoxiana and left Ghazna in 602/ 20 October 1205. Somehow, he seems to have lost contact with the Ghurid cities of Ghazna and Peshawar to the extent that concerns arose that he might have been

238 *al-Kamil fi'l Ta'rikh*, part 3, pp. 89–90

239 Ibid., p. 90

defeated. The Khokhars were camped between the rivers Jhelum and Chenab.[240] Through a series of forced marches, Mu'izz al-Din reached the Khokhar camp. The rebels had not anticipated such a rapid advance, and on the morning of 602/10 November 1205 the sultan's forces closed with the enemy. The battle raged all day and was closely contested. However, the appearance of the Ghurid's Indian forces under the command of Qutb al-din Aybak sealed the rebel's fate. At the onset of evening, the Khokhar forces turned and broke with great loss of life. A number of them sought refuge in thickets and lit fires and immolated themselves, in some cases along with their women and dependants.[241] The leaders escaped, and the numerous captives taken by the Ghurids caused the value of slaves to plummet. Ibn al-Athir mentions five *rukni dinars* for one slave. The spoils taken was by all accounts huge – and would, together with outstanding Indian monies, have gone a long way towards funding the planned campaign against the Qara-Khitai.[242] One of the rebel leaders, Daniyal, the ruler of Mount Judi in the Salt Range, threw himself at the mercy of Aybak who interceded on his behalf with Mu'izz al-Din. The Ghurid sultan acquiesced with the proviso that the citadel of al-Judi was handed over. Having allayed the fears of the people in Lahore, Mu'izz al-Din ordered his forces to return home to make ready for the campaign against the Qara-Khitai. He left Lahore and returned to Ghazna on 603/26 February 1206 to continue preparations for the forthcoming campaign. He would not have long to live. In the meantime, he had already instructed the Ghurid sultan of Bamiyan, Baha al-Din Sam, to be ready to march on Samarkand and that he should construct a bridge, across the Amu Darya, of sufficient strength for the main army to cross, including the elephants and heavy materiel.[243] However, the Khokhars were not the only people causing trouble in the wake of the defeat at Andkhud. The Trahis were another tribal grouping who inhabited the area of mountains west of Kohat. The area is in the Central District of what is the North-West Frontier Province, along the Afghanistan–Pakistan border, south of the Khyber Pass. The Trahis used the opportunity of revolts elsewhere to lead

240 Ibid. Ibn al-Athir mentions between the rivers Jhelum and Sudara. Modern Sodhra is situated a few miles to the east of Wazirabad at a crossing place on the left bank of the Chenab. The Punjab Rivers were serious obstacles to invading armies, *viz* Alexander the Great at the Hydaspes, Mahmud of Ghazna's raids in the early eleventh century and continued to cause problems up to the time of the British particularly, during and after the Sikh wars in the nineteenth century.

241 Ibid., part 3, p. 90. See also *TN*, vol. II, p. 482. '… in the cold season of that year, the Sultan came into Hindustan, and sent that refactory race to hell'.

242 *TN*, vol. I, tr. Raverty, p. 485 note 2 noting comments from Yafa-I that the campaign against the Khokars was 'sufficient to repair the Sultan's finances'

243 *al-kamil fi'l -Ta'rikh*, part 3, tr. Richards, p. 91

an uprising and raid into the middle Kabul river valley and cause widespread disruption.[244] Mu'izz al-Din despatched his senior *mamluk* Taj al-Din Yildiz to deal with the problem and he wasted little time in restoring order, killing many, beheading the leaders and displaying their heads in Islamic held areas. He would have done this, in part, to restore the confidence of those who had converted to Islam earlier in Mu'izz al-Din's reign and as an example to others that the writ of Allah and the Ghurid sultan would always prevail.[245]

As Mu'izz al-Din made his way home to Ghazna he halted at a place called Damyak, whose precise location is not known. Major Raverty goes into some detail, however, and it would seem the most likely spot is somewhere to the west of River Jhelum, but not as far as the Indus. Most authors agree that the camp was in a verdant setting with the sultan's pavilion complex placed close to clear running water, so possibly on a smaller tributary of that river.[246] As Mu'izz al-Din settled into his pavilion unbeknownst to him a plot to assassinate him had been hatched. The assassins were almost certainly Isma'ilis. Mu'izz al-Din was, through his nephew 'Ala' al-Din Muhammad, campaigning against them in Quhistan at that time. He had treated that community harshly and viewed them as deviants. From his early expeditions to Daybul and subsequent campaigns in Quhistan, he had dealt with them mercilessly, so much so that it caused the only rift, we know of, with his brother, Ghiyath al-Din.[247] Ibn al-Athir specifically mentions that two of the individuals, seized after the event, were circumcised men, that is, Muslims. The idea they were Khokhars seems less likely. Although, it is possible, the Isma'ilis could have embedded themselves with Khokhar converts, in order to travel in the sultan's entourage. As Ibn al-Athir tells us, 'God came for him from a quarter he had not anticipated and all the money, weapons and men profited him nothing.'[248] The sultan's retinue had dispersed, to prepare for evening prayer, and he was left in his pavilion with two carpet spreaders and his armour bearer. As Mu'izz al-Din prostrated himself in prayer the assassins struck – there may have been up to four of them. The armour bearer and one of the carpet spreaders were killed. During this commotion, as the armour bearer cried out, the other bodyguards seem to have left

244 Ibid., p. 91 and see also footnotes 6 and 7

245 Ibid, p. 92

246 *TN*, vol. I, tr. Raverty, p. 485 note 3. Possibly the modern Dhamiak, a village in the Jhelum District of Punjab province in Pakistan.

247 *al-Kamil fi'l -Ta'rikh*, part 3, p. 93. The chronicler specifically states that Mu'izz al-Din's operations in Khurasan were the catalyst. 'It is claimed that the Isamailis killed him because they feared his expedition into Khurasan.'

248 Ibid., part 3, p. 91

their posts around the royal pavilion, to come to see what had happened. This gave the other assassins their opportunity. They broke through into the sultan's tent and one or two stabbed him as he prayed. Prostrate in prayer, he would have had no chance to react and received several deep and fatal wounds. In the few seconds it would have taken for his bodyguard to respond he was dead. The murdered sultan's *mamluks* slaughtered the attackers out of hand but it was too late.[249]

Mu'izz al-din's assassination left the Ghurid Empire in a precarious position as he had no son or designated heir. This state of affairs, as in any medieval society, would almost inevitably lead to a succession dispute, particularly in a polity such as the Ghurid Empire, with its disparate power centres. Mu'izz al-Din would have probably been aged sixty-two. He had reigned, as supreme sultan, for just three years and three months before he succumbed to the daggers of the Isma'ilis. He was adjudged to have been a strong and just ruler. Ibn al-Athir tells of an instance of his generosity towards an Alid boy, a community he was not over disposed towards. In another, he made sure that the debt owed to a merchant from Maragha by one his *mamluks* killed on campaign was settled in full. He also mentions his *shafi'i* adherence while commenting on his religious beliefs: '… a follower of the Shafi'i law School, like his brother. However, it is said that he was a Hanafi. God knows best!'[250] It was Ghiyath al-Din who had adopted the *shafi'i* sect in *c.* 595/1199 probably due to its more general appeal. Mu'izz al-Din apparently chose the *hanafi* School, which was the predominant sect of the elite in Ghazna, the centre of his authority. The abandonment of the *karramiyya* sect, which the Ghurids had adopted at their conversion, had led to serious rioting within the empire, notably in Herat and Nishapur and later Firuzkuh. The reasons for the abandonment of the *karramiyya* doctrine probably lie with their evolving place in the Islamic world and their increased status within it. The Ghurids did not wish to be viewed as adherents to an outmoded or ignorant form of Islam and probably thought the *Shafi'i* sect provided a more appealing and sophisticated form of the religion.[251]

Mu'izz al-Din, more than any other Ghurid ruler, through his ability to engender loyalty in his subordinates, particularly in the case of his *ghulams,* and skill as a commander, brought great swathes of territory into the Ghurid orbit making them a world power. He should go down in history as one of the great generals of his own and any age. While it is true he was defeated in three major battles and was lucky to come away with his life in two of those and that his *mamluks* and vassals in India

249 *TN*, vol. I, p. 485 note 3. Taj al-Ma'asir is a contemporary writer.

250 *al-Kamil fi'l-Ta'rikh*, part 3, tr. Richards, p. 95

251 Thomas (2018), p. 314

deserve credit for some of these conquests it is incontestable that his successes were numerous and the second battle of Tara'in was a decisive victory, which altered the political landscape of the Indian subcontinent, opening up India to Muslim rule. It should also be recognised that, from 571/1175–6, he campaigned almost annually and relentlessly across the Indus and as necessary in Khurasan. The result of these efforts was the extensive breadth of the Ghurid Empire at the time of his assassination.[252] If his planned three-year campaign of revenge against the Qara-Khitai in Transoxiana had succeeded, he could have subsequently conquered the Khwarzmian oasis despite the resurgence of the Khwarazamshahs and established Ghurid hegemony in the western Iranian lands. This is all conjecture, however, and even if he had he been successful in these endeavours and restored the *dar al-Islam* in Transoxiana, he would before too long have had to deal with the ramifications of the rise of the Mongols to the east.

The struggle for the succession to the Ghurid throne began immediately after Mu'izz al-Din's death. Various *amirs* gathered around the *vizier* Mu'yyad al-Mulk of Sistan offering support and acknowledging his authority. The primary concern was to protect the substantial treasury travelling with the army and uphold the sway of the *vizier* until such a time as a successor was appointed. The crucial issue in the short term was to maintain calm and discipline in the army and deliver the treasury, which amounted to 2,000 ass-loads of gold, specie and jewels, to Mu'izz al-Din's capital at Ghazna.[253] The dead sultan had his wounds stitched and was placed in his litter surrounded by his servants and an escort with his parasol aloft, as though he were still alive. The plan seems to have been to try to keep his death secret until they reached Ghazna. It did not take long before quarrels broke out among the interested parties. First, the young Turkish *ghulams* rioted, hoping to plunder the treasury. This was swiftly brought under control through the intervention of the senior *mamluks*, in particular Savinj who was the son-in-law of the *malik* Taj al-Din Yildiz, the chief of Mu'izz al-Din's *mamluks*. He is referred to by Juzjani as '…the greatest and most distinguished of the Sultan's slaves'.[254] Those of the rioters who held a fief from Qutb al-Din Aybak, Mu'izz al-Din's senior *ghulam* in India, were ordered to return to it. Money was distributed to encourage them to do so, and they obeyed.[255]

252 *TN*, vol. I, p. 491 for a list of '*victories, successes and Holy-wars*' and note 5

253 *TN*, vol. I, tr. Raverty, p. 492 note 7. Ibn al-Athir says 2,200 either way, a substantial amount, and it would have included spoils from the Khokhar campaign and the delayed tribute from the Indian territories.

254 Ibid., p. 493

255 *al-Kamil fi'l-Ta'rikh*, part 3, tr. Richards, p. 93

As the cortege continued its journey two factions emerged. One consisted of the *vizier* and the *mamluk amirs* who were inclined to support Ghiyath al-Din Mahmud, the son of late supreme sultan Ghiyath al-Din, of the senior Firuzkuh branch of the Shansabanids. He had been allocated the territory of Bust and Zamindawar, where Mu'izz al-Din had made sure that he had little access to the levers of power. The other group consisted of the Ghurid *amirs* who championed the succession of the well respected and powerful sultan Baha al-Din Sam of Bamiyan. The strongest of these factions was the former grouping due to the support of the senior *ghulams.* By the time they reached Peshawar, the dispute was out in the open and the rival parties were close to physical conflict. Ultimately, the *vizier* was able to persuade the Ghurid *amirs* to allow the treasury to proceed via Kurraman as opposed to taking the route towards Bamiyan. Kurraman was situated between Lahore and Ghazna and was the fief of Taj al-Din Yildiz, Mu'izz al-Din's senior *mamluk.* Yildiz seems to have been extremely moved by the death of his master. He would have had a significant force of his own at his disposal including his personal *mamluks.* He demanded that the *vizier* hand over control of the dead sultan's treasury to him due to the insecurity of the situation. He could also rely on the support of the other Mu'izzi *mamluks,* who had been on the campaign against the Khokhars and were returning to Ghazna. Yildiz justified his decision to intervene by telling the *vizier* that his master Ghiyath al-Din Mahmud had appointed him as his deputy in Ghazna and the surrounding areas, as he was currently involved with matters in Khurasan.[256] Ghiyath al-Din Mahmud must have commanded him to act due to his concerns regarding the loyalty of those senior Ghurid *amirs* who had declared their support for Sultan Baha al-Din of Bamiyan.The *vizier* given the circumstances could do little but acquiesce. However, as he was inclined towards the succession of Ghiyath al-Din Mahmud anyway, there was no real reason for him to disagree. The funeral cortege escorted by senior *mamluks,* and others appointed by Yildiz, together with the *vizier* continued on the road to Ghazna. It is unclear whether Yildiz accompanied the cortege. Ibn al-Athir says he did, while Juzjaini implies that he remained in Kurraman.[257] On arrival Mu'izz al-Din was buried in the *madrasa* he had built in memory of his daughter, his only child to survive to adulthood. It had taken three weeks from the time of his murder on 602/13 March 1206 until

256 Ibid., p. 94. Ghiyath al-Din Mahmud as heir to his uncle Mu'izz al-Din's dominions was also heir to his *mamluks* under the laws of Islamic inheritance/succession, hence he was now Yildiz's master. See Raverty p. 398 and note 6.

257 *al-Kamil fi'l- Ta'rikh*, part 3, tr. Richards, p. 94. See also *TN*, vol. I, p. 493. Given that he had taken possession of the treasury, which had accompanied Mu'izz al-Din on behalf of Ghiyath al-Din, Yildiz may have decided to remain in Kurraman.

his burial on 602/3 April 1206. When Ibn al-Athir mentions these dates, it seems clear the sultan's servants would have had to do more than just sew his wounds in order to preserve the body for that length of time – cooler season or not.

Following Mu'izz al-Din's assassination, the Ghurid polity was, for the first time in more than forty years, about to be riven with serious factional conflict. The ensuing instability happened at an unfortunate time and coincided with a resurgent Khwarazmshah who now threatened the recently acquired western parts of the Ghurid Empire. In the first instance there was Ghiyath al-Din Mahmud, heir to the senior Shansabanid line, currently campaigning in Khurasan and about to march on Herat against the governor Izz ud-Din Husain ibn Kharmil. This individual was the *amir* who had deserted Mu'izz al-Din at Ankhud and was now showing signs of coming out in support of the Khwarazmshah. Then there was the son-in-law of Ghiyath al-Din and nephew of Mu'izz al-Din, *malik* al-Haji 'Ala' al-Din Muhammad who had been allocated the Ghurid heartland and Firuzkuh. He was currently fighting in Quhistan obeying the instructions of his late uncle. In Bamiyan, there was Sultan Baha al-Din, supported by his two sons, 'Ala' al-Din Muhammad and Jalal al-Din. In addition to these ruling Shansabanid contenders, there were also Ghurid *amirs,* Shansabanid and otherwise, together with their households who could count as interested parties. Other significant ethnicities included the Khalaj rulers who were able provide troops in relatively large numbers. To these should be added the senior *mamluks* and their own slave retinues. Ultimately, their support was crucial to the success of any of the relevant parties. In the quest for their allegiance Ghiyath al-Din Mahmud, as the son of a supreme sultan, seems to have gained the initial advantage. The two most important cities west of the Indus, for Ghurid purposes, were now Herat and Ghazna.

While this was being played out in the western parts of the Ghurid realm far to the east, Muhammad b. Bakhtiar, the Khalaj commander, had consolidated himself in his capital at Lakhnawti, formerly Gaur, the Pala capital.[258] Following his sack of the Sena capital at Nudiya, he had proceeded to conquer the surrounding areas. By his death in 1206, he had conquered most of Bengal as far as the Brahmaputra. He Islamised the area with the assistance of his *amirs.* They built mosques and established *madrasas* throughout the conquered territory, issuing coins and reading the *khutba* in the name of the sultan Mu'izz al-Din. However, how much control he had over the wider region and how successful the imposition of Islam was is open to question. He continued to send significant spoils he had acquired from his successes as tribute to Aybak in Delhi. Towards

258 *TN*, vol. I, tr. Raverty, p. 559. See note 2 for origins and evolution of Lakhnawti/Gaur name. The name was changed to Lakhnawti in honour of the Sena ruler Lakshmana Sena r. 1178–1206.

the end of 601/1204–05 Muhammad b. Bakhtiar determined to conquer Tibet. The reasons for this, ultimately disastrous decision, are hard to discern. He would be campaigning through an inhospitable region that was largely unsuitable for cavalry operations, his main arm. The likelihood is that the Khalaj general hoped, apart from the acquisition of riches from the raid, to control the main caravan route bringing goods and importantly horses, down the Chumbi valley between Sikkim and Bhutan, into Bengal from the Tibetan plateau and beyond. Juzjaini provides the only near contemporaneous description of these events.[259]

However, this narrative is at times confusing. It would seem that having completed his conquest of northern Bengal by *c.* 594/1197–8 Muhammad b. Bakhtiar had begun to contemplate the invasion of Tibet. On the advice of a convert from one of the tribes who inhabited the proposed route, Ali of the Mej people, Muhammad and his 10,000 horse and assorted infantry departed from Gaur. They reached Devkot, modern Garangampur, another capital of Muhammad b. Bakhtiar's, about fifty-five miles to the north, and probably the most easterly outpost of the Ghurid Empire, more than 1,300 miles from Ghazna. Initially, for ten days the force followed the right bank of River Karotoya, one of the numerous streams flowing through northern Bengal and ultimately joining the Teesta. This river rises in the mountains on the border of Tibet and Sikkim. Of all the rivers of Bengal this watercourse provides the most direct access to Tibet. Today it flows straight, from its source, into the Brahmaputra, but this was not always the case.[260] The river would have bordered the territories of the Rae of Kamrup (Assam). After ten days the Muslim army crossed a twenty arched stone bridge, possibly near Darjeeling. Muhammad b. Bakhtiar left a detachment commanded by a Turkish *mamluk* and a Khalaj *amir* as a guard until their return and crossed over. When the Rae of Kamrup became aware of the Muslim army, he sent messengers to Muhammad b. Bakhtiar advising him to postpone his campaign and to prepare a better equipped force for the next year and that he, the rajah of Kamrup, would mobilise his own forces and help lead the invasion.

The Khalaj leader did not agree with this sage advice and continued towards the high Himalayas and Tibet. After an ardous sixteen days' march, they may have reached the Tibetan plateau and began to pillage the countryside. Unsuprisingly, their approach had not gone unnoticed and within a day or so

259 Ibid., pp. 560–72

260 Ray (2017), vol. I, p. 261. See also *TN*, vol. I, p. 561 and note 3. The author has travelled in western Bhutan and seen river valleys leading into Tibet. An invading army, having struggled through similar country, while coping with different climate zones ranging from tropical to alpine, would not have had an easy time of it. Particularly, in the case of cavalry. Given the distances involved it is not actually certain that Muhammad b. Bakhtiyar's force actually reached Tibet.

a large mounted force attacked the Muslim army causing serious casualties to the invaders. Although they seem to have driven off the attack, the army was badly mauled. After consultation with his *amirs,* Muhammad b. Bakhtiar made the decision to retreat. Their return journey was one of great hardship. The indigenous population had burned everything along the line of march. During the fifteen-day retreat there was no available fodder for the animals, apart from any provisions they carried themselves. The army was reduced to eating its horses. After they left the mountains and entered the territory of Kamrup, they reached the bridge and found it had been rendered unusable. The two *amirs* left to guard the structure had fallen out and abandoned their post, allowing the Assamese to destroy the crossing. Muhammad b. Bakhtiar was now marooned on the wrong side of the river. The Muslims took refuge in '… an idol temple that had been discovered in the vicinity which was … of exceeding height, strength and sublimity, and very handsome, and in it numerous idols of both gold and silver were deposited'.[261] There, they began to discuss how they might obtain suitable materials to construct rafts to cross the river. When the *rae* of Kamrup heard of the desperate straits of the Muslim army, he ordered his people to surround the temple and plant bamboos spiked at each end in the form of a palisade. They effectively walled Muhammad b.Bakhtiar and his remaining force into the temple compound, recognising that if they did not respond quickly, they were going to be imprisoned within the temple precinct. Muhammad B.Bakhtiyar and his men managed, by concentrating their efforts on one part of the bamboo barrier, to break out and reach the river bank. There they were surrounded by the Assamese who did not dare to attack them. In the meantime, the Khalaj ruler and his force endeavoured to construct rafts to ferry themselves to safety. After a number of days, while searching for a crossing, a cry went up from one of the cavalrymen that the river was fordable. For the distance of about a bow shot, possibly up to 500 yards, all was well. Seeing this horseman's progress others joined in. Suddenly, as the large body of cavalry reached the middle of the stream, they were dragged into deep fast moving water with no chance of reaching the far side. The vast majority drowned. However, despite this, Muhammad b. Bakhtiar, accompanied by about 100 of his troops, managed to guide his horse to the opposite bank. There the Khalaj leader was met by members of the Mej tribe who helped him to reach his capital at Devkot. He seems to have been a broken man from this experience and received, wherever he went, the opprobrium of numerous Khalaj women and children whose husbands and fathers had been killed on the expedition. Shortly after his return, he was taken ill and retired to his bed. After three days, an *amir,*

261 *TN*, vol. I, tr. Raverty, pp. 561–9

'Ali-yi Mardan, went in to where he was sleeping, pulled back the bed covering and stabbed the stricken ruler to death.[262] This assassination took place at around the time that Mu'izz al-Din was murdered by the Ismailis.

Muhammad b. Bakhtiar had proved himself to be fearless and resourceful and had gained himself a fief after initial rejection from Aybak, in Mirzapur. Next, through his own tenacity, he subdued Awadh. He then managed to carve out for himself in Bengal, a Khalaj-dominated territory, far to the east of his birthplace in the Garmsir. His remarkable achievements were gained with little outside assistance, if any, and in the face of a hostile reception from the Ghurid establishment. He had gone on to conquer most of Bengal, while remaining loyal to the Ghurid sultan. He had driven the Senas to their territories across the Brahmaputra and established the armies of Islam as the dominant force in that part of India. However, his misjudged expedition to Tibet clearly illustrates some aspects of his character. A total lack of caution, bordering on recklessness, while ignoring local advice and commonsense. Admittedly, it could be said that these traits had served him well in the past. However, in this instance, his overconfidence led to disaster and ultimately his demise.

Meanwhile, in Ghazna and the Shansabani heartlands, the struggle for primacy in the Ghurid world had begun to quicken. Baha al-Din had learned of his uncle's death fairly quickly. A Ghurid *amir* had wasted little time in seeking him out once the news had become common knowledge. Ibn al-Athir states that the ruler of Bamiyan had had designs of succeeding to the Ghurid Empire on the death of his uncle. He had amassed great wealth during his fourteen-year reign to enable him to expedite this ambition. He goes on to say that the sultan was 'loved ... and revered' by the Ghurids.[263] Baha al-Din had gained numerous military successes under the auspices of his uncles, the supreme sultans. His territories, we are told, extended from Bamiyan in the south up to Tirmidh, Balkh and the Oxus frontier beyond. It is reasonable to be wary of Juzjaini's exaggeration regarding Ghurid territorial achievements. However, the areas controlled by or under the influence of the sultan of Bamiyan probably extended to include most of Tukharistan, ancient Bactria, as far as the upper Oxus valley including Badakshan, east to the borders of Kashmir and northeast to the borders of Kashgar via the Wakhan corridor. From here he would have been able to access the wealth of the camel caravans travelling on the Silk Road. Bamiyan itself was located on one of the main routes connecting the Indian subcontinent to China and roads westwards into Iran, and as such was of great strategic importance.

262 *TN*, vol. I, tr. Raverty, pp. 570–72

263 *al-Kamil fi'l-Ta'rikh*, part 3, tr. Richards, p. 95

Coinage was produced and the *khutba* read in Baha al-Din's name, the latter presumably after that of the supreme sultan.[264] However, it is doubtful how much real authority the Ghurids would have exercised in the territories across the Oxus as these were the lands of the Qara-Khitai. Despite this, the financial benefit that accrued to the Bamiyan sultan from being able to access these trade routes would not have been inconsiderable. By any standards Baha al-Din could be classified as a powerful ruler able to draw on significant resources. On learning of the assassination of his uncle, he had written to the Ghurid *amirs* in Ghazna ordering them to hold the city in his name and that he would march with an army to impose his authority. The Ghurid governor of the citadel in Ghazna had already despatched his son to Baha al-Din urging him to come. From this, we can gauge that support for the sultan from the Ghurid *amirs* was strong. Baha al-Din set out with a large army, intent on taking control of the Ghurid Empire as the senior Shansabanid. He had written to *malik* 'Ala' al-Din Muhammad, the ruler at Firuzkuh, demanding his presence.

At the same time, Ghiyath al-Din Mahmud and the governor of Herat, Izz ud-Din Husain ibn Kharmil, were ordered to have the *khutba* read, in his name, in the territories over which they held sway.[265] What is interesting is that he seems to have been oblivious to and not expecting to meet any resistance to his candidature. Nor does he seem to have anticipated or taken into account the power of Mu'izz al-Din's Turkish *ghulams*. The populace of Ghazna are quoted as saying 'we shall not allow anyone other than our lord's son – i.e. Ghiyath al-Din Mahmud – to enter Ghazna', while the Ghurid princes were more inclined to support Baha al-Din.[266] Baha al-Din never reached Ghazna; he was taken ill and died on the road at Kidan. Coincidentally, this was the same location that had already proved fatal, at different times, to two Ghurid princes, Muhammad-i-Suri and Baha al-Din Sam b. Husayn.[267] This was supposed to have occurred only nineteen days after the death of Mu'izz al-Din. Realising he was dying, he declared his son 'Ala' al-Din Muhammad his heir and gave instructions to his sons ordering them to continue to Ghazna. They were to seek the support of the Ghurid factions and use the funds he had amassed to secure their loyalty. He also made sure they understood the importance of reaching an accommodation with Ghiyath al-Din Mahmud, who was soon to defeat and imprison the ruler of Firuzkuh *malik* 'Ala' al-Din Muhammad, in order to continue Shansabanid

264 *TN*, vol. I, tr. Raverty, p. 431

265 *al-Kamil fi'l-Ta'rikh*, part 3, tr. Richards, p. 96

266 Ibid.

267 *TN*, vol. I, p. 432 note 8. The precise modern location is unclear.

authority and sustain the Ghurid Empire.[268] His proposal was that Ghiyath al-Din would have control of the Ghurid heartlands and Khurasan while his sons would be responsible for ruling Bamiyan, Ghazna and the Indian territories. This plan could be viewed as an attempt to replicate and continue the division of Ghurid territorial responsibilities as had been agreed between the late sultan Ghiyath al-Din and his younger brother Mu'izz al-Din.

However, this time there were crucial differences. The original arrangement worked, almost uniquely, between two brothers. Collectively, they came from the senior line of the Shansabanids and formed the dominant force within the Ghurid hierarchy. What Baha al-Din hoped for was an arrangement between cousins with the representative of the senior branch, that is, Ghiyath al-Din Mahmud expected to give up his patrilineal hegemony. It should be remembered that he had been prevented from serious political involvement during his uncle's lifetime and may well have felt embittered consequently and wanted to reassert his primacy and reclaim what he regarded as his inheritance. This plan also omitted, crucially, to address the power of the *mamluk amirs* of Mu'izz al-Din. After all they were the ones who, in some cases, held huge fiefs in India and any solution required their compliance and tacit approval. The death of three senior and respected senior Shansabanids in just over three years left their young and inexperienced successors at a distinct disadvantage and, as a consequence, the Ghurid Empire vulnerable. The Khwarazmshah was showing signs of resurgence in Khurasan at a time when the Ghurid territories required strong and resolute leadership. The party that was going to win out was the one that could guarantee the support of Mu'izz al-Din's senior *mamluks.* It was they who controlled the sources of wealth and materiel from the Indian territories and would be crucial in maintaining the obedience of other Turkish *ghulams.* The support of the Ghurid elites was important but not necessarily the decisive factor. The Khalaj, the Ghuzz and their military contributions would also need to be considered.

'Ala' al-Din Muhammad and his younger brother, Jalal al-Din, continued to Ghazna and took up residence in the sultan's palace. They had been greeted favourably by the populace and the Ghurid *amirs.* However, the *mamluks* were not impressed by the Bamiyani contingent and were prepared to resist. Nevertheless, Mu'izz al-Din's former *vizier*, Mu'yyad al-Mulk, forbade them from doing so. He argued that their forces were insufficient, Ghiyath al-Din Mahmud, having taken the throne of Firuzkuh 602/1206, was now dealing with Ibn Kharmil, the governor of Herat, and that they should bide their time.[269] This

268 Ibid., p. 398

269 *al-Kamil fi'l Ta'rikh*, part 3, tr. Richards, p. 96

line of argument did not convince the *ghulams*. The Bamiyan brothers must have been aware of the *mamluks'* disquiet and their own vulnerable position. But, what they did have at their disposal was Mu'izz al-Din's treasury, which was immense. The hoard wassplit between the two brothers; Jalal al Din's share 'amounted to two hundred and fifty camel loads of pure red gold, jewel studded articles and vessels of gold and silver, this was sent to Bamiyan'.[270] The distribution of largesse by the Bamiyanis persuaded the *mamluks* to swear an oath of allegiance and not to assault the Ghazna citadel. The *mamluks* made it clear that their oath did not supercede their obedience to Ghiyath al-Din. This uneasy state of affairs continued while the senior *mamluks* and Mu'yyad al-Mulk wrote to Yildiz in Kurraman urging him to move on Ghazna.[271] To pre-empt this the two brothers had sent robes of honour to Yildiz asking for his allegiance and offering increased wealth, a senior position in the army with jurisdiction throughout the Ghurid realms and to confer more territory on him personally. Yildiz had already left for Ghazna accompanied by a large force consisting of Turkish *mamluks,* Khalaj and Ghuzz tribesmen. He ignored the emissary sent by the brothers and instructed him to go back and 'Tell them that they should return to Bamiyan. That is enough [for them]. My lord Ghiyath al-Din has ordered me to march to Ghazna and deny it to them. If they do not return to their lands, I shall do to them and those with them what they will not like.'[272] However, according to Ibn al-Athir, Yildiz was more interested in furthering his own career than any allegiance to Ghiyath al-Din Mahmud. His original loyalties lay with the late sultan Mu'izz al-Din who had made certain that Ghiyath al-Din Mahmud was kept out of the Ghurid ruling structure following his father's death. It is doubtful Yildiz ever saw the young Ghiyath al-Din Mahmud as his overlord and would have had little if anything to do with him during the reign of Mu'izz al-Din as supreme sultan. The messenger returned to Ghazna with the gifts and two robes he had been sent with.

Having received Yildiz's uncompromising response, 'Ala' al-Din sent his *vizier* to Bamiyan, Balkh, Tirmidh and other cities under the rule of the Bamiyan Sultanate to collect forces to fight the late Mu'izz al-Din's senior *mamluk.* Yildiz also sent word to the *mamluks* in the city that he had been ordered by Ghiyath al-Din to expel the two brothers. Mu'izz al-Din's *vizier* Mu'ayyad al-Mulk prevented any precipitate action from them and was able to use his authority to control the *mamluks* within Ghazna. 'Ala' al-Din sent out a force of Ghurid and *mamluk* troops, one of which was Savinj, Yildiz's son-in-law. Why

270 *TN*, vol. I, tr. Raverty, p. 494

271 Ibid.

272 *al-Kamil fi'l-Ta'rikh*, part 3, p. 97

he did not wait for the return of his *vizier* with additional forces is unclear. The inevitable happened: the *ghulams* switched sides and put the remainder of 'Ala'-al-Din's force to flight, capturing its commander. In the meantime, Jalal-al-Din had left Ghazna with his entourage for Bamiyan to collect more troops. Yildiz's forces ransacked the Ghuri and Bamiyani owned properties in Ghazna but were prevented from doing more damage. 'Ala' al-Din was beseiged in the citadel and forced to surrender. Humiliated and roughed up by the *ghulams* he was saved through Yildiz's intervention and allowed to depart for Bamiyan.

With Ghazna under his control, Yildiz must have decided that the time was opportune for him to seize power and cast off any pretence that he was acting in the interests of Ghiyath al-Din Mahmud. He probably felt that *mamluks* and other troops he had at his disposal were adequate to maintain and support him in his ambition. This combined with access to a sizeable portion of Mu'izz al-Din's treasury gave him the wherewithal to maintain their loyalty. After four days, all he had done, despite publicly endorsing Ghiyath al-Din Mahmud, was to have the *khutba* proclaimed in the name of the caliph and prayers offered for the murdered sultan Mu'izz al-Din. He summoned the city dignitaries and military commanders together with the caliph's ambassador who happened to be present, having been sent from Baghdad to seek an audience with Mu'izz al-Din. Yildiz informed them of his intention to take up residence in the sultan's palace as ruler. He diplomatically took a subsidiary seat in the throne room rather than that used by Mu'izz al-Din. This move was not universally accepted by the *mamluks*, some of whom had only supported him due to his backing of Ghiyath al-Din Mahmud. Now that he was intent on taking the throne of Ghazna for himself, some withdrew their endorsement, while he managed to persuade others to continue their support through the distribution of fiefs and money. However, some who had campaigned with Mu'izz al-Din, namely Ghurid princes and other nobles from elsewhere including Samarkand, held Yildiz in contempt.[273] The mention of Samarkand is interesting as this city was never held by the Ghurids.

However, the ruler Uthman had intervened with the Qara-Khitai to save Mu'izz al-Din at Ankhud. It is possible he had encouraged his *amirs* to join the *sultan-i-ghazi* in his campaigns beyond the Indus. Yildiz allowed them to depart either to join Ghiyath al-Din Mahmud or the sons of the late Baha al-Din. Ghiyath al-din Mahmud in the meantime thanked Yildiz for his efforts on his behalf and offered him robes of honour while asking for confirmation of his mention in the *khutba* and on any coinage Yildiz should produce. At this juncture, Yildiz ceased any pretence and informed the Ghurid ruler that he

273 *al-Kamil fi'l-Ta'rikh*, part 3, tr. Richards, p. 98

reigned in Ghazna and that as his uncle's *mamluk,* who had no heirs, he should manumit him. Yildiz also demanded that his daughter should marry Ghiyath al-Din Mahmud's son. There was no response from Ghiyath al-Din Mahmud to what he would probably have taken as gross impertinence. It did not take long for the Bamiyan Ghurids to raid Yildiz's fiefs of Kurraman and Suran. Much damage was done and Yildiz despatched his son-in-law, Savinj, with troops who met the invading force, killing many of them. Their heads were put on display in Ghazna. Yildiz then forced a very reluctant Mu'ayyad al-Mulk to be his *vizier*. When congratulated by a friend he replied, 'Yildiz used to come to my door a thousand times until I admitted him. I shall now be at his door each morning! Were it not that with these Turks our lives are preserved, I would have another regime.'[274] This statement is telling as regards the evolving political status quo in the Ghurid Empire at the time. It illustrates the inexorable rise of Mu'izz al-Din's senior *mamluks.* Yildiz, for his part, continued to consolidate his hold on Ghazna, allocating fiefs to the soldiery, while others were free to leave to join Ghiyath al-Din Mahmud or the Bamiyan Ghurids. In public, he still maintained the pretence of loyalty to Ghiyath al-Din Mahmud and saying that on the return of his ambassador to Firuzkuh he would name the Ghurid sultan in the *khutba.* He may have begun to feel that his confidence, at this juncture, in his ability to maintain the loyalty of the general populace and more importantly a large body of the *mamluks* was premature. However, he continued to use the riches he had acquired with Mu'izz al-Din's treasury to recruit further *ghulams* to his standards. After about six weeks, probably around mid-June 602/1206, news arrived that the Bamiyan Ghurids were marching on Ghazna with the intention of sacking the city. Yildiz recacted quickly, sending out a force to intercept the Ghurid army. The vanguard clashed with Yildiz's troops and there were significant losses on both sides. The appearance of the remainder of the army forced the Ghazna contingent to retreat and they were pursued by the main Bamiyan army led by 'Ala' al-Din. Hearing of this, Yildiz took flight towards his old fief of Kurraman hotly pursued by about 3,000 horsemen whom he turned to face and subsequently routed. Having reached Kurraman, he took the opportunity to distribute money and arms, which he must have kept there as a strategic reserve, to his soldiers.[275] The Bamiyan sultans remained hot on his heels, forcing Yildiz to abandon Kurraman. Having captured the place, 'Ala' al-Din assured the populace of his good intents and swiftly returned to Ghazna to execute the original plan. The population fearing what was in store for them prepared to resist. They set about reducing the

274 Ibid., p. 99

275 *al-Kamil fi'l-Ta'rikh*, part 3, tr. Richards, p. 106

size of the gates and narrowing the width of the streets to impede the attackers. Catapults and ammunition were prepared on the walls to meet the invaders. Ghazna was a rich city that had recovered from its sacking more than half a century ago and had prospered under the rule of Mu'izz al-Din.

Ibn al-Athir tells us of the presence there of merchants from Iraq, Mosul, Syria and elsewhere, together with the envoy from the caliph in Baghdad, who had been despatched to see Mu'izz al-Din – the latter probably to seek his support against the Khwarazmshah. These examples serve to illustrate the continuing prosperity and cosmopolitan nature of a city, which was also a significant beneficiary of spoils from the Ghurid Indian territories.[276] The caliph's envoy managed to communicate with a powerful Ghurid *amir*, Sulayaman ibn Sis, who interceded on behalf of the citizenry with the Bamiyani sultans. 'Ala' al-Din and Jalal al-Din returned with their army in 602 /1206. They had with them a portion of Mu'izz al-Din's considerable treasure that Yildiz had seized earlier from Mu'ayyad al-Mulk and that they must have captured when they took Kurraman. Having promised their troops the right to sack and pillage the city, the brothers compensated the soldiery instead with dispersals from Mu'izz al-Din's treasury. The in-demand Mu'ayyad al-Mulk was appointed by 'Ala' al-Din as his *vizier* and in short order the man, against his will, was then forced by Jalal al-Din to become his *vizier* instead. 'Ala' al-Din then had the unfortunate and long-suffering official put in chains and imprisoned. The two brothers then proceeded to divide the treasury and fell out about that and much else: '... dispute over the division arose between them, such as does not arise even between merchants'.[277] In due course, Jala al-Din returned to Bamiyan and 'Ala'al-Din through his *vizier* Imad al-Mulk set about governing Ghazna with indifference to the need of the inhabitants.

Yildiz, in the meantime, had gathered a large army and marched on Ghazna. At Kalu, possibly in modern Helmand province, they captured the town, killing a number of Ghurids in the process while others fled to Kurraman. Yildiz ordered an advance party, led by Aytegin al-Tatar, another of Mu'izz al-Din's senior *mamluks,* consisting of 2,000 assorted cavalry, which included Turksh *mamluks*, Khalaj, Ghuzz tribesmen, Ghurids and other ethnicities to pursue them. Arriving at Kurraman they came upon a force of 'Ala' al-Din's, led by *amir* Abu 'Ali ibn Sulayman ibn Sis, which included other eminent Ghurid *amirs*, all of whom had given themselves up to pleasure and carousing. Despite a warning that the enemy was at hand, they were surprised by Aytegin's force and slaughtered. So

276 Ibid., p. 107. These merchant communities and others like them from across the Islamic world provided essential detail that would have assisted Ibn al-Athir in the writing of his history.

277 Ibid.

comprehensive was the killing that the only survivors were those whom the Turks had singled out for life. Even Yildiz was shocked at the nature of the violence meted out.[278] 'Ala' al-Din when he heard of the destruction promptly crucified the messenger until a superstitious populace begged for him to be taken down when the city was assaulted by a violent hailstorm. Yildiz reinstalled himself at Kurraman where he was well received again by the population following the depradations of 'Ala' al-Din's Ghurids.

Following the defeat, 'Ala' al-Din sent his *vizier* to Bamiyan to update his brother on the situation as regards Yildiz and to seek his assistance. At this juncture Jalal al-Din had been preparing an army to relieve the city of Balkh and drive off the Khwarazamshah. On hearing the news he promptly abandoned that plan and marched on Ghazna. The enduring conflicts with Yildiz seem to have eroded the support for the Bamiyani sultans among their Ghurid *maliks* and *amirs* and increasingly these elements transferred their allegiances to Ghiyath al-Din Mahmud. By August 602–3/1206, Yildiz was again besieging 'Ala' al-Din in the citadel of Ghazna, having guaranteed the safety of the city itself, including the inhabitants, Ghurids and other Bamiyani forces resident there. The arrival of Jalal al-Din and his army of some 4,000 troops in mid-September forced Yildiz to raise the siege. The two forces clashed near Balq, a village near Ghazna in Zabulistan.[279] Yildiz's Turkish *mamluks* confronted the Bamiyan army, consisting of Ghuzz tribesmen and troops from Waksh and Badakshan, and routed it. Jalal al-Din was captured and paraded below the fortress of Ghazna. Yildiz then killed 400 prisoners in front of the citadel when 'Ala' al-Din refused to surrender. Seeing that all hope of relief was lost he handed himself over. Hindu Khan, the grandson of Khwarazmshah Tekish, was also taken prisoner at the same time. Presumably, he had taken up with the Bamiyani sultans as they seemed to offer the most likely avenue to further his interests against his uncle the Khwarazmshah. Yildiz, having given one of his daughters in marriage to Jalal al-Din, hoping to seal a new relationship and prevent any renewed attempts to take Ghazna, sent them back to Bamiyan, where they subsequently fell out. 'Ala'al-Din left to seek the assistance of the resurgent sultan Muhammad Khwarazmshah, without success, and became a virtual prisoner in the process. In their absence, 'Ala' al-Din and Jalal-Din's uncle 'Abbas had installed himself on the throne of Bamiyan, presumably because he had learned his nephews were now prisoners of Yildiz. Jalal al-Din on return wasted little time in putting his uncle to death and flaying

278 Ibid., p. 108

279 *al-Kamil fi'l-Ta'rikh*, part 3, tr. Richards, pp. 108–09

alive his *vizier*, who had previously served the brothers' father Baha al-Din, for disloyalty.

However, according to Ibn al-Athir, Jalal al-Din escaped from Yildiz, which seems unlikely, and on arrival at Bamiyan, his uncle 'Abbas ultimately handed over the citadel and fortresses of Bamiyan. The *vizier* known as the Sahib had gone to seek aid from the Khwarazmshah, which would seem an unwise decision given the relationship between the Ghurids and the Khwarazmshah, to gain support in his attempt to free the nephews from captivity in Ghazna. On learning of the uncle's takeover, the *vizier* further displayed his loyalty to the young sultan by besieging 'Abbas in the citadel until the arrival of Jala al-Din himself. 'Abbas on his surrender explained he had only taken control to protect the Bamiyani territories from the Khwarazmshah and this was taken as an adequate explanation for his actions.[280] The correct turn of events is difficult to ascertain but the killing of 'Abbas and the *vizier* as per Juzjani would seem plausible given what we know of Jalal al-Din's character. He continued to rule in Bamiyan for a further seven years until 612/1215.[281] These events clearly illustrate the growing instability in the Ghurid realms and the difficulties of the Shansabanids in maintaining control of their wider territories.

In the western parts of the Ghurid Empire in Khurasan, the Khwarazmshah proceeded to make inroads to the recently acquired Ghurid territories. At Herat, the governor *malik* al-Husayn ibn Kharmil, a powerful Ghurid *amir*, continued his intrigues with the Khwarazmshah as he beseiged Balkh. Ibn Kharmil ignored a request from Ghiyath al-Din Mahmud to read the *khutba* in his name. On learning of his treachery and that a Khwarazmian army had encamped outside Herat, Ghiyath al-Din Mahmud seized ibn Kharmil's fief, took away his wife and children, confiscated his assets and imprisoned his men at arms. In response, Ibn Kharmil, while still professing loyalty to the Ghurid sultan, despatched a messenger to Firuzkuh, ostensibly to placate Ghurid loyalists in Herat. However, he told the man that on the approach of darkness, he was to abandon this mission and pursue the Khwarazmshah's forces, which were now marching towards Nishapur, and urge them to return. On arrival, the Khwarzmian troops were installed as the garrison. Ghiyath al-Din Mahmud despatched an army under 'Ali ibn Abi 'Ali, the former lord of Talaqan, who had lost his fief to one of the sultan's father's *mamluks,* due to his initial hesitation in offering support to Ghiyath al-Din Mahmud. The sultan remained in the relative security of Firuzkuh in the knowledge that while the Khwarazmshah was besieging Balkh

280 Ibid., p. 115

281 *TN*, vol. I, tr. Raverty, pp. 267, 434 and 495

he could make an attempt to seize the Ghurid heartlands. Why Ghiyath al-Din Mahmud would choose to entrust his army to a disaffected *malik* to bring to heel another overtly disloyal and disgruntled *malik* seems a strange decision. However, he may have had little choice and could not afford to delay and risk losing Herat, the most significant Ghurid city in the west. His commander let him down and connived with ibn Kharmil who attacked the force slaughtering many, although the Ghurid contingents seemed to have been largely spared.[282] Meanwhile the Khwarazmshah continued in his attempts to capture Balkh. He had on learning of Mu'izz al-Din's assassination freed a number of Ghurid prisoners captured during that sultan's disastrous campaign that culminated in the battle of Andkhud. One powerful Ghurid prince, Muhammad ibn 'Ali ibn Bashir, had opted to take up service with the Khwarazmshah and was rewarded with a fief. He was to be used as an intermediary with the Ghurid governor of Balkh, Imad al-Din 'Umar al-Ghuri, and was instrumental in persuading a number of other Ghurid governors to give up their cities.The governor of Balkh continued to resist the Khwarazmshah's forces while awaiting a relief force from his overlords in Bamiyan.[283]

However, the young sultans' involvement with Ghazna prevented them from intervening and their ultimate capture by Yildiz put paid to any chance of relief. On learning of this through Muhamamd ibn 'Ali ibn Bashir and being put under pressure by this fellow Ghurid, the governor finally agreed to surrender and make the *khutba* in the name of the Khwarazmshah. He was given a robe of honour and restored to his position.[284] However, shortly afterwards, he was sent as a prisoner to Khwarazm and the city, that had only been in Ghurid hands for eight years 594–602/*c.* 1198–1206, was given to the Khwarazmian appointee Ja'far al-Turki. Next the Khwarazmshah turned his attention to Kurzaban, which had been a fief of Ibn Kharmil. The governor was persuaded by Muhammad ibn 'Ali to surrender the place and the fief was returned to Ibn Kharmil. Next to fall was Tirmidh, which was ruled by the son of Imad al-Din and already under pressure from the Qara-khitai, so much so that the Khwarazmshah, having taken the city, was forced to cede it to them as his overlords.[285] The Khwarazmian sultan

282 *al-Kamil fi'l- Ta'rikh*, part 3, tr. Richards, pp. 103–04

283 *TN*, vol. I, tr. Raverty, p. 401 note 3 continued from p. 400, referring to the chronicler Yafa-i, Ghiyath al-Din Mahmud attempted to interevene at Balkh, but the Ghurid forces were surprised and routed by the Khwarazmshah's troops

284 *al-Kamil fi'l-Ta'rikh*, part 3, p. 105

285 Ibid., part 3, p. 106. This act of ceding Tirmidh, a piece of the *dar al-Islam*, to the infidel incurred much criticism and Ibn al-Athir defends the Khwarazmshah, suggesting that the action formed part of a stratagem to prepare for his later revolt against the Qara-Khitai.

then proceeded to the city of Talaqan, ruled by Savinj, the *amir* of the hunt as deputy of Ghiyath al-Din Mahmud, who after a brief show of force surrendered.[286] Ghiyath al-Din Mahmud was incensed. No doubt it must have begun to dawn on the Ghurid sultan that the loss of these territories and those in Khurasan combined with the disloyalty shown by a number of his Ghurid lieutenants left the Ghurid Empire in a precarious state. This was largely due to internal feuding following the death of Mu'izz al-Din combined with the lack of a strong and experienced paramount ruler and the inability of the young Ghurid sultan to control Mu'izz al-Din's senior *mamluks*. Ghiyath al-Din Mahmud needed to impose his authority on them swiftly, to have an effective army at his disposal that could be deployed in the west to uphold Ghurid interests. The territories to the west of Ghur were now under pressure from the Khwarazmshah. However, given Yildiz's ambitions and suspect loyalty, this was looking increasingly unlikely. For Ghiyath al-Din Mahmud reimposing Ghurid rule in Herat, utilising the troops he had was essential if he was to maintain any significant hegemony west of Ghur. The Khwarazmshah had brought his army to Herat and was camped outside the city when an emissary arrived from Firuzkuh bearing gifts. Ibn al-Athir's comments on the Ghurid sultan's current status are clearly illustrated.

> *The Khwarazmians used to refer to Ghiyath al-Din the elder, father of this present Ghiyath al-Din, as they used to refer to Shihab al-Din his brother, when they were both alive, merely as 'the Ghurid' or 'the ruler of Ghazna'. At this time however, the Khwarazmshah's vizier, despite his powerful position and this Ghiyath al-Din's weakness, only ever referred to him as 'our lord the sultan', although he was weak and feeble and his lands were few.*[287]

The ruler of Sistan, Harb ibn Muhammad, who had recognised the suzerainty of Ghiyath al-Din the elder, providing troops for his campaigns and had made the *khutba* in his name, chose not to do so for his son when this was requested of him. Instead, he selected to shift his allegiance to the Khwarazmshah.[288] And so yet another territory in the west slipped from the Ghurid orbit.

Yildiz, having recaptured Ghazna and taken the young Bamiyani sultans and Hindu Khan prisoner, still made a pretence at recognising Ghiyath al-Din's sovereignty by sending various standards and a number of prisoners to

286 *al-Kamil fi'l-Ta'rikh*, part 3, tr. Richards, p. 116

287 Ibid.

288 Ibid., p. 117

Firuzkuh by way of tribute.[289] This seems to have happened despite Yildiz's earlier proclamation, before his expulsion by the Bamiyan Ghurids that he ruled in Ghazna. The Ghurid sultan again responded, insisting he make the *khutba* in his name in the mosque in Ghazna. Despite his prevarication, the arrival of another emissary from Ghiyath al-Din Mahmud forced Yidiz's hand and he ordered the *khutba* to be made in the name of Taj al-Din Yildiz following prayers for the soul of the late Mu'izz al-Din. This move, it seems, did not go down well with the populace and was probably why Yildiz had not attempted to implement it earlier. A number of the *mamluks* in Ghazna also expressed their unhappiness with the decision. It is quite obvious that to them the Ghurid sultan deserved their allegiance rather than one of their own number, no matter how senior and respected Yildiz had been under Mu'izz al-Din.[290] Ghiyath al-Din Mahmud, now nominally the senior Ghurid sultan, was in a particularly weak position. The idea of a coordinated Shanabanid response from Firuzkuh and Bamiyan to the threats posed to the Ghurid Empire had proved a failure. The Ghurid *maliks* and *amirs* were too independently minded for the young sultans and their loyalty was often suspect. The Khwarazmshah was proving to be an increasingly powerful and destabilising influence in the west. The Bamiyan sultans had failed in their attempts to conquer Ghazna and impose their rule on the Indian territories, while at the same time losing control of cities in Khurasan. The fighting against Yildiz had achieved little except to illustrate their ultimate impotentcy against the Indian *mamluks* and their armies. Mu'izz al-Din's *mamuks* were simply too strong to ignore and accommodation with Yildiz, had it been a primary aim, might have prevented the Ghurid denouement in the west. However, this opportunity, had it even been a fleeting possibility, was lost. Yildiz, in his correspondence with the sultan in Firuzkuh, makes the situation from his perspective very clear.

> *On what basis do you plague me and claim authority over the treasure here? We collected it with our swords. You seized this royal power of yours. Around you have gathered those who are the root of dissension and you have awarded them with fiefs. You have promised me things that you have not kept to. If you free me, I shall acknowledge you in the khutbah and present myself at your service.*[291]

The manumission of Mu'izz al-Din's senior *ghulams* and Taj il-Din Yildiz and Qutb al-Din Aybak in particular had become a major issue. This was in

289 Ibid., p. 109

290 Ibid., p. 117

291 Ibid.

contrast to events following the death of Ghiyath al-Din where these issues had not arisen. His Turkish slaves would automatically have become the property of Mu'izz al-Din, as his heir, and given the sultan's unchallenged authority there was no dissent, and the issue of manumissions did not arise. It is also likely that the individuals involved were not promoted to the levels of authority of Mu'izz al-Din's *ghulams* as Ghiyath al-Din preferred to use Ghurid *maliks* and *amirs* in these positions. Ghiyath al-Din Mahmud, as heir of Mu'izz al-Din, had inherited his uncle's *mamluks*, who would practically all have been of Central Asian Turkish origin. Recent events had shown that some of these individuals were now more powerful than the Ghurid sultans and held territory, as fiefs in India, probably in excess of what Ghiyath al-Din Mahmud and the Bamiyan sultan Jalal al-Din now ruled in the west. However, the status of these *mamluks* was not equal. Yildiz seems to have been among the most senior and with the resources at his disposal able to launch campaigns in his own right. While Aybak, who at the time of his posting to Khuram and Samanah *c.* 593/1196–7 by Mu'izz al-Din would have been a relatively junior *mamluk,* had since then become a person of major significance.[292] The world of the *ghulam* was a meritocracy and while it could be ruthless, success in a position or endeavour tended to be rewarded. Aybak had been left as the sultan's deputy and a senior commander of his forces in India, when Mu'izz al-Din was recalled to fight in the west. He is the Ghurid servant in those territories whose activities we know most about. From relatively early in his career he was in the position to appoint Turkish *mamluks* and his own *ghulams* to certain strategic strongholds, for example, Iltutmish to Gwalior and subsequently Baran and Bada'un and other Turkish slaves to Kalinjar and Kol.[293] In addition, it was to Aybak that the Khalaj adventurer Muhammad b. Bakhtiyar sent his tribute acknowledging him as Mu'izz al-Din's representative. The episode of the fall of Gwalior and Aybak failing to hand the fortress over to Baha al-Din Toghril, one of Mu'izz al-Din's other senior *ghulams,* when the sultan had stipulated that that was to be the case, does illustrate the nature of Ghurid rule in India at that point in time and in particular the power devolved to senior *mamluks*.[294] While he may not have been Mu'izz al-Din's viceroy at this juncture, Aybak was by now his senior lieutenant in the Indian territories and had earned this position through his military ability, which was evidently considerable. He must have been confident in his authority as it would have taken a brave and assured man to have gone against the sultan's writ. However, his relationship

292 *TN*, vol. I, tr. Raverty, p. 516 note 2

293 Jackson (2003), p. 26

294 *TN*, vol. I, p. 546 note 7

with other senior *mamluks*, for example, the ruler of Uch, Nasir al-Din Aytemur killed at Andkhud fighting beside Mu'izz al-Din is unclear.[295] Nor do we know exactly how far Aybak's authority ranged at the time of Mu'izz al-Din's death. Perhaps Uch marked the boundary of the Indian territories. Peshawar, Lahore and Multan had all been conquered from the Ghaznavids. However, Mu'izz al-Din did use Lahore as a base for his Indian campaigns and at times wintered there. Professor Jackson refers to Aybak's eulogist Fakhr-i-Mudabbir who says that his status as viceroy 'from the gates of Peshawar to the furthest parts of India' only happened a matter of weeks before his master's assassination.[296] This does not seem impossible and could have been brought about by the Khokhar rebellion. After the concerted effort required to put down this revolt Mu'izz al-Din realised that he needed to further delegate powers and responsibilities east of the Khyber Pass while he dealt with the threats to Ghurid rule in the west.

Ghiyath al-Din Mahmud, after receiving Yildiz's response giving his views on his position, made the decision to free him – the sultan having earlier stated that he would make an accomodation with the Khwarazmshah, effectively agreeing to the terms for peace set by him.[297] Through these decisions, Ghiyath al-Din Mahmud was probably hoping to introduce some stability in the Ghurid territories, which would in turn serve to protect his own position, which was looking increasingly insecure. He also agreed to manumit Aybak around the same time. As Mu'izz al-Din's de facto ruler in India, he was too powerful to ignore and could provide a counterbalance to Yildiz. Each of the *mamluks* received great riches, including robes of honour, arms, 100 horses and two parasols, a sign of royal status in the medieval Islamic world. It is interesting to note the replies of the two *mamluks* to these gifts. Yildiz responded 'we are slaves and mamelukes. The parasol is for rulers.' From Aybak, the reply was broadly similar. 'The parasol is not suitable for mamelukes, but manumission is very acceptable. I shall repay it with everlasting service.'[298] From their responses, it would seem that the two *mamluks* were not necessarily requesting to be raised to the position of sultan. They were more than aware of the significance of the gift of the parasol having seen it deployed before. They were most interested in being freed and having their territorial positions ratified. For them, the issue of the position of sultan, if and when required, could be dealt with at a later date. It would seem at this juncture that Aybak was still prepared to continue his allegiance to Ghiyath al-

295 Ibid., p. 531

296 Jackson (2003), p. 27. Fakhr-i-Mudabbir was writing shortly after Aybak's elevation to sultan.

297 *al-Kamil fi'l-Ta'rikh*, part 3, tr. Richards, p. 118

298 Ibid., pp. 117–18

Din Mahmud. By now, he had moved up to Peshawar from Lahore and was involved in restoring law and order in the surrounding regions. He was arguably the most powerful of Mu'izz al-Din's *mamluks* at this juncture *c.* 603/1206–07.[299] The forces at his disposal had been further augmented by the earlier despatch of the younger *ghulam* elements to their *iqtas* in India. These holdings had been allocated to them previously by Aybak. However, the peace plan hatched with the Khwarazmshah shows signs of desperation on the part of the Ghurid sultan. The Khwarazmshah proposed a marriage alliance with Ghiyath al-Din Mahmud and that Herat, under the rule of Ibn Kharmil, should be allowed to fall into his orbit. He further suggested a joint expedition to attack Ghazna in concert with him. Both parties agreed that if they managed to disposess Yildiz, they would split the spoils with a third going to the Khwarazmshah, a third for Ghiyath al-Din Mahmud and the remainder to the soldiery. By continuing to connive with the Khwarazmshah Ghiyath al-Din Mahmud was only serving to undermine his own position. It seems that by now, he had resigned himself to the Ghurid loss of Merv and other cities in Khurasan and accepted to only be left with Ghur itself and those districts he held to the south in the region of Garmsir, part of what is now Helmand. Agreeing to give up his right to Herat and to campaign openly with the Khwarazmshah in Ghurid territory, as a junior partner, was tantamount to accepting vassalage from the Khwarazmshah.

Yildiz, when he learned what was happening, was extremely bitter. Ghiyath al-Din Mahmud argued, 'I was brought to this by your rebellion and disobedience.'[300] Yildiz reacted by invading Tekin Abad and Bust and capturing those territories. He cancelled the *khutba* for Ghiyath al-Din Mahmud there and ordered the ruler of Sistan to do the same and to reinstate the prayers for Mu'izz al-Din. He also took the opportunity to cancel the *khutba* for the Khwarazmshah and ordered Ibn Kharmil in Herat to do the same. For good measure, he threatened to invade their territories if they failed to comply.[301] He was doubtless willing to carry this out, thus adding to the general instability in the wider region. According to Ibn al-Athir, it was at this juncture that Yildiz freed Jalal al-din, giving him his daughter in marriage. He despatched him to Bamiyan, to regain his throne from his uncle, accompanied by 5,000 horses led by Aytegin al-Tatar, one of Mu'izz al-

299 *TN*, vol. I, tr. Raverty, pp. 398–9, p. 502 note 6 and p. 526 note 8 for discussion of chronology regarding the two *mamluks* and their elevation to sultan. It is possible that Aybak received his investiture as sultan prior to Yildiz but not before mid-1206.

300 *al-Kamil fi'l-Ta'rikh*, part 3, p. 118

301 *TN*, vol. I, p. 504. Juzjani says Ylidiz did lead an expedition into Sistan possibly to dissuade the ruler Harb ibn Muhammad from recognising the Khwarazmshah.

Din's *mamluks.* This was the man who had led the force of Turkic cavalry that had annihilated 'Ala'al-Din's troops in an earlier engagement in Kurraman. Aytegin was critical of this arrangement. He tried, unsuccessfully, to persuade Jalal al-Din to return and challenge Yildiz in Ghazna where there was support for this among the other *mamluks.* 'You were not content to don Ghiyath al-Din Mahmud's robe, although he is older and from a more noble line, but you put on the robe of this catamite' he said referring to Yildiz.[302] Aytegin refused to go on and returned to his fief in Kabul. There he was met by an emissary from Aybak who told him that he had been sent to restore Yildiz to Ghiyath al-Din's obedience. Aybak had ordered Yildiz to reinstate the *khutba* for the senior Ghurid sultan, just as he had done in his own territories, and that if he did not, he would attack him. The messenger from Aybak had also visited Firuzkuh, and had advised Ghiyath al-Din Mahmud to go along with the Khwarazmshah's peace proposals. Aybak seems to have been confident that once the issue of Ghazna had been resolved, it would be easy to manage the Khwarazmshah and, by inference, Ibn Kharmil and other dissenters to accept the authority of the senior Shansabanid ruler and reimpose Ghurid rule. The most interesting point of this exchange is that Aybak, despite his undoubted power and increasing independence, was still issuing coins in the name of the Ghurid sultan, Ghiyath al-Din Mahmud, in the territories under his control – a sure sign of his continuing allegiance to the Ghurid Sultanate.[303]

On learning of Yildiz's behaviour, Aybak ordered Aytegin to attack Ghazna. The plan was for him to capture and hold the citadel until Aybak came to relieve him. If he was unsuccessful, he was to withdraw either in the direction of Ghiyath al-Din Mahmud or Aybak himself and failing that, to return to Kabul.[304] Yildiz had been forewarned by Jalal al-Din and consequently Aytegin failed to take the citadel, which was held by the *vizier* Mu'ayyad al-Mulk. He then ordered his men to sack the city, which they proceeded to do. The *qadi* in Ghazna managed to interevene and a compromise was reached before too much damage had been done. Fifty thousand *rukni* dinars was handed over from the treasury and more money was provided by the merchant community, who would have been only too happy to contribute, to avoid ruination at the hands of marauding *mamluks.* He replaced the name of Yildiz with that of Ghiyath al-Din Mahmud in the *khutba*. Yildiz learned of this from Aybak's messenger and made for Ghazna with Aytegin departing as he did so. Ghiyath al-Din, on receiving the funds from Aytegin that he had taken from Ghazna, manumitted him and returned the

302 *al-Kamil fi'l-Ta'rikh*, part 3, p. 118

303 Ibid., p. 119

304 Ibid.

monies to him. Those from the treasury were to be for his own use but the sultan stipulated that the sums obtained from the merchant community were to be given back. The *qadi* returned the funds to the appropriate people while informing Yildiz of what was happening. He advised Yildiz to acknowledge Ghiyath al-Din Mahmud and seek accommodation with the Ghurid sultan and he offered to mediate between them. However, Ghiyath al-Din Mahmud, when informed of this, prohibited the *qadi* from acting as a go-between, saying, 'Do not petition on behalf of a runaway slave.'[305] This is another example, even if Yildiz had received his manumission by this time, of what Ghiyath al-Din Mahmud really thought of this errant *mamluk* and his behaviour. The idea of Yildiz being acknowledged as sultan is most unlikely. Yildiz proceeded to attack Ghurid territory while Ghiyath al-Din Mahmud, after assigning an army to Aytegin, reconquered Bust and the surrounding regions. The political situation in Ghurid lands was now splintering into disagreements over the primacy of the legitmate Ghurid ruler, the interference by and increasing influence of the Khwarazmshah and the competing loyalties and ambitions of Mu'izz al-Din's senior Indian *mamluks*. Of the latter, the most powerful, at this juncture, were Qutb al-Din Aybak and Taj al-Din Yildiz.

305 Ibid.

CHAPTER THREE: 1206–1236

THE LAST GHURIDS, THEIR *GHULAMS* AND THE ESTABLISHMENT OF THE DELHI SULTANATE

QUTB AL-DIN AYBAK – 1206–1210: INDEPENDENT RULER IN INDIA

In the first few months following the death of Mu'izz al-Din, it was becoming increasingly clear that the fortunes and survival of the Ghurid Empire depended on the power of the late sultan's *mamluks.* They were the *Diadochi,* the rival generals, of Mu'izz al-Din who were to fight among themselves for control of the late sultan's possessions from Ghazna to the Bay of Bengal. These Turkish slaves, *ghilman* – sing. *ghulam,* or *mamalik,* sing. *mamluk* – should not be confused with our interpretation of slave in the sense of someone working cotton fields, sugar plantations or more modern iterations. These disciplined soldiers were of almost exclusively Turkish extraction recruited from Turkic tribes converted or unconverted to Islam beyond the Oxus/Amu Darya. The early eleventh century had witnessed the arrival of the Turkish confederacy known as the Qipchak who established themselves in the area extending from the lower Syr-Darya/Jaxartes west to River Dneiper. They came to be known variously as the Cumans, Polovtsy and Pechenegs. The eastern area between the Ural and Syr-Darya rivers fell under the control of the Qangli, another grouping of Turkic peoples, whose relationship with the Qipchak is uncertain. The entire region became known as the Qipchak steppe – *dasht-I Qipchak-.* By the first quarter of the twefth century another mainly Turkic tribal confederation, the Olberli, had migrated from the eastern steppes and established themselves between the Volga and the Jaxartes. This grouping was to become a significant power among the eastern sector of the Qipchak-Qangli confederation.[306] It was *mamluks* recruited from these peoples who supplied the raw materials for a significant element of the Ghurid armies. They were sought after above all for their military prowess as heavy cavalry and for their use of the bow. They could also be acquired as captives in war and be bought in the slave markets of the cities of the Islamic world, as boys or youths. Here, they would be purchased by slave traders to be sold on, having sometimes been educated to a high level by their masters and, ultimately, could become the servants of powerful princes and sultans.

Frustratingly, although we sometimes learn the origins of these special slaves, our sources very rarely provide details of the prices paid for them. The most talented became viceroys, governors and generals commanding armies. The powerful among

306 P. Jackson *The Mongols and the Islamic World from Conquest to Conversion* (New Haven and London 2017) pp.54–5. See also Chapter 2, 'The Islamic World and Inner Asian Peoples down to the Mongol Invasion', for further details on the evolution of the Asian Steppe and the interaction of its peoples with the *Dar al-Islam.*

them could acquire *mamluks* in their own right. Mu'izz al-Din was particularly enthusiastic in his purchase of these slaves, and he was rewarded for the most part with great loyalty from them.[307] At Ankhud, they were the ones who remained to fight and die around him and who, ultimately, led him to safety. Mu'izz al-Din's former commanders benefitted uniquely from this patronage. Unlike the historic Ghurid lands and the conquests in the west where Ghurid *amirs* and princes were preferred, in the territories conquered by Mu'izz al-Din it was his *ghulams* who were promoted to high military and gubernatorial positions. Mu'izz al-Din is portrayed as having no sons. In fact as far as we know he had a number of children but only one daughter survived him.[308] When a favourite commented on his lack of sons to continue his Empire, Mu'izz al-Din responded, '-Other monarchs may have one son, or two sons: I have so many thousand sons, namely, my Turk slaves, who will be heirs to my dominions, and who, after me, will take care to preserve my name in the *khutba* throughout those territories.'[309]

It was these *mamluk* soldiers who formed the spine of Ghurid armies in their conquests across the Indus. In just over a decade, these troopers had made great progress, striking inroads into the Indian subcontinent mainly in the Ganges plain. The Ghurids' ability to recruit and deploy large cavalry armies put their Indian counterparts at a disadvantage. Mu'izz al-Din is referred to in one of the Hindu sources as 'lord of the north-west where horses abound'.[310] This apparent abundance of cavalry combined with the historic reputation of Ghur as a place to mine metal, particularly iron, and the Ghurid's ability to produce significant quantities of weapons and coats of chainmail, may have given them a military advantage. These commodities had been provided in the past as tribute to both their Ghaznavid and Seljuk overlords by the rulers of Ghur. This resource and the ability to deploy light and heavy cavalry, combined with horse archers, gave the Ghurid forces mobility and firepower on the battlefield that their Indian opponents lacked. It may also be the numbers of horsemen that the Ghurid sultan could deploy that provided the strategic advantage. In Indian armies, on the other hand, the cavalry arm was less numerous and while the elephant could confer military advantages, it could also be a more complex animal to manage and deploy in the field. This is not to say that they were not militarily effective and that the Ghurid sultans were to employ these animals extensively themselves in their own campaigns. Elephants also conferred

307 *TN*, vol. I, tr. Raverty, p. 497: 'and he had a great fancy for purchasing Turkish slaves, and he bought a great number of slaves of that race'

308 Ibid., p. 496 note 1

309 Ibid., p. 497

310 P. Jackson (2003), p. 15 note 41

great prestige on their owners and reference to the number owned by a particular ruler was used to denote his status. They were often provided as gifts between the powerful or in tribute. However, with the arrival of the Ghurid armies it was the horse and *mamluk* cavalry, in particular, that became the dominating factor in conflict in the subcontinent.

Despite the significant successes achieved on the battlefield by Mu'izz al-Din and his *mamluk* generals, their victories did not necessarily result in a change of ruler and an accomodation was often reached with the defeated potentate. Mu'izz al-Din was in many ways a supreme ruler with the conquered *rais* and *ranas* as tributary princes who came 'to rub the ground of the exalted court of Aybeg'.[311] Not all conquests, however, were permanent and given the disparity in numbers between the conquerors and conquered a *modus vivendi* was needed. As Professor Jackson states, 'Whatever the Muslim *literati* wanted people to think, the hallmark of these years was not one of uncompromising iconoclasm.'[312] No doubt the Ghurids in their campaigns did at times wreak destruction on a large scale, and if we are to believe Juzjani, this was all down to *jihad*. However, the major aim was conquest and above all plunder to fund the fight against the Khwarazmshah in the west. The conflict should not be viewed as one of Muslims against Hindus and in the course of events, Hindu soldiers served in the armies of Ghurid generals. Aybak when he moved up to Lahore in 602/1206 was accompanied by Hindu potentates with their own soldiers, all of whom were in the employment of a Turkish *mamluk*.[313]

Yildiz and Aybak were the first of the *Diadochi* to come to blows. We do not know much about Yildiz's origins, just that he was purchased as a young man by Mu'izz al-Din. Over a period of time he became head of Mu'izz al-Din's Turkish *mamluks* and was ultimately appointed as governor of the fief of Sankuran and Karman. This was a large area consisting of long valleys running from the White Mountains the Safed Koh or Spin Ghar, a fertile region, mainly watered by Kurram River, which joins the Indus at Isa Khel, and its tributaries. It encompassed a region that extended as far as the southwest slopes of the Salt Range in the north and towards Gomal River in the south. The ruler of this territory held an important post as it covered the lower route from Lahore to Ghazna.[314] When Mu'izz al-Din made his annual journey from Ghazna to Lahore to prepare for his Indian campaigns he would halt at Yildiz's headquarters. There, he would be presented with a thousand quilted tunics and headresses as yearly payment for the fief. On

311 Jackson (2003), p. 19 quoting Hasan-i Nizami

312 Ibid., p. 20

313 Ibid., p. 21

314 *TN*, vol. I, tr. Raverty, p. 498 and note 7

his final expedition into India, Mu'izz al-Din chose one tunic and headdress for himself and gave Yildiz his own 'princely robe' as well as conferring on him a black banner for his own use[315] – the inference being that the sultan by conferring the black banner of Ghaznin on Yildiz was nominating him as heir to the territory of Ghazna. He had previously ordered that Yildiz should give a daughter in marriage to Aybak and another to Nasir al-Din Qubucha, a senior *mamluk,* who had been entrusted with the government of Uch following the death of Nasir al-Din Aytemur. He was to play a significant part in the struggle of the successors to the Ghurid lands in the east over the following decades.[316] With these arrangements, Mu'izz al-Din may have been hoping to instil a sense of kinship among his senior officers in the hope that they might be able to find an accommodation among themselves and not resort to conflict on his demise.

Compared to Yildiz, we know rather more about Aybak's origins, and they provide a good example of how a *mamluk*'s career could progress.[317] Aybak was probably of Cuman-Qipchak descent and purchased beyond the Oxus. He was trafficked to the slave market in Nishapur and there bought by the chief *qadi* of that city, Fakhr al-Din, who was a descendant of the eminent Imam Abu Hanifah of Kufa, in Iraq. Abu Hanifah was a jurist, theologian and founder of the eponymous school of Islamic jurisprudence. Fakhr al-Din was the governor of Nishapur and its surrounding territories. In this environment, Aybak, along with the sons of his master, was taught to read the Koran and horsemanship as well as the use of the bow. He must have been quite young when he was first sold as riding proficency would have been a basic requirement in nomadic Turkic society. Showing promise and having mastered these skills, Aybak was sold on as a youth to merchants who bought him to Ghazna. Whether he was sold by the *qadi* or by his sons on their father's death is unclear. When he arrived at the court of Ghazna, Mu'izz al-Din, hearing of his great qualities, purchased him. His only blemish was a paralysed little finger on one hand.[318] His purchase led to an illustrious career in the service of the Ghurid sultan. From 602/1206 Aybak had based himself in Lahore and this seems to have been the catalyst for conflict with Yildiz. While Aybak had probably situated himself there for strategic reasons, to protect the Indian territories he held, Yildiz seems to have considered Lahore and the Punjab as the territory of Ghazna. It was to him that Mu'izz al-Din had given the black flag of Ghazna in his own right and Sultan Ghiyath al-Din Mahmud had subsequently recognised his position in

315 Ibid., p. 500

316 Ibid., p. 532. Qubacha was also a son-in-law of Aybak. Twice over after the first daughter died.

317 Ibid., pp. 512–28

318 *TN*, vol. I, p. 513 and notes 8, 9 and 1. 'Ibak-i-Shil-*the weak fingered.*'

Ghazna, albeit reluctantly. He considered Aybak at best a usurper and that he was the rightful ruler of all Mu'izz al-Din's eastern conquests. However, Aybak was in a strong position in India and his authority was acknowledged in Bengal. There, his appointee, the assassin of Muhammad b. Bakhtiar, Ali-yi Mardan, now ruled the entire Muslim conquest in Bengal from the capital Devkot.[319] For all intents and purposes, Aybak was now supreme ruler in Muslim India. What is unclear, as the sources concentrate on his disputes with Yildiz, is the status quo as regards Indian subject rulers. There is a lack of evidence for campaigns undertaken by Aybak against them or neighbouring Hindu states.

Sometime in 605/1208–09 Yildiz reacted. He despatched Mu'yyad al-Mulk his *vizier* in Ghazna with a force to expel Qubacha from Lahore, which he held at that time on behalf of Aybak. Major Raverty comments that some authors say that Yildiz went himself.[320] Qubacha was driven from the city and Aybak wasted little time in responding. He mobilised a large army from his Indian territories and marched against Yildiz. A battle took place somewhere in the Punjab and Yildiz was defeated and retreated into the inaccessible country surrounding his fief in Karman and Sankuran originally given to him by the late sultan Mu'izz al-Din. Aybak moved quickly to occupy Ghazna. Once there, he resorted to revelry and anarchy prevailed. He only held the place for about forty days, by which time the populace had had enough and beseeched Yildiz to return. Aybak and his forces were taken unawares and forced to retreat to Lahore via the Sang-i-Sarak, one of the routes between Ghazna and the Punjab. He never returned to Delhi but remained in Lahore, to protect his Indian territories from Yildiz. He died when his horse slipped during a game of *chaugan,* similar to modern polo, and the pommel of his saddle was forced into his chest killing him instantly.[321] This took place in 607/1210. He had ruled for four years and was buried in Lahore. He had managed to rise through his considerable abilities from ordinary *mamluk* to Mu'izz al-Din's generalissimo in the Indian territories and die as a sultan and the acknowledged ruler of the Muslim lands in the subcontinent. He was recognised as running a just and competent regime. His rule was renowned for encouraging Sunni religious orthodoxy and largesse while continuing Ghurid policies. Aybak's pragmatism and lack of prejudice also gained him the respect of his Hindu subjects. The relative peace and stability of his regime encouraged trade and agriculture, while his reputation for munificence also attracted clerics, poets and scholars to his court at Lahore. These individuals were to contribute to the spread of Persian culture in

319 Ibid., p. 578

320 Ibid., p. 526 note 6

321 Ibid., p. 528

India.[322] Despite this reputation it should not be forgotten that Aybak ruled as a despot as was expected of him. A contemporary chronicler at his court in Lahore approvingly states of his rule 'his gifts were bestowed by hundreds of thousands, and his slaughters likewise were by hundreds of thousands'.[323] Aybak also left behind an architectural legacy in Delhi that resonates even today in the Qutb complex. His greatest creation was the Qutb Minar – the tallest minaret in the world standing at 72.5 metres. Inspired by the minaret of Jam, the construction was begun by Aybak sometime in 595–1199 and later completed by Iltutmish. Built in mainly red sandstone, the minaret is adorned with beautiful Quranic calligraphy and in recent times has become the leading symbol of Delhi tourism.

After the death of Aybak, further to the west, the Khwarazmshah in alliance with the ruler of Samarkand was engaged in a series of inconclusive skirmishes and battles with the Qara-khitai 'some of them Khwarazmshah won and some he lost'[324] In the meantime, he had finally had enough of Ibn Kharmil the governor of Herat and Ghurid renegade who had taken it upon himself to imprison Khwarazmian troops for their behaviour against the populace. The Khwarazmshah despatched 'Iz al-Din Jaldik ibn Tughril, the lord of Jam, whose father had been governor of Herat during the reign of the Seljuk sultan Sanjar, with 2,000 cavalry. The Khwarazmshah had told Ibn Kharmil that he was despatching Jaldik because of his skills as an administrator. In fact, he had ordered him to arrest Ibn Kharmil at the first opportunity. Ibn Kharmil rode out to meet Jaldik, counting on his position to protect him. This turned out to be wishful thinking and he was promptly taken prisoner. Ibn Kharmil's *vizier,* Khwaja al-Sahib, when threatened by Jaldik that if he did not surrender Ibn Kharmil he would be put to death, responded, 'I shall surrender the city neither to you nor to the traitor Ibn Kharmil. It belongs only to Ghiyath al-Din and his father before him.'[325] He refused to surrender, and Ibn Kharmil was executed. Thus ended the career of a powerful Ghurid *malik* who had treacherously seized Herat and used it as a bargaining chip to further his own interests. Herat for now remained a Ghurid city, despite being further invested by an army of 10,000 led by the governor of Nishapur and Amin al-Din Abu Bakr, lord of Zuzan. Subsequently, the *vizier* informed the besiegers that their status was inadequate for him to surrender the city to them, but that he would hand it over to the Khwarazmshah. It was around this juncture that the Khwarazmshah was captured by the Qara-Khitai following a defeat somewhere in Transoxiana. His

322 *Encyclopedia Iranica*, www. Iranicaonline.org, entry for Qotb al-din Aybak

323 G.H.R. Tillotson, *Mughal India* (London, 1990), p. 34

324 *al-Kamil fi'l-Ta'rikh*, part 3, tr. Richards, p. 128

325 Ibid.

imprisonment appears to have been short lived, as his captors were unaware of his identity, and he was able to make his escape.

However, in the interim, Kuzlik Khan, governor of Nishapur, rebelled along with 'Ali Shah, the brother of the Khwarazmshah, who dropped his brother's name from the *khutba* and proclaimed himself ruler. Muhammad Khwarazmshah returned to a state in turmoil, Kuzlik Khan promptly fled to Iraq and his brother left via Quhistan to take refuge with Ghiyath al-Din Mahmud in Firuzkuh. Given his precarious position, one wonders why Ghiyath al-Din Mahmud decided to offer sanctuary to 'Ali Shah, as it was only likely to enrage the Khwarazmshah and further imperil his own position. Having reasserted himself, the Khwarazmshah marched on Herat via Nishapur. On arrival, he demanded that the *vizier* surrender the place to him as he had promised. The *vizier* Khwaja al-Sahib now had cold feet and was worried that the Khwarazmshah would put everyone to the sword and refused to surrender to anyone but Ghiyath al-Din Mahmud. The citizenry, fed up and exhausted by the constant military threats and the resulting instability and ruination of their livelihoods, rioted when the *vizier* failed to handover the city. The Khwarazmshah took advantage of the situation and captured Herat and put the *vizier* to death. This took place in 605/1208–09 and the city remained in the possession of the Khwarazmshahs until their defeat at the hands of the Mongols.[326] The last major conurbation in the western Ghurid lands had been finally lost to the ruler in Firuzkuh. Ghurid power and influence in the west was at an end. The position of Ghiyath al-Din Mahmud had become one of virtual vassalage to the Khwarazmshah following his earlier agreement to a joint campaign against Yildiz in Ghazna. The Khwarazmshah wasted little time in demanding that he imprison his brother 'Ali Shah. Ghiyath al-din Mahmud complied and imprisoned 'Ali Shah in a building referred to as the *Kasr*, which could be perhaps best described as a fortified complex with buttresses, domed towers and balconies, a Ghurid Ghormengast according to Juzjani, within the confines of Firuzkuh. The building was obviously of significance having been embellished with gold items, some taken at the capture of Ajmer and sent by the late sultan Mu'izz al-Din to his brother.[327]

'Ali Shah had arrived in Firuzkuh with a substantial number of retainers and dependents, which included Iraqi's, Khurasanis, Khwarazmians and his

326 *al-Kamil fi'l-Ta'rikh*, part 3, tr. Richards, p. 131

327 *TN*, vol. I, tr. Raverty, p. 404, regarding the building's description and ornamentation, which included two gold *humae*, the mythical bird of Iranian legend, the size of a camel and p. 331 note 2. Regarding the definition of *kasr* see A. Patel, *Iran to India: The Shansabanis of Afghanistan, c.1145–90 CE* (Edinburgh, 2022) pp. 136–46, for a contemporary interpretation of Firuzkuh's archaeology and Juzjani's description.

own Turkish *mamluks,* together with his sons, wives and women. Numerous influential figures among them wrote to Ghiyath al-Din Mahmud reminding him of his obligations to those who had sought his protection. There were veiled threats, which, given the number of 'Ali Shah's followers, the Ghurid sultan should have taken seriously. and this he failed to do. Some of 'Ali Shah's retainers were in the habit of climbing the hill of *Koh-i-*Azad under the cover of darkness. This hill apparently faced the *Kasr* and from this vantage point, it was possible to look into the private apartments where the sultan slept. The Khwarzmians noted this and one night four assassins climbed up onto the roof of Ghiyath al-Din Mahmud's quarters, accessed his private apartments, killed him and made their way across the Har-i-Rud. The killers made good their escape and proclaimed their deed from the heights of the *Koh-i-Azad,* the names not coming down to us. The Ghurid sultan was killed in 607/July 1210 and initially buried within the *kasr* itself. Firuzkuh was now in a state of tumult with various competing parties vying for dominance while the followers of Ali Shah contrived to gain his release. Following the assassination, the Ghurid *amirs* and Turkish *amirs* agreed to raise Ghiyath al-Din Mahmud's son Baha al-Din, Sam to the Ghurid throne. The new sultan was fourteen years old and had a ten-year-old brother, Malik Shams al-Din, Muhammad. Neither of them would have any say in future proceedings. The power lay with the Shansabanid elite and the Turkish *amirs.* Juzjani specifically mentions Turkish *amirs,* who would have been senior manumitted slaves of Ghiyath al-Din and probably of Mu'izz al-Din. These *amirs* were powerful in their own right and for their influence among other lesser *ghulams.* The mother of Baha al-Din, titled the Malikah-i-Mu'izziah, realising the precarious nature of her son's position incited the Turkish *mamluks* to kill various senior Shansabanid *maliks* who might try to compete with her son for the sultanate. In the end, his supporters and Turkish *amirs* prevailed, and Baha al-Din's throne was secure for the moment. Meanwhile, 'Ali Shah still remained a prisoner, and his retinue waited for Firuzkuh to calm down before launching a bid to free him. What is strange is that if they were known to be the sultan's assassins, how had they not been rounded up and 'martyred' or imprisoned by the Ghurids? It is plausible that they had hoped the assassination would precipitate a succession crisis, which it did, giving 'Ali Shah the opportunity to put forward his candidature? The plotters planned to re-enter Firuzkuh with the men hidden in treasure chests, possibly as part of a caravan, but were betrayed by one of their number. Three of the assassins were captured, humiliated and put to death; two other individuals were thrown off a hill within the city; while another seventy-five were trampled under elephants before a baying crowd. Given the high state of alert that would have prevailed in the Ghurid capital it is extraordinary they thought they could succeed.

Within three months of the murder of Ghiyath al-Din Mahmud, the Khwarzamshah Muhammad agreed to support the candidature of the Ghurid prince 'Ala' al-Din Astiz, son of *jahan-suz*. Astiz had come to his court, approximately eighteen months earlier, to solicit support for his claim to the Ghurid throne.[328] The governor of Herat, Amir Malik of Turkic descent, was detailed to support him with an army that duly set out from Khurasan. The approach of this force to the Ghurid heartland caused the Ghurid elites to decide to free 'Ali Shah, perhaps anticipating that he might be able to persuade some of the approaching Khurasani army to side with him.

However, other sources give a different chain of events. It is possible that somehow 'Ali-Shah was directly involved in the assassination of Sultan Ghiyath al-Din Mahmud. He was after all already in the *kasr* and the idea he was plotting to take the Ghurid throne for himself is not beyond the bounds of possibility. The Ghurid *amirs* may have decided at some juncture that 'Ali Shah was a better bet than the young Baha al-Din, and offered him the throne,[329] hoping the Khwarazmshah would ratify this. The Khwarazmshah had other ideas and despatched 'Ala' al-Din Astiz with the support of the governor of Herat. The Ghurid *amirs* and *maliks* prepared to defend Firuzkuh, and after a day and half of fighting the Khwarazmians broke into the city and any pretence of an independent Ghurid Sultanate was over. 'Ali Shah is said by Juzjaini to have escaped. Whatever the chain of events, both 'Ali Shah and Sultan Ghiyath al-Din Mahmud died in 607–1210.[330] With 'Ala' al-Din Astiz on the throne as a Khwarzmian vassal the Ghurid heartland belonged to the Khwarazmshah. Sultan Baha al-Din Sam and his younger brother together with their sisters and mother, an aunt, the daughter of Ghiyath al-Din Muhammad-i-Sam, and other dependents were led off to Khurasan. The litter of the assassinated sultan Ghiyath al-Din Mahmud was placed in the catacombs of the Mosque in Herat. Other dependents were sent to Khwarazm. The young Ghurid sultan and his brother survived in Khwarazm until the Mongol invasions. Then, on the orders

328 *TN*, vol. I, tr. Raverty, p. 399

329 Ibid., p. 407 notes 5, 7 and p. 411 note. Juzjani seems to tacitly confirm, albeit reluctantly as a Ghurid champion, that 'Ali Shah was offered the throne. He was probably living in Firuzkuh by this stage, so his version of events does have some credibility.

330 *al-Kamil fi'l – Ta'rikh*, part 3, tr. Richards, p. 132. Ibn al-Athir states that Sultan Ghiyath al-Din Mahmud was alive and captured at the fall of the city and later put to death, on the orders of the Khwarazmshah, which was not the case. However, he also comments that 'Ali Shah was captured and put to death shortly afterwards on the orders of his brother, which seems entirely likely. The idea of his escaping to Ghazna seems far fetched; it is doubtful he made it that far, and if he had what would Yildiz's reaction have been?

of Muhammad Khwarazmshah's mother, they, along with other political prisoners, were drowned in the Oxus *c.* 612/1220.[331]

With the Ghurid heartland firmly under his control, the Khwaramzshah Muhammad was free to concentrate on his campaigns against the Qara-Khitai, ignoring his father Tekish's wise advice 'never to embroil himself with the Khita, if he desired to preserve the safety of his dominions'.[332] The Gur-Khan and his vassals provided a bulwark against other Central and East Asian nomads who might covet the riches of the settled lands of the Khwarazmian oasis, the fertile valley of the Amu Darya and the wealthy cities of Transoxiana. Within a year of the death of Sultan Ghiyath al-Din Mahmud, the Khwarazmshah had managed to free himself from his obligations to the Qara-Khitai and had added a number of Qarakhanid city-states to his territory, including Samarkand, which he made his capital.[333]

SHAMS AL-DIN ILTUTMISH – 1210–1236: FROM MAMLUK'S *MA MLUK* TO SULTAN

By 607/1210, in the former Ghurid lands west of the Indus, Ghazna and Bamiyan were the only areas retaining their independence. The others had all succumbed to the Khwarazmshah. Taj al-din Yildiz in Ghazna must have realised with a certain inevitability that it would not be long before the Khwarazmshah turned his attention to these territories. If the murder of Ghiyath al-Din Mahmud in Firuzkuh prompted a succession crisis in Ghur, the accidental death of Sultan Qutb al-Din Aybak in the same year produced a similar upheaval in the Ghurid lands in India. The main players in this tussle for supremacy were the following: the remaining *Diadochi,* the former Ghurid *ghulams,* Yildiz in Ghazna coveting Lahore, Nasir al-Din Qubacha in Uch, competing with Yildiz for control of Lahore and with designs on Sind. In the Gangetic plain, Shams al-Din Iltutmish, a former slave of Aybak, based at his *iqta* in Bada'un, would need to assert himself in Delhi and the surrounding territories in order to compete. The immediate problem he would face would be other *amirs* who had also received *iqtas* in India from Mu'izz al-Din and Aybak. Initially his position was far from secure. In

331 *TN*, vol. I, p. 412. According to Juzjani at the time of his writing his history two daughters of sultan Ghiyath al-Din Mahmud were still alive – one in Bukhara and the other married and living in Balkh.

332 Ibid., p. 244

333 Jackson (2017), pp. 56–7

Bengal, the Khalaj Ali-yi Mardan had declared his independence. While Aybak had been recognised by fief holders in the region as ruler of Muslim lands from Lahore to the Bay of Bengal, this acknowledgement of unified territorial control expired with his death. It was to take years of hard fighting before one of the former Ghurid *ghulams* came out on top. The first major problem that Itutmish was forced to confront was the raising of Aram Shah to the throne in Lahore.

Who exactly Aram Shah was remains something of a mystery. He is referred to as Aybak's son by Juzjani but only in a chapter heading referencing his brief appearance on the stage.[334] However, elsewhere we are told that Aybak only had three daughters as offspring. Two were married to Qubacha and one to Iltutmish. Chances are he was a Turk *amir*. It is just possible he was the adopted son of Aybak, put on the throne by former *mamluks* of Mu'izz al-Din as a continuity candidate to preside over an orderly transition of power. This was not acceptable to those ruling in Delhi. Consequently, the military justiciar of the city, 'Ali-yi-Isma'il summoned Iltutmish from his fief in Bada'un to take up power. Following this decision and unhappy with the installation of Iltutmish, the former Mu'izzi *amirs* and possibly a minority of Qutbi *amirs,* that is Aybak's former *mamluks* left for Lahore to join Aram Shah. However, ltutmish seems to have enjoyed the support of the majority of the Qutbi *amirs*.[335] Aram Shah and his forces marched on Delhi and were defeated at Bah-i-Jud, a plain now forming part of a public park, in the city. Those leaders of the Aram Shah party who had not been killed in the battle were put to the sword and Aram Shah was martyred.[336] Whether he was killed during the fighting or executed later is unclear. Following this defeat, Juzjani says Hindustan – the Ghurid Indian territories – were sub-divided into four parts.[337] Qubacha took the opportunity to annexe Sind and occupy the city of Multan on River Chenab. Iltutmish now established in Delhi would have to campaign in the outlying areas dependent on that city to establish his authority in the wider area. The Khalaj-controlled territory to the east in Bengal was ruled by 'Ali-yi Mardan, the former vassal of Aybak who on hearing of his death, had assumed royal status and declared himself Sultan 'Ala' al-Din. Yildiz, in Ghazna, was to dispute control of Lahore with Qubacha and Iltutmish.

334 *TN*, vol. I, tr. Raverty, pp. 528–9

335 P.Jackson (2003), p. 29 and p. 42 states there was more of a definitive split between the *mamluks* with the Mu'izzis leaving to support Aram Shah and the Qutbis remaining loyal to Iltutmish, while also referring to Iltutmish's chronicler Hasan-i- Nizami who reports that the whole revolt was engineered by Turks led by the *sar-i-jandar* Berki and disregards Aram Shah.

336 *TN*, vol. I, tr Raverty, p. 530

337 Ibid.

1. Qutb Minar a minaret and "victory tower" of the Qutb complex, Delhi's oldest fortified city, Lal Kot, India *(Alamy)*

2. Intricate detail of the Qutb Minar red sandstone tower (minaret), Delhi, India *(Alamy)*

3. Minaret of Jam, Ghor Province in Afghanistan. View of the Minaret of Jam from below showing detail of the geometric decoration. *(Jonathan Wilson / Alamy Stock Photo)*

4. Minaret of Jam and the Hari River in the Shahrak District, central Afghanistan's Ghor Province. The Minaret of Jam, along with its archaeological remains, was inscribed on the World Heritage List by the United Nations Educational, Scientific and Cultural Organization (UNESCO) in 2002.
(Saifurahman Safi/Xinhua/Alamy Live News)

5. Iltutmish's tomb in Qutb Minar complex in Delhi (13th century).
(Sergii Rudiuk / Alamy Stock Photo)

6. Copper and silver inlaid brass ewer, Herat *c.*1180–1200. The ewer's decoration features classical, figural and celestial imagery emphasised in silver. This includes lions, parakeets and signs of the zodiac accompanied by benedictory inscriptions in Arabic script. The object illustrates Herat's status as a major cultural hub and centre for the production of high quality metalwork. H: 40 cm. *(© The Trustees of the British Museum)*

7. Footed bronze dish with elephant in the centre, eastern Iran or Afghanistan, end of 12th–early 13th century. The elephant depicted in the central medallion makes it probable that the the dish was made under the Ghurids whose art shows the influence of Indian models. H: 9.8 cm; Diam: 31.8 cm. *(David Collection Inventory No. 43/1998, photographer Pernille Kemp)*

8. Earthenware bowl with incised decoration in a white slip and painted in green and manganese in a yellowish glaze (Bamiyan type), Afghanistan *c.*1200. H: 8.5 cm; Diam: 18 cm. *(David Collection Inventory No. 14/1989, photographer Pernille Kemp)*

9. Hexagonal table, poplar, covered in paper and coloured laquer and with incised decoration, Afghanistan 11th–12th century. H: 26 cm; Diam: 38 cm. *(David Collection Inventory No. 33/1997, photographer Pernille Kemp)*

10. Gold coin of Mu'izz al-Din as vassal of his brother Ghiyath al-Din, 597/ Dec 1200–Jan 1201, Ghazna mint. This 'bull's eye' type was modelled on contemporary Ayyubid coinage of Egypt. 26mm. *(David Collection Inventory No. C 480, photographer Pernille Kemp)*

11. Gold coin of Mu'izz al-Din, 600/1203–4, probably Ghazna mint. 35 mm. *(David Collection Inventory No. C 132, photographer Pernille Kemp)*

12. Greenish Limestone matrix for stamping leather, Afghanistan end of 12th–beginning of 13th century. The name of a Ghurid general is found in one of the matrices – he died *c.*1210 as governor of Herat. H: 33.5 cm; W: 18.5 cm. *(David Collection Inventory No. 4/2000, photographer Pernille Kemp)*

Of all these individuals, Iltutmish is the one who we know most about, and his early life provides a good example of the opportunities available to those *mamluks* with the ability and perspicacity to seize them. According to Juzjani, who in Iltutmish's service would have had the opportunity to learn about the sultan's origins, he came from the Ilbari or Olberli tribe in Transoxiana. His father, I-lam Khan, was a chief among one of that tribe's sub-clans. He seems to have been sold into slavery by some of his brothers and uncles, who were apparently jealous of him, at a very young age. This was engineered by using the excuse of taking him to a horse fair where he was sold to merchants from Bukhara. Once at the slave market there, he was sold again, this time to the *sadr-i-jahan*, the chief religious authority of the city in whose family he was brought up with great care. He received the same education as the *sadr's* sons. He was then sold to the Bukhara Haji who may have been a kinsman of the *sadr-i-jahan*. The reason for his sale has not come down to us. The Haji then sold him on to Jamal al-Din Muhammad, of the tight tunic, who took him to Ghazna. By now, Iltutmish was recognised for his abilities, good looks and intelligence. Mu'izz al-Din who was always on the look out for *mamluks* asked for the price of this prodigy. Iltutmish formed part of a lot with another slave called I-bak. Jamal al-Din and the sultan were unable to agree an amount for the pair and, consequently, Mu'izz al-Din forbade any sale in Ghazna. After a year, the merchant left for Bukhara where he remained for three years and then returned to and spent another year in Ghazna, probably hoping that the sultan's ban on the sale would be rescinded. However, it was not until the arrival of Aybak from India, following his victory over Bhimadeva II at Mount Abu, that any progress was made with regard to Iltutmish's future. The successful *mamluk* managed to persuade Mu'izz al-Din to let him buy the young slaves. The sultan relented and agreed but only if the sale took place in Delhi away from his direct jurisdiction. Aybak returned to Delhi, leaving another *malik* Nasir al-Din i-Khar-mil, who had shared a command with him on campaign against the ruler of Benares. He was instructed to bring Jamal al-Din of the tight tunic with him when he returned to Delhi.[338] This was done and Aybak bought Iltutmish and I-Bak who received the name Tam-ghaj. In due course, he became *amir* of Tabarindh and was later killed in a battle between Yildiz and Aybak. The sum paid must have been high and certainly more than the amount Mu'izz al-Din had refused to consider.[339] What these episodes indicate is the financial investment and time taken on nurturing some of these *mamluks*. In this instance, the broker or dealer had to bide his time over a period of years

338 Ibid., p. 516

339 Ibid., p. 603 and note 6

before being able to profit from any sale. They illustrate the potential high value of the commodity in general and, more particularly, if the slave in question was deemed to have exceptional qualities.

We do not know Iltutmish's age when he was purchased by Aybak but early twenties would seem possible. He became *sar-i-jandar*, that is, chief of Aybak's personal guards. According to Raverty, the *Mamluk* Sultanate in Egypt had a class of officers with this title whose roles were to guard the entry to the sultan's quarters, give and implement the sultan's orders to his *amirs* and guard the persons of standing held prisoner by the sultan.[340] From this position, he was promoted to *amir-i-shikar* – chief huntsman – and with the surrender of the great fortress at Gwalior, he became the *amir.* Next, he was offered the town of Baran and its dependent areas as a fief, and, finally, Aybak endowed him with the territory of Bada'un.[341] Following the defeat at Ankhud and the frantic mobilisation to deal with the Khokhar revolt, Iltutmish arrived with a significant force from his fiefs in India to support his master, Aybak. In the ensuing campaign, his valour was noted by Mu'izz al-Din who gave him a robe of honour and instructed Aybak to free him. Given this glittering career, it is perhaps unsurprising that the *amirs* and other members of the governing class in Delhi approached him to take the throne. However, Iltutmish's position still required bolstering, and he took steps to ensure this, shortly after he had dealt with the immediate challenge to his accession. He acknowledged Yildiz as sultan in Ghazna and Lahore and in return received insignia confirming his own royal status. Yildiz sent him a *chatr* or canopy of state and other regalia as part of their agreement. His earliest known inscription dated 608/October 1211describes him as king – *malik al-muazzam* – and not sultan.[342] However, we learn nothing from Juzjani during Iltutmish's early reign or about him having to enforce his position among *maliks, amirs* and Indian potentates alike. Hasan-i-Nizami mentions a single expedition against the Chauhan ruler of Jalor sometime between 608/1211 and 613/1216. Iltutumish, we are told, assembled a large army and invested the fortress there. The *rai* Udi Sah was forced to surrender the stronghold that was slighted. Having prostrated himself before the Delhi ruler and handed over one hundred camels and twenty horses as tribute, he was reinstated in his position. However, this incident provides our only knowledge of Iltutmish's activities up to 612/1215.[343]

340 *TN*, vol. I, tr. Raverty, p. 603 note 7

341 Ibid., p. 604 and note 5. The fief of Bada'un was acknowledged as the most prestigious in the Delhi territories at the time.

342 P. Jackson (2003), p. 30

343 H.C.Ray (2017), vol. II, p. 1,130

By the beginning of 613/1216, the last of the former Ghurid territories in the west had fallen to Muhammad Khwarazmshah. In 612/1215, he had made a lightning strike against the Ghurid sultan in Bamiyan. Jalal-al-Din was taken unawares, captured and put to death. The accumulated treasure there fell into the hands of the Khwarazmshah. He had earlier consolidated his position in Kirman, Makran and part of Sind where the *khutba* was now read in his name as far as the straights of Hormuz and beyond into coastal Oman following an expedition to the region led by an *amir* Abu Bakr, lord of Zuzan. The rulers across the straights were subordinate to the ruler in Hormuz and for trade reasons wished to shelter under his protection. According to Ibn al-Athir, the harbour at Hormuz accommodated ships from 'the furthest parts of India, China, Yemen and other countries'.[344] It is possible that the Khwarazmian *amir* was just reinstating an arrangement that had previously existed when the *khutba* had been read on behalf of the supreme Ghurid sultan Ghiyath al-Din and that his writ had also extended across the Straights of Hormuz. Having conquered Bamiyan and its associated territories and removed the remaining Ghurid *amirs* from their fiefs in Khurasan, the Khwarazmshah turned his attention to Ghazna. Yildiz had defended his territory robustly over the years and had despatched an army against the Khwarazmshah's vassal in Ghur sultan 'Ala' al-Din Astiz. This army was led by one of his *amirs, malik* Nasir al-Din Husain, his *amir-i-ishikar* – chief huntsman. There was no love lost between the two parties. Yildiz, the former *mamluk* of Mu'izz al-Din, and other former *mamluks* were facing off against the Ghurid *amirs* who now represented the opposing side. The battle took place somewhere near Ghazna, and the Ghurid sultan was mortally wounded in the fighting. He had reigned for four years. This engagement took place sometime in 611/1214.[345] Yildiz, having garrisoned Firuzkuh, then had the former ruler in Ghur, *malik* 'Ala al-Din Muhammad, who had been installed there previously by Mu'izz al-Din, reinstated. He had been released from the fortress of Siva-Khanah in Gharjistan, having been imprisoned there by 'Ala'-al-Din Astiz.[346]

344 *al-Kamil fi'l-Ta'rikh*, part 3, tr. Richards, p. 162. Ibn al-Athir mentions the coastal town of Qalhat, p. 161.

345 *TN*, vol. I, tr. Raverty, p. 416

346 Ibid., p. 396. During intra-Ghurid fighting following Ghiyath al-Din Mahmud's assassination an *amir* sought out and killed 'Ala al-Din Muhammad's son, Muhammad -i-Iran Shah, who was under house arrest with the Ghurid *amir* Umr-i-Shalmati for leading an earlier rebellion. He would have been considered a potential threat to the young sultan Baha al-Din. The eighteen-year-old Juzjani witnessed the return of the assassin with the bloodied head. 'Ala al-Din Muhammad, when the opportunity arose, slew Umr-i-Shalmati in revenge for his son's murder, for which he was reincarcerated.

When 'Ala al-Din Muhammad reached Ghazna, Yildiz treated him with great fanfare. Mu'izz al-Din's canopy of state, which now decorated his mausoleum, was produced and placed over the head of 'Ala al-Din Muhammad who was given the title of sultan by Yildiz. He would have been only too happy to support the nephew of his former master and to reinstate him as ruler in Firuzkuh. 'Ala al-Din Muhammad only reigned for a year, although the *khutba* was read for him and coinage issued in his name. However, he was to all intents and purposes a vassal of the Khwarazmshah who had tactfully reminded him of his obligations under a previous treaty between the two of them. 'Ala-al-Din Muhammad required Yildiz's support and with his demise he was forced to abdicate and went to live out his days in Khwarazm.[347] In (612/late1215) the Khwarazmshah had sent a request, more likely an ultimatum, to Yildiz that he make the *khutba* for him and issue coins in his name while also requesting an elephant in tribute.[348] He explained that if he did this he would confirm the former *mamluk* in his possession of Ghazna. Yildiz called a meeting of his senior *amirs* and Qutlugh Takin, his governor in Ghazna, and another of Mu'izz al-Din's former *mamluks* who advised that there was nothing to be gained from further fighting and that the Khwarsazmshah was too strong to resist. The decision was made to agree to the Khwarazmshah's terms. With this resolved, presents were despatched with the Khwarazmshah's envoy. Yildiz then set out on a hunting expedition into the Punjab.[349] However, in his absence the situation in Ghazna started to unravel. The Turkish *mamluks* and *amirs* conspired and put to death the former *vizier* Mu'ayyad al-Mulk, now described as *khwajah* – literally a man of distinction – and Muhammad-i-'Abdullah, Sanjari who is named as *vizier* and *malik* Nasir al-Din Hussein, the *amir-i-shakar*. The latter had previously come to blows with Yildiz but had returned in his absence.[350] There seems to have been a coup d'état engineered by Qutlugh Takin who sent a message to the Khwarazmshah asking him to come and accept the surrender of the citadel in Ghazna. Muhammad Khwarazmshah reacted quickly and, after a series of forced marches over forty days from Transoxiana, he arrived before Ghazna. He entered the city killing a number of soldiers and Turkish *mamluks*. When Qutlugh Takin was bought before the Khwarazmshah, he was asked why he had had betrayed his friend although his fate, as a traitor and former *mamluk* of Mu'izz al-Din, was probably already sealed. He was arrested and put to death, despite handing over enough treasure and goods for thirty baggage loads. A further 400 *mamluks*

347 Ibid., p. 418

348 *al-Kamil fi'l-Ta'rikh*, part 3, tr. Richards, p. 166

349 *TN*, p. 504

350 Ibid., p. 504 and note 4, p. 505

were brought before the Khwarazmshah – and one assumes executed.[351] This mass execution reflected their suspect loyalty and the threat they would continue to pose. The cities of Ghur and Ghazna and their dependent territories were made over to Jalal-al-Din. The Khwarazmshah's son and governors were installed to administer them in his name. The citadel at Ghazna fell in 612/January1216 and Yildiz was left with no choice but to retreat towards Lahore. With the most direct road via the Karah Darah pass held by the Khwarazmshah's troops he was forced to take a more southerly route.

Before Lahore, another former Mu'izzi' *mamluk* barred his way. Qubacha was now ruler of Lahore and a large part of Sind, including the cities of Multan, Uch and Daybul. Yildiz was confronted by a substantial army consisting of 15,000 cavalry. According to Ibn al-Athir, he only had 1,500 mounted *mamluks* and a number of elephants at his disposal, which is possible given his forced departure from Ghazna – however, looking at the outcome the numerical disparity does seem unrealistic.[352] Initially, the battle went badly for Yildiz. His left and right wings were swiftly put to flight, and he lost the majority of his elephant force. Despite these setbacks, and by using his two remaining elephants, he made a do or die attempt to reach Qubacha. With the elephants seizing Qubacha's *chatr* and standard the victory was his. Qubacha retired to Sind and continued to consolidate his hold on his territories there. His rule now extended from the Arabian Sea to the Indus Delta and north to Peshawar and the fort at Nandana on the eastern slopes of the Salt Range in the Punjab.[353] After securing Lahore, Yildiz wasted little time in assembling a sufficient force to march on Delhi. This move was an attempt to impose his authority on his erstwhile subordinate and son-in-law who had previously accepted the *chatr* and regalia from him. However, by now, five years on, Iltutmish was powerful enough to dispute the matter with his former protector. In 612/late January 1216 the two armies clashed at Tara'in, the battleground where so many significant engagements had already been fought for control of the upper Gangetic plain. Yildiz was comprehensively defeated, captured and sent to Buda'un Iltutmish's fief where he could be closely held, and put to death. Although we have no time frame for his execution it must have happened shortly after his arrival. He had ruled in Ghazna as sultan for nine years. Only two of Mu'izz al-Din's former *mamluks,* now sultans, remained to dispute control of the former Ghurid Indian lands. The Khalaj rulers in Bengal had never been *mamluks.*

351 *al-Kamil fi'l-Ta'rikh*, part 3, p. 167. Ibn al-Athir does not mention their fate but that must be the inference given the earlier comments regarding *mamluks.*

352 *al-Kamil fi'l-Ta'rikh*, part 3, tr. Richards, p. 167

353 P. Jackson (2003), p. 30

The defeat of Yildiz may have increased Iltutmish's security and status but little more. Lahore was swiftly recoccupied by Qubacha. The two sultans continued to dispute Tabarindh, Kuhram and Sarsati in the eastern Punjab. During the winter of 613/1216–17, Iltutmish captured Lahore and installed his son Nasir al-Din Mahmud as ruler only for it to change hands again. Qubacha also had his supporters among former Ghurid lieutenants in the Delhi sultan's territory and proved a formidable opponent to Iltutmish.[354] On a wider perspective, the power of the Khwarazmshah meant that there was no guarantee that the Ghurid-conquered territories east of the Indus would survive as independent entities should Sultan Muhammad decide to intervene. He had already created a territory for his son Jalal al-Din, which encompassed all the former Ghurid lands from Ghur itself to the Indus. His troops had also seized Peshawar from Qubacha.[355] However, the Khwarzmians were shortly to encounter serious problems of their own and when Jalal al-Din, son of Muhammad II Khwarazmshah d.618/1221, did appear, it was as a fugitive not a conqueror. The great Khwarzmian Empire had fallen prey to the armies of Chingiz Khan who had first invaded Islamic lands in 616/1219. We are told by Juzjani that following the depradations of the Mongols 'a great number of men of Khurasan, Ghur and Ghaznin presented themselves before him', that is Qubacha. These arrivals formed part of a wider exodus from Islamic lands, now under Mongol rule, to the relative safety of former Ghurid India.[356] Jalal al-Din the Khwarazmshah had witnessed first hand the ferocity of a Mongol attack when he suffered a crushing defeat in the battle on the banks of the Indus 618/1221. Jalal al-Din had only managed to escape by driving his horse over a thirty-foot drop into the water and having survived storms of Mongol arrows somehow managed to reach the opposite bank of the fast-flowing river. Chingiz Khan had watched with great admiration and amusement Jalal al-Din's brave escape.[357] The Khwarazmian sultan was gradually joined by stragglers from his army until he had a reasonable force at his disposal. Soon he began an aggressive campaign in northern India to try to establish a territory for himself, which was to last for the best part of three years. His presence was to cause immediate problems for Qubacha and also provided a dilemma for Iltutmish. The Delhi sultan with his newfound independence did not wish to jeopardise this, by offering support to the fugitive Khwarazmshah, and give the Mongols any excuse to move beyond the Indus valley and Punjab as they continued a fruitless search for Jalal al-Din.

354 Ibid., p. 31

355 Ibid., p. 32

356 *TN*, vol. I, tr. Raverty, p. 534

357 *CHI*, vol. 5, p. 320

Unfortunately, our main sources, Juzjani and Ibn al-Athir, tell us next to nothing about Khwarazmshah Jalal-al-Din's activities in India. His father, by this stage, was dead, having succumbed on an island in the Caspian Sea during their flight from the Mongol armies.[358] It may be that Juzjani glosses over the events; he was certainly in a position to comment, due to Iltutmish's reluctance to assist a fellow Muslim ruler against the pagan Mongols and the bad example this set in Muslim eyes. Jalal al-Din seems, at this stage, to have been able to assemble a force of between 3,000 and 4,000 men, consisting mainly of survivors from his defeat on the Indus. He appears to have clashed with Indian elements in the Salt Range with some success. However, news of the pursuing Mongol army forced him to withdraw towards Delhi. He halted a few days march from the city. The Mongols by this stage had reached Rawalpindi but subsequently decided to abandon their pursuit.[359] Jalal al-Din despatched an emissary to Iltutmish to request asylum and proposed that they enter into an alliance against the Mongols. Iltutmish would not have wanted to assist Jalal al-Din for a number of reasons, partly with regard to his own security. He had after all begun his journey as the slave of a slave and there was the possibility of a potential threat to his position as sultan posed by the status of Jalal al-Din as ruler of a long-established dynasty. Nor did he wish to encourage the Mongols to launch a full-scale invasion across the Indus to take Delhi as a reprisal. Iltutmish had the envoy killed and then sent presents to mollify the Khwarazmshah with a non-commital reply. By this stage, Jalal al-Din may have had in the region of 10,000 men at his diposal, his army augmented by more refugees escaping from the ravaged Khwarazmian territories, but certainly not enough to deal with the substantial forces at the disposal of the Delhi Sultanate. Had his incursion happened earlier when Iltutmish was still consolidating his hold on Delhi and dealing with rival Qutbi and Mu'izzi *amirs,* the outcome might well have been different. The Khwarzmshah might have been able, through his own Turkic ancestry, to persuade some of the former *ghulams* to join him. Hence Iltutmish's reluctance to become involved. Instead, Jalal al-Din turned back towards Lahore and Iltutmish sent troops to support Qubacha.The Khwarazmian force, which had been joined by the Khokhars following another successful expedition by Jalal al-Din against the tribes of the Salt Range, defeated Qubacha near Uch. Qubacha then sought refuge in Multan.[360] He was forced to become a tributary of the Khwarazmshah. His son who had earlier rebelled against him at Lahore was also forced to accept Jalal al-Din's overlordship. Iltutmish then mobilised against Jalal al-Din and the opposing

358 Ibid., p. 317

359 Ibid., p. 322

360 Ibid.

vanguards clashed but both leaders sent conciliatory messages and withdrew. The Khwarzmshah having pillaged Uch set about securing the submission of the lower Indus by occupying Sehevan and Daybul and despatching an expedition to Nahrwala in Gujerat in search of plunder.[361] Meanwhile, Iltutmish had managed to organise an alliance between himself, Qubacha and various Hindu potentates who had gathered on the banks of possibly River Sutlej, intending to cut off Jalal al-Din's retreat. It was probably this and favourable reports from the western Khwarazmian territories that decided the Khwarazmshah to leave and to return to western Persia via the Makran desert in late 620/1223.[362]

However, the threat of the Mongols had not gone away. Chingiz Khan considered trying to return to Mongolia by a more direct route through the foothills of the Himalayas and is supposed to have sent envoys to Iltutmish to seek his permission to travel through his territories. We do not know what happened to this embassy. Nevertheless, either due to unfavourable omens or the lack of any suitable route, the Great Khan abandoned his attempt and made his way back via Peshawar.[363] The departure of the Khwarazmshah for the west did not signify the end of Khwarazmian presence in the Indus valley. One of Jalal al-Din's lieutenants, Jahan- Pahlawan Ozbeg-bei, was entrusted with his Indian conquests, while those parts of Ghur and Ghazna that had not been devastated by the armies of Chingiz Khan were entrusted to Sayf al-Din Hasan Qarluk. The Mongol general Dorbei sacked the strategic fortress of Nandana, in the Salt Range, which was held by another of Jalal-Din's lieutenants and at the end of the winter in 621/1224 laid siege to Multan.[364] Juzjani tells us that 'for a period of forty-two days, closely invested that strong fortress'.[365] Qubacha himself launched a courageous defence. The Mongols with the onset of the hot season decided they had had enough and retreated. However, Mongol pressure west of the Indus, in Ghazna and Ghur, continued to erode the Khwarazmian position there, and Firuzkuh finally succumbed in 623/1226. There is no doubt that Qubacha had been seriously weakened and that his empire had suffered more compared to Iltutmish's as a result of the depradations of the Khwarazmshah and the Mongols. In the same year that Ghur fell to the Mongols, Qubacha was forced to deal with

361 P. Jackson (2003), p. 33. See also p. 35 note 55. At this stage the Sumra ruler of Daybul acknowledged the sovereignty of Iltutmish, illustrating that Qubacha's territories were already under pressure from Delhi.

362 Ibid., p. 33

363 Ibid., p. 34

364 Ibid.

365 *TN*, vol. I, tr. Raverty, p. 536

a force of Khalaj in Khwarazmian service who had established themselves in Mansura in Siwistan, modern Sehevan. The Khalaj were led by one Malik Khan who probably answered, at least in theory, to the Khwarazmian appointee Hasan Qarluk. Qubacha moved against the Khalaj and defeated them, and Malik Khan was killed in the battle. The survivors then sought refuge with Iltutmish and were subsequently to support him in his campaign against Qubacha.[366]

However, all this activity on the western frontier of his territories did not mean that Iltutmish had neglected the eastern parts of the former Ghurid Empire in Bengal. There, the government of Ali-yi Mardan, who styled himself as Sultan 'Ala' al-Din following the death of Aybak, had descended into tyranny. Juzjani refers to him as a 'bloodthirsty and sanguinary man' and he seems to have lived up to his reputation.[367] In his belligerence, he despatched armies in all directions and the local *raes* were quick to fall in line and to send him tribute. It was not just the Indian potentates who suffered at his hands. A large number of Khalaj *amirs* were put to death and it would seem that, as time went on, the sultan spent more and more time at the capital Lakhnawti while becoming increasingly psychotic. Finally, the arbitrary terror became too much and a group of Khalaj *amirs* killed him and placed Husam al-Din Iwad on the throne. This probably took place in 609/1212–13. Ali-yi Mardin is supposed to have reigned for two years. His successor, who took the title Sultan Ghiyath al-Din, originated from and had apparently been a minor chief in the Garmsir and had served Muhammad b. Bakhtiar. During his reign, he issued coinage and had the *khutba* read in his own name. Having chosen Lakhnawti as his capital, he built the fortress of Basan-kot to protect it. Ghiyath al-Din also initiated the construction of large embankments across his territory. These stretched from Lakhnawti south to the city of Lakhnor in the region of Rarh on the route to Katisin in the southwest of the Ganges Delta and north to Devkot in the district of Varendra. Devkot had served as a former capital until Ghiyath al-Din's accession. These constructions were extensive and, by all accounts, impressive. Some of the causeways could be as much as ten days march from end to end. Not only did they serve to consolidate Muslim control and protect infrastructure but they also facilitated transport and trade across the state during the rainy season.[368] For a period of ten

366 Ibid., p. 542 and end of note 5 and p. 615 note 1

367 Ibid., pp. 578–80

368 *TN*, vol. I, tr. Raverty, p. 585 and note 6, pp. 586–7. When Iltutmish finally conquered Lakhnawti and the eastern Muslim territories he was so impressed with the construction and good works done by Ghiyath al-Din Iwad that 'he would style him by the title "*sultan* Ghiyas-ud-Din Khalji", and from his sacred lips he would pronounce that there could be no reluctance in styling a man sultan who had done so much good'.

years or so, we have very little detail of the goings on in the eastern lands of the former Ghurid Empire.

We do not possess a contemporary account, as Juzjani did not arrive at the Delhi court until 625/1227–8. From his closely held domain, Ghiyath al-Din campaigned over a huge area. He pressured the Sena rulers in eastern Bengal (Bang) and extracted tribute from them. The same method was applied to the *rae* of Jajnagar on the borders of Jajnagar (Orissa), also rich in elephants, as well as the regions of Kamrup (Assam) and Tirhut (part of Bihar) – all of which provided Ghiyath al-Din with great wealth. Later one of Iltutmish's representatives, Sayf al-Din Aybeg, continued in this vein and was known by the sobriquet *yaghantut* due to the large number of elephants he acquired in his raids in Bang and sent back to the sultan.[369] Inevitably, Ghiyath al-Din's western borders, particularly Bihar, came under attack from Iltutmish. It seems that around 616/1219, following a series of campaigns, Iltutmish prevailed and acquired Bihar installing his own *amirs* to govern the region. At around this time, another sultan, Mu'izz al-Din 'Ali-yi 'Iwad, comes into the picture. He was almost certainly the son of Ghiyath al-Din and may have ruled jointly with his father.[370] What is clear is that the Khalaj sultans had established a rich and powerful entity in western Bengal centred on Lakhnawti. According to Juzjani in 622/1225 Iltutmish marched into the Lakhnawti district to try to bring Ghiyath al-Din to heel. The Khalaj sultan responded by moving his war vessels upriver, to prevent Iltutmish from crossing the Ganges to the Lakhnawti side.[371] It is likely that this incursion was the result of Iwad and his forces contesting control of Bihar and Awadh with Iltutmish's *amirs*. After a possible skirmish, an agreement was reached between the two sultans, and Iltutmish received thirty-eight elephants and eighty *laks* of silver and it was agreed that the *khutba* would be read for him and coins issued in his name.[372] Following this rapprochement Iltutmish returned to Delhi, leaving *malik* 'Izz-al-Din Jani to administer Bihar. However, this arrangement seems to have been shortlived, as the Khalaj sultan marched into Bihar and imposed a harsh rule in the region with Iltutmish's representatives driven out, *malik* Jani seeking refuge in Awadh. For the next couple of years, sultan 'Iwad maintained control in Bihar. Iltutmish, however, had not given up. Having appointed his son Nasir al-Din Mahmud, who had previously been governor in Lahore to the *iqta* of Awadh, they bided their time. In due course, Ghiyath al-Din departed on a plundering raid into Assam and Bang with a large army. This

369 Jackson (2003), p. 141 and *TN*, vol. II, p. 589 and note, p. 732

370 Ibid., p. 36

371 *TN*, vol. I, p. 593 note 6

372 Ibid., p. 593 note 7

was the opportunity that Nasir al-Din Mahmud had been waiting for. Sometime in 624/1227, without warning, he invaded Lakhnawti in force, with troops for the purpose provided by Iltutmish, which included contingents from unknown Hindu feudatories.[373] Ghiyath al-Din, on learning of this, returned post haste to deal with the invaders. However, the problem he would have had was that having transhipped his forces across the Brahmaputra into Assam or the delta of the Ganges/Brahmaputra rivers to Bang, any swift return was going to be logistically challenging. Timely reinforcement from the west was not probable, which would have had to cross the territory of the Delhi Sultanate to reach him, unless he could persuade local Indian potentates to support him. Given his historic relations with them that would seem unlikely. With all the forces he could gather he made for his capital only to discover that Nasir al-Din Mahmud had beaten him to it. A major battle was fought outside the gates of Lakhnawti and Iwad was defeated and taken prisoner. He and his surviving *amirs* were put to death. Juzjaini informs us that Sultan Ghiyath al-Din 'Iwad had reigned for twelve years.[374] Iltutmish installed his victorious son as viceroy and sent him a red *chatr* together with a beautiful robe from a number he had received from the caliph in Baghdad in congratulation of hisson'svictory.[375]

In 623/1226, Iltutmish, following his intial success against Ghiyath al-Din, had launched a campaign against the Chauhan rulers of the great fort of Ranthanbor situated southwest of Gwalior. Despite its renowned impregnability the Delhi army took the fortress. The following year, he capured the stronghold of Mandor. These raids not only served to keep Hindu rulers in check, but also provided sustenance for Iltutmish's treasury and combined with the monies he had extorted from 'Iwad in Bengal provided the funds for additional recruitment in his campaign to eliminate Qubacha.[376] Qubacha had been badly mauled in confrontations with the Khwarazmians, the Mongols and Iltutmish. He would have found himself at a numerical disadvantage as compared with the formidable forces now at the disposal of the Delhi sultan. Relations between the two former Ghurid *ghulams* had been fraught and Qubacha, for the reasons explained, seems to have had the worst of it. There is the possibility that Iltutmish had agreed to support Qubacha in his struggles with the Khwarazmians and Mongols, and possibly in his struggle with Yildiz, as it was patently in his interest to do so. However, this support probably came at a price, possibly the acknowledgement of the sovereignty of the Delhi

373 *TN*, vol. I, tr. Raverty, p. 629

374 [67] Ibid., p. 594

375 Ibid., p. 630

376 Jackson (2003), p. 39

sultan and the ceding of territory. It could be that Qubacha's failure to observe his commitments under any agreement led to the conflict with his rival ruler in Delhi. Iltutmish had campaigned against Lahore in 613/1216–17, possibly with success.[377] We know that his son Nasir al-Din Mahmud was appointed governor of that city and that by the time of the surrender of Multan, Nasir al-Din Aytemur was Iltutmish's appointee there.[378] Subsequently, Qubucha lost the district of Ganjrut or Wanjrut near Multan. The territorial integrity of his empire in the Indus valley was being constantly eroded by Iltutmish. By the end of 625/1228, the Delhi sultan had also acquired Tabarindh, Kuhram and Sarsati where he installed one of his *mamluks* as ruler.[379] Iltutmish arrived before Uch with his Delhi army in 625/1228 while Qubacha had set up camp outside the town of Ahrawat, a place unknown to us, but likely to have been on the Indus not far from Uch. Juzjaini tells us 'the whole of his fleet and boats, on board of which the baggage and followers of his army were embarked, were moored in the river in front of the camp'.[380] Given his dispositions, it would seem that Qubacha realised that the writing was on the wall and that the forces now ranged against him made it impossible to dispute with Iltutmish in open conflict. He swiftly learned that the Lahore army under Aytemur had arrived before Multan and that Uch was under siege from Iltutmish. Consequently, he made the decision to set sail downriver with his army to the island fortress of Bhakkar, having instructed his *vizier* in Uch to despatch the treasury to the same destination. On learning of this, Iltutmish sent a force under his *vizier* Muhammad Junaidi in pursuit. Uch was besieged by the Delhi army for three months in the end, terms were agreed, arranged by Qubacha's son *malik* 'Ala al-Din Bahram Shah, and the city surrendered in early May 625/1228. At the end of the month Qubacha threw himself into the Indus to avoid being taken alive. As Juzjani puts it, 'subsequently to that the treasures and the remainder of the followers of Malik (Sultan) Nasir-ud-Din, Kabajah, reached the presence of the court, the Asylum of the world'.[381]

It is interesting that he describes the court of Iltutmish in Delhi as the asylum of the world, as it was increasingly the chosen destination of Muslims escaping the onslaught and destruction wrought to Islamic lands west of the Indus by the

377 Ibid., p. 35. Professor Jackson mentions the possibility, referring to Juzjani, of Qubacha's capture and release by Iltutmish's forces in a campaign prior to the final assault on Sind. However, if this were the case would Iltutmish have allowed his rival to go free?

378 *TN*, vol. II, p. 728

379 Ibid., p. 723 and note 1

380 *TN*, vol. I, tr. Raverty, p. 612

381 Ibid., p. 614

Mongols. Delhi was becoming the capital of Persianate culture and the most important Islamic city of the east – Juzjani himself was just one of numerous exiles. On the appearance of Iltutmish's forces before Uch, he expediently abandoned his position in Qubacha's and his son's employ, as *qadi-yi lashgar*, realising that they were not going to be the winning side. He fawned before Iltutmish's entourage and reached Delhi in Ramadan – the ninth month – 625–1227/8.[382] Shortly after the fall of Qubacha, the Sumra ruler of Daybul, Chanisar sent his submission to the Delhi sultan via the latter's *vizier.* Iltutmish's writ now extended beyond the mouth of the Indus along the coast of the Arabian Sea. Qubacha's empire in the Indus valley, despite the manifest efforts of its ruler, had proved difficult to defend. Although there is no doubt of the commercial and mercantile opportunities the territory offered, it was vulnerable. The area in the years following the demise of Mu'izz al-din had become a disputed zone. First, in the conflicts between Mu'izz al-Din's *Diadochi,* and subsequently, it had had to weather the Khwarazmian invasion and partial occupation as well as Mongol incursions. These invasions encouraged political instability and although he could call on some Indian allies, Qubacha was at a distinct disadvantage and ultimately unable to resist the power and resources of the nascent Delhi Sultanate.

With the demise of Qubacha, Iltutumish was free to address what remained of the Khwarazmian occupation following Jalal al-Din's departure. He had established in the northwestern borderlands what was to be a short-lived principality whose territorial scope is unclear but encompassed the areas where the Khwarazmshah had operated.[383] Iltutmish, whose western border by this stage probably reached River Jhelam and north as far as the borders of Kashmir, wasted little time in defeating Ozbeg-bei, one of Jalal al-Din's appointees who fled to Iraq while others including Hasan Qarluk submitted to the Delhi sultan. Binban, which had been ruled by Ozbeg-bei, became the fief of Hasan Qarluk who later ruled in Ghazna, Binban and Kurraman.[384] Iltutmish's successes elicited a positive response from the new caliph al-Mustansir 623–640/1226–1242 who thought the emerging Delhi Sultanate was a force worth cultivating in a way that his father had endorsed the Ghurids as a counterbalance to the powers of the Khwarazmshah. Juzjani witnessed the arrival of the caliph's embassy, bringing

382 Ibid., p. 615 note 9

383 Jackson (2003), p. 36. The territory is thought to have included Nandana, Kujah (Gurjat), Sodra and Siyalkot.

384 Ibid., p. 36. See also Jackson (2017), p. 82. The Mongols under Qaghan Ogodei had despatched a force under Mongeddu who based himself in Kunduz-Baghlan in northern Afghanistan to campaign against Khwarazmian remnants in the upper Punjab. In the end it seems Iltutmish's actions pre-empted their involvement at this juncture.

robes of honour and diplomas confirming Iltutmish's position as conqueror of the territories he now held, and was present at the celebratory dinner. The titles on offer included *yamin khalifat Allah* – right hand of God's Deputy – and *khalifa-yi amir al mu'minin* – Deputy of the Commander of the Faithful – and probably others.[385] Iltutmish, the former *mamluk*, had achieved recognition from the highest levels of the Islamic world. He was now accepted as one of the elite among Muslim rulers, no small achievement for somebody who had once been a *ghulam's ghulam*. Shortly after these celebrations, in early winter 626/1228–9, news reached Delhi of the death of Iltutmish's son and heir and a subsequent revolt in Lakhnawti. Nasir al-Din Mahmud had reigned for under two years, although how much control he actually exercised is open to conjecture. How he died and where is unknown, although Raverty seems to suggest Awadh and not Lakhnawti itself.[386] The rebellion was led by a former official of Iltutmish, Ikhtiar al-Din Dawlat Shah, otherwise known as Bilge Malik.

In 628/1230–31 the Delhi sultan invaded Bengal with a substantial army, including Indian contingents and the rebel was defeated and according to Juzjani 'secured' and one assumes martyred.[387] Having brought the eastern territories to heel, Iltutmish was now the undisputed Muslim ruler in the subcontinent and for the remainder of his reign and a period beyond the Muslim held regions in the east remained subject to Delhi. He installed as his deputy and ruler in the east *malik* 'Ala' al-Din Jani before returning to his capital. Iltutmish, having reimposed his authority in Bengal, took the opportunity brought about by the newly won stability in the lands under his authority to launch a new currency. This was based on the pure silver *tanga* rather than imitations of billon coins, such as the horseman type, issued by Hindu rulers.[388] In 629/1232–3 Iltutmish set out for the great fortress of Gwalior, which had been captured by Aybak but had fallen into Hindu hands again during the upheaval following his death. The Indian ruler in question is referred to as 'Mangal Diw, the accursed, son of the accursed Mal Diw'.[389] Iltutmish besieged Gwalior for eleven months, and, in the

385 P. Jackson (2003), p. 38 and see also *TN*, vol. I, p. 616 and note 4

386 *TN*, vol. I, tr. Raverty, p. 617 note 5. Al al-Din Jani was succeeded by Saif al-Din Aybak *Yaghantut* the elephant hunter who ruled until (631/1234–5) followed as governor by *malik* 'Izz al-Din Toghril-i-Toghan Khan who was in post at the time of Iltutmish's death.

387 Ibid., p. 618 and note

388 Jackson (2003), p. 37

389 *TN*, vol. I, p. 619

end, the *rae* Mangal Diw abandoned the fort.[390] A number of the inhabitants, possibly as many as 700, were summarily executed, and Iltutmish appointed various *amirs* to administer his new conquest. Juzjani was appointed to the positions of '*khazi, khatib and Imam*' in the city. The sultan then left the walls of the fortress and set up camp a few miles away where he remained for a few days as he made his way back to Delhi. While at the encampment, he inaugurated the imperial *nawbat* five times a day presumably, as he felt this display was now appropriate with his unchallenged sovereignty. The Ghurid sultan Ghiyath al-Din had assumed the same dignity when he received robes from the caliph.[391] Later, the Delhi sultan campaigned against the city of Ujjain on Khshipra River, in modern Madhya Pradesh, destroying the place and plundering its temple. He carried off various idols, and booty at the same time. By now, in failing health, Iltutmish's last campaign took place in 633/1235–6. This expedition was to the northwest borders against Binban and the lands of the Khwarazmian legatee, Hasan Qarluk, who had previously submitted to Iltutmish. The catalyst seems to have been a desire to impose his authority on Hasan Qarluk's territories, which could be used as a dropping off point for the invasion of India and therefore posed a potential threat to the Delhi Sultanate. Qarluk had been forced to accept a Mongol resident and this coupled with concern of increasing Mongol activity on his northwest borders, including an invasion of Kashmir, decided Iltutmish to gather his forces and march towards the Indus – Binban is situated on the west of the middle Indus.[392] The expedition was aborted due to Iltutmish's ill health, and he returned to Delhi where he lingered for a further nineteen days, dying on Shaban 633 (29 April 1236). He, unlike many of his contemporaries and rivals, had managed to die in his own bed, a rare achievement. We do not know his age but around sixty-five might be a reasonable estimate.

Iltutmish was undoubtedly the greatest of the Ghurid *mamluks,* among the successors to the Ghurid imperium, and his achievements speak for themselves. He had triumphed over his competitors and established a dynasty. While his ability is unquestionable, the scale of his success could not have been foreseen. He was fortunate in the way events unfolded. The Khwarazmshahs, who certainly posed a very real threat to the emerging rulers of the former Ghurid Indian territories,

390 H.C.Ray (2017), vol. II, p. 829 note 1. These rulers were probably members of the Parihara dynasty of Gwalior who had ruled the city for 103 years prior to the extinction of the line with Iltutmish's conquest.

391 *TN*, vol. I, pp. 620–01 and p. 383. The quintple *nawbat* consisted of 'kettledrums and other instruments sounded, at stated periods, before the gate of sovereigns and great men'.

392 P. Jackson (2017), p. 246 and (2003), p. 105

became embroiled with the Mongols. Chingiz Khan, following his victory over Jalal al-Din on the banks of the Indus, did not pursue him aggressively, as he might have done, thus allowing the survival of Muslim India. Iltutmish then managed to avoid any alliance with the exiled Khwaramzshah, keeping him at arm's length and, in so doing, avoided encouraging any Mongol interference. He had been careful to keep himself out of politics west of the Indus while establishing his own state in Delhi. He did not intervene in the struggles between Qubacha and Jalal al-Din until late in the day, allowing his rivals to weaken themselves. All the while he was building up his own military establishment. His expeditions against Hindu potentates and the Khalaj Sultanate in Bengal further enhanced his exchequer, enabling him to field larger armies. Qubacha had been forced to expend considerable financial resources resisting the Mongol siege of Multan and with these exhausted following the Mongol departure, he was then at the mercy of Iltutmish's fresh and formidable armies and not in a position to resist. The availability of specie, from his various *razzias,* enabled Iltutmish to recruit and pay his *mamluks* and soldiers of fortune fleeing eastwards from the Mongol eruption into Islamic lands from 617/1220 onwards. Qubacha's empire may have been the closest safe haven for the refugees from eastern Iranian lands, Khurasan, Khwarazm, Transoxiana, and former Ghurid territories, but ultimately many chose Delhi as their final destination. Both Jalal al-Din and Qubacha suffered from changing allegiances with many exiles ending up at the court of the Delhi sultan.[393] It is possible that Delhi being further away from the contested borderlands offered a more secure prospect of employment to both military adventurers and scholars alike. Iltutmish actively pursued the cream of these immigrants through generous gifts.[394] However, it was not just free agents that Iltutmish relied on to fill military and administrative positions within what had become a sizeable territorial empire. Like Mu'izz al-Din before him he created a substantial force of Turkish *ghulams* answerable to him alone. Some of these Shamsis as they came to be known are listed by Juzjani at the end of his chapter on Iltutmish in a list of nobles of Iltutmish's court.[395] A number of these personal *ghulams* are given biographies in the *Tabaqat-i-Nasiri*.[396]

393 Jackson (2003), p. 40. Mentions two of Jalal al-Din's envoys deserting to Iltutmish following the recent hardships they had endured in the Khwarazmshah's service.

394 *TN*, vol. I, tr. Raverty, pp. 598–9

395 Ibid., pp. 625–6

396 *TN*, vol. II, pp. 702–802. Juzjani would have met or known of most of them.

Iltutmish's *Mamluks*

Iltutmish had learned early, as the slave of a slave, that Mu'izz al-Din's policy of acquiring *mamluks* who were loyal to him alone was something to be emulated. The Mu'izzi and Qutbi *ghulams* had all played an important role in the establishment of Aybak and later Iltutmish himself. He may have paid particular attention to recruiting Turks of a similar background to his own origins from the Cuman/Qipchak/Qangli confederation and the subgroup of the Olberli who were his people.[397] Utilising these connections made sense. It is possible that Aybak singled out Iltutumish not only for his impressive qualities, but due to his origins and their similarity to his own. Many of the Shamsi *ghulams* originated from the Steppe peoples beyond the Black and Caspian seas. As sultan, Iltutmish sent merchants to the great emporia of Central Asia, including Bukhara and Samarkand, in search of these slaves.[398]

He began this activity when he was the *ghulam* of Aybak, purchasing Sanjar-i-Gajz-Lak Khan from a trader, Ali Bastabadi, whose origins are unclear, while he was still fiefholder of Baran. Iltutmish initially gave the slave to his son Nasir-al-Din Mahmud Shah. Gajz-Lak Khan's loyal sevice was ultimately rewarded with charge of Uch and its dependent territories following the demise of Qubacha. He died at his *iqta* in 629/1232.[399] The next individual on Juzjani's list is referred to as 'Mu'izzi', that is, he had originally been the *ghulam* of the Ghurid sultan Mu'izz al-Din. Kabir Khan-i-Ayaz is referred to as a 'Rumi' or Roman Turk, that is, from Byzantine lands in what had become the Seljuk Sultanate of Rum. Another option for the 'Rumi' origins of *mamluks* could refer to a person of Greek or Slav origin from within Byzantine territory itself. How Kabir Khan-i-Ayaz came to be a Ghurid slave we do not know. It is possible that he was a Muslim, if indeed he was from Seljuk Anatolia. He may have been captured and sold into slavery unlawfully and trafficked eastwards along the network of caravanserais to the markets of Central Asia. On the death of Mu'izz al-Din, he seems to have become the property of Nasir al-Din Husain *Amir-i-Shikar* – Chief Huntsman – of Ghazna, who was killed along with the *wazir* of Ghazna during a revolt against Yildiz who at the time was marching on Dehli against Iltutmish.[400] Following this turn of events, Khabir Khan-i-Ayaz fled with his children to India.

397 Jackson (2003), p. 63

398 Ibid.

399 *TN*, vol. II, tr. Raverty, p. 725

400 *TN*, vol. I, pp. 504–05

He was by now a renowned warrior and was purchased by Iltutmish from Sher Khan-i-Surkh – the red – and his brother, the sons of Nasir al-Din Husain, and made governor of Multan and its dependent districts. Latterly, he seems to have fallen out with Iltutmish and was recalled to Delhi and given the city of Palwal in Haryana as an *iqta*. However, he was to hold significant positions during the following reigns. Under Iltutmish's successor, sultan Firuz Shah r. 633–4/1236, he was appointed to Sunam in the northern Punjab. Firuz Shah appears to have had great difficulty in managing Iltutmish's *mamluks* and their expectations and it did not take long for open dissent to emerge. When the governor of Lahore, 'Ala al-Din Jani, a free Turkish noble, and Saif al-Din Kuji, the feudatory at Hansi, revolted, Kabir Khan joined them, causing great trouble to the sultan who was killed in the ensuing insurrection. On the accession of Iltutmish's daughter Radiyya 634–7/1236–40, who may have been originally selected by Iltutmish to succeed him, these *ghulams* were still in open rebellion against the central authority.[401] They marched on Delhi, attacking the city and the surrounding regions. Ulltimately, Sultan Radiyyya, with promises of positions of authority under her regime, managed to detach Kabir Khan along with *malik* Izz al-Din Muhammad Salari, a Ghurid *amir* from the uprising. Following this, the other rebels withdrew, disconcerted with Kabir Khan's sudden change of allegiance.[402] True to her word, Radiyya appointed him to the strategically important governorship of Lahore and its dependencies. However, it was only two years later in 636/1238 that Kabir Khan was in open revolt, forcing Radiyya and her army to march on Lahore. There, Radiyya appointed Qarash Khan Ikhtiyar al-Din, formerly at Multan, to that city. Kabir Khan again chose to submit and was surprisingly offered, depite his persistent disloyalty, the fiefdom of Multan. It was not long, however, before he had declared himself independent again, offering himself a *chatr* and taking possession of Uch. He died a rebel in 639/1241during the reign of Bahram Shah r. 638–40/1240–02 and was succeeded by his sonTaj al-Din Abu Bakr-i-Ayaz. At the time of the new sultan's succession, it would appear that both Sind and Lahore were not under the authority of the Delhi sultan.

Another recruit from the generation of Mu'izz al-Din's rule was Nasir al-Din Aytemur al-Baha-i -Ayatim – one of Baha al-Din Toghril's *mamluks*. Toghril had been one of Mu'izz al-Din's most respected slaves and Iltutmish purchased Ayatim from Toghril's heirs. This *mamluk* proved himself to be a capable servant and following the capture of Uch and Qubacha's remaining territories he was invested with the governorship of Ajmer. This fief was considerable and consisted

401 Jackson (2003), p. 46. Apparently, he predicted that none of his sons would make a suitable sultan.

402 Jackson (2003), pp. 67–8

of the area known as Sivalik by the Muslims, centred on the northern area of the Aravalli range. The territory in question stretched from Sarsati and Hansi in the north to Nagor, Ajmer and Mandor in the south and possibly as far as Jalor.[403] Ayatim also received the unique honour of an elephant from Iltutmish, which distinguished him from the other *maliks*. Juzjani tells of his campaigns and 'making holy war against infidel Hindus and devastating their country.'[404] These Hindu potentates would have included the Chauhan heirs of Prthviraja III. However, these expeditions were not a series of one-sided Islamic victories and were closely fought. On one such raid in the Bundi region, probably against the Chauhans of Ranthanbor, Ayatim came to grief. He was ambushed in a defile while fording a river, possibly the upper Chambal; forced to cross in full armour, he drowned.[405] Another *mamluk* who is just described as a Turk, Saif al-Din Aybak was bought from a man described as Jamal al-Din, an armourer at Bada'un, between the Ganges and Rahab rivers. How he ended up there is not known. He began his career as the sultan's personal cupbearer, and later received the fief of Narnul and then those of Baran and Sunam. He took part in the expedition to Lakhnawti and was subsequently assigned the fief of Uch following the death of its incumbent Gajz-Lak Khan. His career provides a good insight into the progression of a *mamluk* of ability. From there, he became a significant figure, and following Iltutmish's death, was instrumental in thwarting Jalal al-Din Khwarazmshah's former appointee Hasan Qarluq's incursion into the Punjab. Juzjaini tells us it was an important victory for the Delhi Sultanate in the turmoil following Iltutmish's death. Saif al-Din Aybak died shortly after this victory following a fall from his horse, which kicked and killed him.[406] *Malik* Saif al-Din Aybak-i- Yaghantut was a Qara-Khitan whom Iltutmish purchased from the heirs of a merchant and slaver, Ikhtiar al-Din of the tight-fitting vest. He is not to be confused with the slave dealer of a similar name who sold Iltutmish himself.[407] He rose to a high position and was given the *iqta* of Sursuti and used this appointment as an opportunity to spread largesse, in the form of a horse to his peers and other notables of Iltutmish's administration. What is striking here is the example of a senior *mamluk* using patronage, distributing gifts for which he would not only be remembered, but also through the act hoping to acquire

403 Ibid., p. 130 for explanation of the historical geographical terminology versus moden usage of Sivalik as a sub-range of the Himalayas

404 *TN*, vol. II, tr. Raverty, p. 728

405 Ibid.

406 Ibid., pp. 730–01

407 Ibid., p. 731

influence that would serve him well in the future. Juzjani specifically mentions the episode possibly implying that it was unusual behaviour. Iltutmish obviously thought highly of him and entrusted him with the fief of Bihar. Ultimately, he was promoted to the fief of Lakhnawti in Bengal. He is remembered for his proactive rule there and in particular the capture of elephants, in Bang. The animals were then despatched to Delhi. For these exploits, he received the title *Yaghantut*, taker of elephants, from Iltutmish. He died in 631/1234 of causes unknown.

The next slave mentioned by Juzjani is the Turk Nusrat al-Din, Tayasai who had been bought by Mu'izz al-Din. We learn from Juzjani that at the time of his arrival at Iltutmish's court, this *ghulam* held the fiefs of Jhind, Barwalah and Hansi. What we do not know is how he came to be serving Iltutmish. At his accession, the Mu'izzis had chosen to support Aram Shah. He rose to be governor of the Gwalior territory using that fortress as his residence. From there he was instructed to raid into the Kalinjar and Chanderi regions in the Chandella kingdom of Jejakabhukti or Bundelkhand as the area is now called. He was provided by Iltutmish with troops from Qinnawj, Mahir and Maha'un for these undertakings. The impression we have from Juzjani is that he was given a substantial force to deal with resurgent Hindu rulers, particularly the Chandellas on the southern borders of the sultanate. At this time, the Chandella capital was Kalinjar, situated at the end of the Vindhaya Range. The place had been captured during Qutb al-Din Aybak's reign following the death of Paramardideva r. 560–99/1165–1203 but must have been lost subsequently. Trailokyavarman r. 599–642/1203–45, Paramardideva's son, never reoccupied Kalinjar, seemingly content to rule from Ajayagarh. Trailokyavarman was heavily defeated by Tayasai and lost his ceremonial parasol and standards in the process. The plundering during this campaign was so extensive that in the space of fifty days, Iltutmish's fifth share alone was valued at twenty-five *laks.*[408] One assumes that numerous shrines and temples in the Chandella territories, such as Khajuraho, had recovered from Aybak's earlier depredations, provided the spoils. Despite this, the Chandellas carried on ruling in Jejakabhukti, where they continued to flourish and to style themselves as kings of Kalinjar.[409] Perhaps, the extra distance of Ajayagarh from Muslim territory and its location persuaded them to abandon Kalinjar. The Chandellas seemed to have held their own against the Muslim incursions. An inscription of Trailokyavarman's son Viravarman compares his father to Vishnu 'in lifting up the earth immersed in the oceans of the Turuskas'. The inscription also mentions Trailokyavaraman as 'a very creator in providing strong places'. The use of these *durggapravidhana-veddah* is possibly referring to the way he conducted his

408 *TN*, vol. II, tr. Raverty, pp. 732–3

409 P. Jackson (2003), p. 143

warfare against the Muslim invaders. The fortresses provided a refuge from which to sally forth and retreat to as necessary. Either way, he seems to have consolidated the Chandella position after the disastrous reign of his predecessor Paramardideva. His campaigns were not just against the Delhi Sultanate but also included other neighbouring Hindu rulers, including the Kalachuri kings of Chedi.[410] On another occasion returning from an expedition, laden with plunder and heading for the safety of Delhi territory Tayasai was ambushed by the Ranah of Ajar. Juzjani describes him as the 'greatest of all Raes of that tract of country'. He is better known as Chahadedeva of the Yajvapala or Jajapalla dynasty ruling from Narwar and a rival of the Chandellas.[411] The episode, despite Juzjani's attempts to put a gloss on it, was a close run thing and Tayasai did well to extricate himself and return with his plunder intact to Gwalior.[412]Juzjani had been appointed *qadi* of Gwalior at this time, and so heard the details of this incident first hand. Tayasai, a veteran *mamluk*, died early in Sultan Radiyya's reign. He had been appointed to the *iqta* of Awadh by her and was marching to Delhi in response to her appeal to assist in the struggle against the rebel subordinates of Lahore and Hansi. Having crossed the Ganges, he was confronted by the rebels and captured by the *malik* Saif al-Din Kuji of Hansi and died of illness in captivity shortly afterwards.

The following two *ghulams*, Toghan Khan and Temur Khan, are described as Turks. *Malik* 'Izz-al-Din Toghril-i-Toghan Khan was a Qara-Khitan. His early competence saw him progress through various positions in the imperial household. While promoted to *sar-dawat-dar*, chief keeper of the private writing case, he managed to lose the bejewelled item and suffered his owners' wrath in consequence.[413] This was only a temporary setback, however, and after a series of further appointments by 630/1232 he had been given the *iqta* of Buda'un and later that of Bihar. On the death of Saif al-Din Aybak *yaghantut*, Toghan Khan was appointed to Lakhnawti. Following Iltutmish's death, he disputed the possession of the town of Basankot, within the jurisdiction of the city of Lakhnawti itself, with the *mamluk* Aor Khan, feudatory of Lakhnawti-Lakhnahor, whom he killed. We are told, 'Toghan Khan's name became great (in consequence), and both sides of the

410 Ray (2017), vol. II, pp. 727–8

411 *TN*, vol. I, p. 691. See also Jackson (2003). p. 144 and note 127 for indentification of 'Chahar'.

412 Ibid., vol. II, ppp. 733–4

413 Blair, Sheila S., *Text and Image in Medieval Persian Art: Edinburgh Studies in Islamic Art* (Series editor R. Hillenbrand) (Edinburgh, 2019), p. 83 Fig. 3.18. The illustration is of the cast brass pen box inlaid with copper and silver belonging to Majd al-Muzaffar, the penultimate vizier of the Khwarazmshahs. It is a fine and substantial example of Herat metalwork, measuring 5 x 31.4 x 6.4 cm. It is reasonable to imagine that the example made for a sultan would be even more ornate hence Iltutmish's great displeasure at its disappearance.

country of Lakhnawti ... became one and came into *malik* Tughril's possession.'[414] It seems that Iltutmish's successors were unable to control him. He raided along the north bank of the Ganges into the region of Tirhut, gaining significant spoils as he did so. Despite Toghan Khan's unorthodox activities, Raddiya and Bahram Shah recognised him as a tributary sovereign, awarding him a canopy of state and standards, probably implying that they were unable to reign him in. Following the accession of Sultan 'Ala' al-Din r. 640–44/1242–6, a grandson of Iltutmish, Toghan Khan ceased to pretend that he had any loyalty to the sultan in Delhi and effectively declared himself an independent ruler. He raided into Awadh, attempting to annexe it, despite it being held by another *mamluk*. However, in 641/1244, he came badly unstuck in a campaign against Hindu potentates in Jajnagar/Orissa and was forced to ask the sultan for reinforcements. The Hindu army under the ruler of Jajnagar captured Lakhnor killing Toghan Khan's lieutenant, Fakhr-al-Mulk, Karim al-Din, Laghri, in the process and reached the gates of Lakhnawti. The Hindu victory is commemorated in an inscription from the reign of the eastern Ganga ruler Narashima II r. 656–83/1278–1305 celebrating the victory over the *'yavanas'* – westerners.[415] Toghan Khan sent a minister, the *sharf al-Mulk,* to Delhi and a relief force was despatched by the sultan to support the beleaguered rebel *mamluk*. This army, led by the feudatory of Awadh, Temur Khan and other *amirs* entered Bengal. However, on arrival, fighting broke out, not with the Hindus, who had by this stage withdrawn from Lakhnawti, but between the two Muslim armies.[416] It would seem that the central government in Delhi had decided it was time to bring Toghan Khan back into the fold. The recalcitrant *ghulam* was forced to come to terms and surrendered Lakhnawti to Temur Khan. Accompanied by a number of *amirs,* Toghan Khan returned to Delhi where he was greeted with great pomp and perhaps more surprisingly awarded Temur Khan's old fief of Awadh. Why the sultan decided to adopt this policy is hard to gauge. It is possible that the power wielded by these *ghulams* made it essential that they possessed an *iqta* rather than being in Delhi itself where any revolt could have serious consequences for the sultanate. What Temur Khan's retainers in Awadh made of this sudden change of feudatory is not recorded. By coincidence, the rivals died on the same day in 644/1247. Temur Khan is described by Juzjani as being of Qipchak origin and Iltutmish had acquired him early in his career, while he was still a slave of Qutb

414 *TN*, vol. II, tr. Raverty, p. 737 note 7. Raverty explains that there were two great fiefs in that region of Bengal Lakhnawti and Lakhnahor, one on each side of the River Ganges. To distinguish them the right bank was referred to as Lakhnawti-Lakhnahor.

415 Jackson (2003), p. 142

416 *TN*, vol. II, p. 740

al-Din Aybak, and, for once, we learn that he was purchased for the sum of 50,000 *dhirams*. He is mentioned as distinguishing himself on Mu'izz al-Din's expedition to Chandwar against the Ghadavala ruler Jayachandra and had personally captured his son Laddah. He was later appointed *amir -i-akhur* – deputy lord of the stable – when the incumbent Toghan Khan was promoted to the fief of Buda'un. He was subsequently appointed to the *iqta* of Awadh and campaigned as far as the territory of Tirhut against Hindu rulers 'obtaining great booty' and also raided south into the Chandella territories towards Kalinjar.[417] Later, he married the daughter of Aybak-i-Yaghantut. He died in *c.* 644/1247, on the same night as his rival Toghan Khan, while in rebellion at Lakhnawti. He had served from (590/1193), a period of at least forty-four years that spanned the apogee and fall of the Ghurid dynasty and the establishment of the Delhi Sultanate. His service encompassed the reigns of Iltutmish and four of his successors.

The next entrant in Juzjani's list is notable for not being a Turkish tribesman from Central Asia. He is remembered for his administrative rather than martial qualities. Mu'izz al-Din and his *mamluk* successors would have relied on native Indians to assist in the administration of their conquered territories and particularly for dealing with the local rulers. They must have been numerous but *malik* Hindu Khan is the only one singled out in Juzjaini's list. Iltutmish purchased him, early in his career, while he held the *iqta* of Baran, during the reign of the sultan Qutb al-Din Aybak. He was bought from Fakhr-al-Din the Safahani, presumably a slave dealer. Otherwise, his origins are obscure. Where and how he was originally acquired and when he converted is not known. He had a close relationship with Iltutmish and was treasurer, a position he continued to hold in the administration of his daughter Sultan Radiyya. His first significant position was as *yuz-ban*, the 'keeper of the hunting leopards', that is, cheetahs. During a campaign in Aybak's reign against unspecified 'independent tribes of Hindu infidels', he unhorsed and killed a Hindu warrior. For this deed, Iltutmish promoted him to 'ewer-bearer', a position that would have involved personal attendance on the sultan and a post he did not relinquish for the rest of Itutmish's life despite his appointment as treasurer. Juzjani makes it clear in this biography that he was beholden to Hindu Khan for his kind treatment when he was appointed as *qadi* in Gwalior.[418] Hindu Khan was made feudatory of the extensive territory of Uch. He was subsequently appointed by Radiyya's successor and probably half-brother Sultan Mu'izz al-Din Bahram Shah to Jalandhar, where

417 *TN*, vol. II, p. 743

418 Ibid., p. 746

he died, date unknown. He was another *mamluk* with more than forty years of service to Iltutmish and his Shamsid successors.

Among the other early recruits was the Qara-Khitan, Ikhtiyar al-Din Aytegin, Qarakush Khan, who was immediately appointed as Iltutmish's cupbearer. After ruling a series of fiefs, including Tabarhindh, he became feudatory of Multan in succession to *malik* Kabir-Khan and received the title Qarakush Khan. He held various appointments in the subsequent reigns. The instability of the rule of Sultan Bahram Shah and the ensuing fighting among *ghulams* and *amirs* led to his imprisonment by that sultan. He was released on the accession of Sultan 'Ala' al-Din and was killed in 644/1246 under unknown circumstances. The next two *mamluks* on Juzjani's list were heavily involved in the upheavals of Radiyya's reign. *Malik* Ikhtiyar al-Din Altuniya/Altunapa was purchased by Iltutmish although the circumstances and his origins are not given.[419] He was appointed *sharab-dari* – the office involved the care of liquors. They were not necessarily alchoholic and could be classified as medicinal. From there, he progressed to *Sar Chatar-dar*, head of the state canopy bearers. Following her accession, Sultan Radiyya appointed him to the fief of Baran and subsequently that of Tabarhindh. However, his actions and those of the next *ghulam* on Juzjani's list, Ikhtiyar al-Din Aytegin, were to fatally undermine the rule of Radiyya whose accession as a woman was unprecedented in the Muslim world if not among that of the Qara-Khitai. Despite her competency, she was to face objections to her rule from some of the Turkish *mamluks* and the Shamsid ruling classes. Juzani describes her as 'a great sovereign, sagacious, just, beneficient, the patron of the learned, a dispencer of justice, the cherisher of her subjects and of warlike talent'.[420] The latter accolade is not something he ascribes to the other Shamsid sultans. The Shamsi *mamluks* began to undermine Radiyya ostensibly due to her favour for Jamal al-Din Yakut, an Abyssinian – *Habashi* – Yakut was one of a cadre of non-Turkish officers she had promoted.[421] This group also included the Ghurid *amir* Qutb al-Din Hasan b. 'Ali' as commander of the army – *na'ib-i lashgar*, as she sought to build her own powerbase outside that of her father's *ghulams.* Her preferment of this new group saw a number of Iltutmish's *mamluks* turn against her as they perceived a potential threat to their positions. The *amir-i-hajib* – the military chamberlain, who fulfilled the role as field commander, Ikhtiyar al-Din Aytegin, a Qara-Khitan, purchased by Iltutmish from the *amir*

419 P. Jackson (2003), p. 67. Professor Jackson argues persuasively that the correct pronunciation of Altuniya or Altuniah as Raverty has it should be Altunapa pointing to a Qipchak/Polovtsy origin for this *mamluk.*

420 *TN*, vol. I, tr. Raverty, p. 637

421 Jackson (2003), p. 62 note 4. *Habashi* meaning Abyssinian.

Aybak Sanna-I, was one of them. The governor of Tabarindh, Altunapa was another and both were instrumental in Radiyya's downfall. Altunapa engineered a mutiny and after defeating one rebellion, Radiyya moved against him. However, her troops revolted, and she was defeated, Yakut was killed and Radiyya imprisoned in the fortress of Tabarhindh. There, she agreed, almost certainly unwillingly, to marry Altunapa, who no doubt saw this as an opportunity to further his own position against the other rebels and changed sides. With this last throw of the dice to regain her throne, Radiyya and Altunapa marched on Delhi. They were defeated by her half-brother and successor's detachments and escaped only to be captured by Hindu forces and put to death.[422] Ikhtiyar al-Din Aytegin was assassinated having overreached himself. He had insisted on being made in effect deputy of the young sultan and to rule on his behalf for a year in conjunction with the *wazir* Muhazzab al-Din. He insisted on being awarded the *naubat* and being permitted to station an elephant at his gate. He also married one of Bahram Shah's sisters. In the end, the sultan succeeded in having him killed by 'Turks' while he was conducting government business in the audience hall.[423] The *wazir* was wounded and escaped.

The next *ghulam* on the list, Badr al-Din Sonqur is also described as of 'Rumi' origin, but of Muslim birth, implying possible origins in the Seljuk Sultanate of Rum or the former Byzantine ruled territories in Anatolia. How he fell into slavery is not revealed. He received various appointments from Iltutmish leading to his appointment as *amir-i-akhur* – lord of the stable. During the siege of Gwalior, Juzjani comments on his kindness to him.[424] He was enfeoffed with Bada'un by Sultan Radiyya. Her successor, Bahram Shah, appointed him *amir-i-hajib* following the assassination of Ikhtiyar al-Din Aytegin. He had been instrumental in defeating his former sovereign in her attempt to regain her throne. Ultimately, he fell foul of palace intrigue and with *Khwaja* Muhazzab-al-Din, the *wazir* in particular. He was martyred, as Juzjani would have it, on Bahram Shah's orders for reasons unknown. Taj al-Din Sanjar-i -Qabaqulak was another *mamluk* Juzjani held in high esteem.[425] He was a Qipchaq and was purchased by Iltutmish early in his reign from the *Khwaja*, Jamal al-Din-i-Nadiman, about whom we know nothing. At the time of Iltutmish's death, he was superintendent of the stable and

422 *TN*, vol. I, tr. Revrty, p. 648. Ikhtiyar al-Din was the first *ghulam* to be raised to the position of *na'ib*, that is, viceroy or deputy see Jackson (2003), p. 68 note 15.

423 *TN*, vol. II, p. 751

424 Ibid., p. 752

425 P. Jackson (2003), p. 63. See note 16 for the origins of this *mamluk*'s name, *sanjar* one who pierces and *qubaqulak* sticking out ears. Reference to Clauson, *An Etymological Dictionary of Pre-thirteenth Century Turkish* (Oxford, 1972). See also list of Turkic words, pp. 13–14, *Gold Khan and Other Siberian Legends* (Trans. Norman Kohn) (London, 1946).

under Radiyya, was appointed to the fief of Baran and was later despatched with troops to the fortress of Gwalior to relieve the garrison and install a governor loyal to Radiyya.[426] He returned with Juzjani to Delhi where another office was offered to Juzjani in addition to the position of *qadi* he held in Gwalior. Juzjani was particularly grateful as 'he carried two chests of books, the property of this servant upon one of his own camels ... and upon other occasions he treated the author with manifold kindness...'[427] Taj al-Din Sanjar-i-Qabaqulak campaigned with up to 8,000 men against Hindu tribes with great success, subduing and annexing Kalinjar and Mahobah. In addition, it is noted he founded numerous mosques. He could count on substantial military support and was held in high esteem for the power he could deploy and his abilities as a war leader.

However, his accomplishments led to envy from a certain 'party' although Juzjani does not elaborate as to who they were. Sanjar-i Qabaqulak was ultimately assasinated succumbing to poison. Juzjani had good reason to be thankful to him following an earlier incident during the turmoil at the end of Bahram Shah's reign. He was attacked by a sword-wielding mob funded by dependents of the *Khwaja* Muhazzab-al-Din, following Friday prayers in the *Jami' Masjid*. Fortunately, he was armed and with the help of his own slaves managed to escape. It was obvious he could not remain in Delhi, and he left for Lakhnawti, sending his family in advance to Buda'un where Sanjar-i Qabaqulak provided refuge and a stipend for them and, ultimately, for Juzjani himself. Another Qipchak was Taj al-Din Sanjar-i Kuret Khan, a great horseman and accomplished warrior with incomparable skills in arms, particularly the bow, and the only man in Juzjani's list who was not a slave. He was appointed as *shahnah* – superintendent of rivers and vessels. This is a position that has not been mentioned before in the list of appointments and raises a number of questions. The post seems to imply control of shipping in whatever sense, throughout the sultanate, on the Indus, Ganges and their tributaries. What sort of ships and what sort of navy if any the Ghurid successors and nascent Delhi Sultanate possessed is hard to gauge. We know 'Iwad in Bengal was able to deploy war vessels on the Ganges. The Ghurids' armies and the campaigns of their successors involved horses and cavalry and the idea of operating a fleet of vessels for logistics and to protect trade on these great rivers is likely. The only littoral port the Ghurids and their immediate successors controlled was Daybul on the Arabian Sea. Did Kuret Khan's writ extend to ports and, if so, what did it involve? Unfortunately, we have no further detail about this role. He is another individual that Juzjani says he has great affection for and by this inference must have known him well. Some of

426 *TN*, vol. I,p. 643 note 4

427 *TN*, vol. II, p. 755

the reasons for his esteem are fairly obvious. The senior Shamsid *ghulams* became tired of the *wazir, Khwaja*, Muhazzab-al-Din's intrigues and decided to act. In the ensuing fracas, one of his slaves wounded Kuret Khan with a sword slash across his face. He bore the resulting scars for the rest of his life. The *wazir* was killed and Juzani for one would not have been unhappy at this outcome, given the suffering and threats to life he had endured at the hands of this man and his acolytes. These events took place in 640/1242 during the turmoil at the end of Bahram Shah's reign, which included a Mongol invasion of the sultanate 639/1241–2 and their sack of Lahore. Ultimately, Kuret Khan received the important fief of Awadh and from there he plundered Bihar and the surrounding territories. The area was lost to the Ghurid successors following the death of Iltutmish along with Kalinjar and Mahoba. Kuret Khan was struck by an arrow and killed outside Bihar on one of his raids by which Hindu potentate and on what mission, Juzjani does not elaborate. It is possible that Kuret Khan's death outside Bihar was connected with the sultan in Delhi's attempt to regain control of the city after it had been appropriated by Toghan Khan.[428]

The next biography is that of Saif al-Din Bat Khan-i-Aybak a Khitan bought by Iltutmish at the start of his reign. Whether the Khitan or Khita'is – from northern China – were of different ethnicity to the Qara-Khitais is open to debate.[429] He continued to serve Iltutmish's heirs in various capacities and was killed in a fall from his horse late in the reign of Nasir al-Din r. 644–64/1246–66 after at least thirty-five years of service as a *mamluk.* Another of Iltutmish's *ghulams,* the *malik* Taj al-Din Teniz Khan was a Turk from Transoxiana, possibly from the areas between the Amu Darya and Syr Darya, corresponding to ancient Sogdia.[430] He had a long and successful career under Iltutmish and his successors and was ultimately appointed to the fief of Awadh '… and brought that territory under his control; and gave the independent communities of infidels of Hindustan a thorough chastisement, and extorted tribute from them'.[431] Teniz khan was still serving in Awadh when Juzjani completed his history. Given this timeframe it is likely he was purchased late in Iltutmish's reign.

The next *ghulam* on the list, *malik* Ikhtiyar-al-Din Yuzbeg Toghril Khan, was a Qipchak.[432] Under Iltutmish, he had already risen to the position of *ib chashni-*

428 P. Jackson (2003), p. 91

429 Ibid., p. 62

430 *Encyclopedia Iranica*, www.iranicaonline.org, describes the area in question as Ma Wara'al-Nahr

431 *TN*, vol. II, tr. Raverty, p. 760. See also Jackson (2003), p. 71 for etymological origins of Teniz Khan.

432 Ibid., p. 761

gir – deputy comptroller of the royal kitchen – by the time of the seige of the fortress at Gwalior. Later during the short reign of Firuz Shah, he became close to that ruler and was promoted to *shanagi* – superintendent of the elephants. Yuzbeg Toghril Khan was among those who instigated the coup that brought Sultan Radiyya to the throne. She rewarded him with the position of *amir-i-akhur* – lord of the stable. In his subsequent career under Bahram Shah, he fell foul of the courtier Fakhr al-Din Shah Farruki who encouraged the sultan to expel the Turkish *mamluks* from Delhi. Unwisely, Bahram Shah began by imprisoning Qara-Kash Khan i Aytegin and Yuzbeg Toghril Khan. The *mamluks* revolted against the rule of Bahram Shah and took the city. The sultan was killed as was the *wazir* Muhazzab al-Din who had also attempted to sow dissent between the sultan and his *mamluks*. The new sultan, 'Ala' al-Din, son of Sultan Rukn al-Din Firuz Shah, may have been complicit in the downfall of Bahram Shah, as the leading *mamluks* responsible for the coup went unpunished and were even rewarded.[433] Toghril Khan was one of them. He was appointed to the fief of Tabarindh and subsequently made governor of Lahore where he was soon feuding with Nasir al-Din Muhammad of Bindar, who is also mentioned in the list of *maliks* at the end of Iltutmish's reign. Toghril Khan was brought back to Delhi by another of Iltutmish's slaves, Baha al-Din Balaban later Ulugh Khan, who had only been acquired in 630/1232–3. He was another example of Iltutmish recruiting *mamluks* from a similar background to his own, namely from the Olberli sub-group of the Qipchak or Qangli conferderation. Others from this group included his brother Sayf al-Din Aybak Kishli Khan and their cousin Nusrat al-Din Sanjar Shir Khan.[434] Toghril Khan, following the intercession of Ulugh Khan, was absolved and given the *iqta* of Qinnawj. However, it did not take him long to revert to type. An army was despatched under the command of Kutb al-Din Husain whose father Abi 'Ali, a Ghurid *malik*, had found service under Iltutmish. Toghril Khan was forced to come to terms and removed to Delhi. Despite his continual disobedience, he was later appointed first to the *iqta* of Awadh and then to Lakhnawti. He quickly began raiding into Jajnagar/Orissa. Having been victorious in two earlier engagements he gained a major success over the eastern Ganga ruler Narashima I r. 638–64/1238–64, the builder of the great shrine to the sun god Surya at Konark, or his son-in-law Sabantar.[435] According to Juzjani, this occurred in 652/1254, more than ten years after Toghan Khan's

433 P. Jackson (2003), p. 68

434 Ibid., p. 63 and note 17. Sayf al-Din Aybak was later entitled Kishli Khan, and Nusrat al-Din Sanjar was to be become known as Shir Khan.

435 T. Donaldson, *Konark* (New Delhi, 2003), pp. 17–18

defeat to the same ruler.[436] Following his victory Toghril Khan captured and sacked the *rae* of Jajnagar's capital at Umurdan. Unfortunately, the location of this city is unknown. It was probably on the borders of Orissa and situated on one of the tributaries in the Ganges Delta somewhere to the north and west of Calcutta. The Ganga king abandoned the city in a hurry and retreated further into the fastness of Orissa. Toghril Khan captured the ruler's family and numerous dependents and acquired much spoil and a number of elephants. Emboldened by this success, he rebelled against the sultan Nasir al-Din, awarding himself three canopies of state coloured red, black and white. He then wasted little time marching his army into Awadh. He captured the city of Awadh itself declared the *khutba* in his name and styled himself Sultan Mughith al-Din. A few weeks later a Turkish *mamluk* loyal to the central government marched on Awadh. Toghril Khan did not wait to discover the size of the forces ranged against him and took flight on a boat downriver to his capital at Lakhnawti. The underlying reason for his precipitate departure was the response of the inhabitants of Awadh.

There seems to have been a general feeling among the population that his behaviour had become unacceptable. Juzjani doesn't specify any particular event that triggered Toghril Khan's withdrawal. This reaction was not just confined to the Muslim population but also the Hindus. That Juzjani mentions the latter illustrates that they were by this juncture of some consequence regarding the affairs of the sultanate and that their opinion, at least in the conquered territories, now mattered.[437] Having been baulked in Awadh, Toghril Khan was soon marching recklessly into Kamrup. He captured the capital city of Komatapur situated on River Dharla, a tributary of the Brahmaputra.[438] This endeavour yielded, if Juzjani is to be believed, a vast treasure amassed by the local rulers over a considerable period of time. The territory conquered is likely to only have involved some of the main river valleys in the region. In Kamrup, the *khutba* was read, a mosque built and the imposition of Islam on the populace attempted. The *rae* tried to persuade Toghril Khan to reinstate him as a vassal, promising not only a substantial annual tribute but also to retain the *khutba* and utilise Muslim coinage. All these offers were rejected by the *mamluk*. The Hindu ruler reacted by gradually limiting the availability of rice and other foodstuffs to the invaders. By the time of the spring harvest, presumably after it had been gathered, he ordered his subjects to open the water dykes, leaving Toghril Khan's forces marooned and starving. Toghril Khan had not taken precautions regarding food security, and his men were forced to retreat

436 *TN*, vol. II, tr. Raverty, p. 763

437 Ibid., p. 764

438 Ibid., p. 764 note 6

to Lakhnawti. However, with the land flooded or occupied by hostile Hindus, the invaders with the aid of local guides sought the uplands to return to Bengal. After suffering continuous harassment along their route and as the terrain became more precipitous, they were ambushed. While riding on an elephant, Toghril Khan was hit by an arrow in the chest and fell to the ground where he was taken prisoner along with his family and the remainder of his force. He died shortly afterwards in the presence of his son and the *rae*.[439] Like Mohammad Bakhtiar before him, the lure of Assam had proved his undoing.

Juzjani informs us that *malik* Taj al-Din Arslan Khan was bought by Iltutmish from an Abyssinian slaver, Ikhtiyar al-Mulk, Abu Bakr who had purchased him in Aden.[440] He was bought on an embassy sent by Iltutmish to Egypt in 629/1231/2, then ruled by the Ayyubid sultan Al-Kamil r. 615–25/1218–38.[441] Sayf al-Din Aybak later Kishli Khan was probably purchased at the same time.[442] Both Baha al-Din Balaban purchased in 630/1232–3, late in Iltutmish's life, and Arslan Khan had begun their careers as falconers *kasadar* – under the sultan.[443] Later under the sultan Radiyya, Arslan Khan was given the *iqta* of Balaram. This example of Radiyya's patronage of her father's junior *mamluks* and the resulting competition between them would cause serious problems for the emerging Delhi Sultanate and Iltutmish's successors. They would clash not only with the high-ranking free Turkish *maliks* but also with the powerful grouping of the late sultan's senior *mamluks*. Arslan Khan had been given the daughter of Baha' al-Din Toghril, one of Mu'izz al-Din's senior *ghulams*, in marriage by Iltutmish. Presumably, she had become the charge of Sultan Aybak on her father's death and thence, to Iltutmish. During the reign of Nasir al-Din he received Bhiyana as a fief and later Tabarhindh. The city was held by supporters of Shir Khan whose fief it had been until the upheaval caused by the fighting between Ulugh Khan Balaban, his supporters and other Shamsi *mamluks* and Sultan Nasir al-Din. Shir Khan, in the meantime, had retired to the Mongol court. On his return from the Mongol territories, having made up with the powers in Delhi, Shir Khan began to have designs on his old fief, and it was not long before he and Arslan Khan came to blows. The court intervened and Shir Khan was reinstated at Tabarindh. In due course, Arslan Khan, who had been a staunch supporter of

439 Ibid., p. 765

440 *TN*, vol. II, tr. Raverty, p. 766

441 A. Wink, *The Making of the Indo-Islamic world c.*700–1800 CE (Cambridge, 2020) p. 219. The Ayyubids in Yemen (1174–1229) provided naval escorts for merchant shipping on the routes to India.

442 P. Jackson (2003), p. 70

443 Ibid., p. 71

Ulugh Khan Balaban over the previous two years, was given the fief of Awadh. This area had become increasingly problematic for the central government. It was not long before Arslan Khan was dealing with incursions into his territory from another powerful Shamsi *ghulam*, Qutlugh Khan. He was the enemy of Ulugh Khan Balaban, who despite his influence and importance Juzjani does not provide us with a biography. Qutlugh Khan was sufficiently powerful to marry the sultan Nasir al-Din's mother – a move that probably did not help his relationship with the sultan.[444] In the increasingly fractious environment of the late 1240s and 1250s, which witnessed Mongol incursions in the northwest and fighting between the Shamsi aristocracy, the central control of Iltutmish's territorial empire waxed and waned.[445] In 652/early 1255, the now reconciled Balaban and the sultan had returned to Delhi. Qutlugh Khan and the sultan's mother were expelled from court and directed to Awadh, which had become his new *iqta*. There, Qutlugh Khan continued to plot against the sultan. He and his allies besieged Delhi for a short time only to be driven off by the arrival of the *na'ib* Balaban's army. At this juncture Qutlugh Khan seems to have left Indian territory entirely, possibly for the Mongol court.[446] He cannot have remained there long as Arslan Khan was appointed to Awadh in 654/1256 and it was only a short time before Qutlugh Khan and his allies began to threaten Awadh and Kara. Arslan Khan was successful in driving off Qutlugh Khan. He was forced to seek refuge in the mountains to the north of Delhi, in Sirmur now part of Himachal Pradesh, with the *raja* of Santur, Ranpal. The latter was the leading Hindu potentate in the region. In response, Balaban Ulugh Khan mounted an expedition in 655/1257 and sacked that ruler's capital, gaining great riches in the process.[447] Following his success against Qutlugh Khan, Arslan Khan's attitude changed towards the Delhi government. He and the *muqta* of Kara, Qilich Khan, failed to appear at a muster with their contingents in the capital in early 656/1258 to participate in a campaign to drive the Mongols out of Sind. Balaban wasted little time in reigning in the mutinous *mamluks*. In 657/1259, Arslan Khan had his fief transferred to Kara and Qilich Khan was re-appointed to Lakhnawti. However, this appointment was shortlived and by 657/June 1256 the *iqta* had been reallocated, this time to 'Izz al-Din Balaban i-Yuzbegi, the son-in-

444 P. Jackson (2003), p. 72 note 69

445 *TN*, vol. II, tr. Raverty, p. 723. The enemies included Qutlugh Khan and his wife, Kushlu Khan, and his son-in-law 'Izz al-Din Balaban-i Yuzbegi and the Indian eunuch Rayhan, slave of sultan Nasir al-Din and probably supported by him.

446 Jackson (2003), p. 75 note 64

447 *TN*, vol. II, pp. 839–40

law of Qutlugh Khan, who had recently put himself in favour with the sultan by sending 'treasure, valuables and elegancies to a large amount, with two elephants, reached the sublime threshold from the Lakhnawti territory'.[448] He must have been raiding from Bengal at the time, even if his appointment to the *iqta* of Lakhnawti had not been formally ratified. Qilich Khan vanishes from history. However, Arslan Khan seems to have felt that Kara did not satisfy his ambitions. Ostensibly, he prepared his army for a campaign into Malwah and Kalinjar, but his real ambition was to take control of Lakhnawti. Acting on his own authority and without informing even his own sons, *amirs, maliks* and *mamluks* of his real intentions, he marched directly to Lakhnawti. According to Juzjani, his officers and sons were extremely reluctant to pursue this venture when they discovered its true nature.[449] However, having ventured so far, there was little option but to continue. Conveniently, Balaban- i Yuzbegi was campaigning in eastern Bengal/ Bang presumably against one of the Sena kings. He had left the city of Lakhnawti weakly garrisoned. Arslan Khan took and comprehensively sacked the city for three days. Balaban– i Yuzbegi on learning what had happened returned from his expedition and was defeated, captured and killed. Arslan Khan seems to have remained at large and unpunished in Lakhnawti until his death *c.* 664/1266.

Another of the Qipchak *mamluks,* 'Izz al-Din Balaban Kushlu Khan, had been purchased by Iltutmish from a merchant at the siege of Mandor in 624/1227. At the time of his master's death, he was the fief holder of Baran. He was one of the ring leaders at Tara'in in the revolt against Sultan Rukn al-Din Firuz Shah and involved in Radiyya's accession. The rebels were primarily made up of junior *mamluks* still holding positions within the imperial household and Balaban among them suffered a short period as a prisoner – before returning to favour under Radiyya. Under Bahram Shah, open hostility arose between the sultan and his *amirs* resulting from the machinations of the *wazir* Muhazzab al-Din leading to a *mamluks'* revolt. The rebels advanced on Dehli led by Balaban Kushlu Khan. As has been mentioned, they besieged the city, which fell after five months, and Bahram Shah was killed. Balaban Kushlu Khan on reaching the royal palace announced his candidature for the throne. This brought an immediate reaction from the senior Shamsi *mamluks,* Ikhtiyar al-Din Aytegin, Nasir al-Din Ayitim, Qabaqulak and others hostile to this turn of events. They met at Iltutmish's mausoleum and rejected the proclamation.[450] The episode illustrates not only the disenchantment of the Ghurid *amirs* with this arrangement but also the

448 *TN*, vol. II, p. 769 and p. 849

449 Ibid., p. 769

450 Ibid., p. 780

continuing loyalty of the senior Shamsis to the descendants of their former master and their rejection of the aspirations of the more junior of Iltutmish's *ghulams*. The sons and grandson of Iltutmish were released from the *kasr-i-safed-* – the white castle – which Raverty states was being used as virtual state prison and 'Ala' al-Din was duly set up as sultan.[451] It is likely loyalties and links among the elite *mamluks* also played a part.[452] However, some compromise must have been made between these ruling factions and 'Ala' al-Din was chosen as the successor. It was at this juncture that Balaban was awarded with the new title of Kushlu Khan and appointed to the fief of Nagawr. He was also further rewarded with the gift of an elephant.[453] Nagawr while extensive was relatively far from Delhi and possibly chosen to keep this relatively junior *mamluk* away from the centre of government. Later, he supported 'Ala' al-Din in his campaign against the Mongol incursion around Uch. Following these events, he was also given the *iqta* of Multan 643/1246. Not entirely satisfied Kushlu Khan angled to be given Uch as well as the fief of Multan. From his perspective one can see why, as it would give him an extensive and contiguous territory forming a large part of Sind. In the end, the court acquiesced on the understanding that his fiefs in the Siwalik and Nagawr were to be given up in order that they might be reallocated to other *maliks* and government servants. But when Kushlu Khan acquired Uch, he did not relinquish his hold on Nagawr, inviting the wrath of the sultan.

Finally, the sultan accompanied by his *ghulams* and *maliks* including Ulugh Khan, his lieutenant, marched on Nagawr.[454] Kushlu Khan prevaricated but, in the end, he was forced into submission and left for his *iqta* at Uch. Shortly afterwards, Hasan Qarluq, the former deputy of the Khwarazmshah Jalal-al Din, arrived from the territory he had carved out for himself centred at Binban on the middle Indus. This region was the target of Iltutmish's last campaign during which he was taken ill and forced to return to Delhi where he died. Previously, Hasan Qarluq had been fighting the *mamluk* Kabir Khan Ayaz who had set up an independent principality encompassing Uch and Multan and was later succeeded there by his son Taj al-din Abu Bakr. They had successfully defended their fledgling state until the death of Abu Bkr in the early (1240s).

451 *TN*, vol. I, tr. Raverty, pp. 660–01 and note 1. This Ikhtiyar al-Din Aytegin is not the same *mamluk* as the one assassinated in the upheavals following the death of sultan Radiyya.

452 Jackson (2003), p. 69

453 *TN*, vol. I, p. 660 note 1. The gift of an elephant was considered to be the equivalent of his being considered as part of the royal family.

454 *TN*, vol. II, p. 781 and note 1. Ulugh Khan's description of *Khilafat* refers to the position of deputy or lieutenant of the sultan. Juzjani's gushing prose confirms that Nasir al-din was still alive when this was written.

Subsequently, Multan had fallen to Hasan Qarluq.[455] It is likely that Multan was already in Hasan Qarluq's possession at this juncture. Hasan Qarluq was killed in the ensuing battle with Kushlu Khan's forces before Multan. Kushlu Khan then entered the citadel of Multan. However, it seems Hasan's Qarluq's men agreed to a peace treaty and persuaded Kushlu Khan to give up the city to them. Possibly, he agreed because he feared being trapped and besieged in the city by the Qarluq force? Juzjani says he did so unawares of the death of Hasan Qarluq and would not have done so otherwise. Whatever the reasons he lost the city and retired to Uch.[456] Subsequently, the *malik* Shir Khan forced the Qarluqs out of Multan and appointed one of his retainers to govern it. Kushlu Khan tried again to capture the city but was forced to give up. Shir Khan in the meantime had arrived from his fief in Tabarindh and Lahore with an army and invested Uch. Kushlu Khan thinking he could negotiate with Shir Khan as a fellow *mamluk* entered his camp and was promptly placed under guard in Shir Khan's pavilion. There, he was forced to order his garrison to surrender Uch. After doing so, he made his way to Delhi where he was assigned the fief of Buda'un and its dependencies. The sultan and an army set out to deal with the rebel Shir Khan who fled to the Mongol court of the Great Khan Mongke. Tabarindh was brought under control and Multan and Uch were captured and returned to Kushlu Khan. However, it was not long before he, too, was in open rebellion. He chose via the Ghurid *malik* Shams al-Din Kart, ruler in Herat, to approach the Mongol Ilkhan Hulegu 654–63/1256–65 in Iran sending one of his grandsons as a pledge of his good intentions. At the same time, he requested a Mongol representative or *Shihna* be allocated to his court, effectively throwing off his allegiance to the sultan in Delhi.[457] Having failed in his attempt with Qutlugh Khan to seize Delhi he retreated into the Siwalik with a retinue of about 300 troops and returned to Uch. From there Kushlu Khan seems to have continued into Khurasan in person to Hulegu's court, which resulted in a strong Mongol force being sent into Sind. Kushlu Khan returned to Uch, which he lost in unknown circumstances towards the end of Sultan Nasir al-Din's reign. What happened to him subsequently is open to conjecture and may have been associated with the intra-Mongol conflicts between Hulegu and Jochi, one of Chingiz Khan's grandsons, whose commander, Neguder, had taken refuge in Afghanistan.[458]

455 P. Jackson (2003), p. 89

456 *TN*, vol. II, tr. Raverty, p. 782

457 Ibid., p. 785

458 P. Jackson (2003), p. 94 and pp. 115–16

In the short biography of *malik* Nusrat Khan, Badr al-Din Sonqur, another Rumi and a *sufi,* it is noted that he served Iltutmish and every one of his descendants. He was the leader of the rebellion that led to the assassination of the *wazir* Muhazzab al-Din. Following this, he was given the *iqta* of Kol near Aligargh and later under Nasir al-Din received Bhayana. During Kushlu Khan's attempt on Delhi, he arrived post haste with his forces driving off the rebels and was subsequently rewarded with the fiefs of Tabarindh, Sunam, Jhajar and Lakhwal.[459] This occurred in 657/1259. Shir Khan, the previous fiefholder of these *iqtas*, was given Bhayana in return. Tabarindh at this juncture was on the frontier of the sultanate and Nusrat Khan's command extended as far as the fords across River Beas. His job was to avert conflict with Kushlu Khan and deter his Mongol allies, for which he was provided with a large army.[460] He still held this position when Juzjani completed his work.

The *malik* Sayf al-Din Aybak Shamsi-yi Ajami was from one of the Qipchak tribes and had been sold into captivity as a result of kindred strife, the exact circumstances of which we are not told. He became the slave of *khwajah* Shams al-Din the 'Ajami who is described by Juzjani as *malik-ut-Tajjar* – chief of the merchants – of 'Ajam-Iran-, Iraq, Khwarazm and Ghazna, a man of some significance. Shams al-Din reached Delhi and sold Sayf al-Din to Iltutmish. He was deemed competent and trusted enough by the sultan to be despatched as an emissary throughout his realm on matters of importance. Under Sultan Radiyya, he was appointed *shah al-Hasham* – marshal of the retinue, which sounds similar to the position of steward in a household. Subsequently, under Bahram Shah, he became *amir-i-dad* – military justiciar – of Karah and later held the same position in Delhi under Sultan 'Ala' al-Din. When Nasir al-Din came to the throne, he was also appointed to the *iqtas* of Palwal and Kamah and later Baran.[461] This position he still held at the time Juzjani completed the *Tabakat-i-Nasiri.*

Malik Nusrat al-Din Shir Khan has already been mentioned. He was Ulugh Khan Balaban's first cousin both of whom's fathers were tribal leaders among the Olberli. He was purchased by Iltutmish and continued to serve his descendants. At the time of the Mongol siege of Uch and Sultan 'Ala' al-Din's march on Lahore he was awarded the fief of Tabarindh and all its dependent territories. It did not take long for him to become embroiled in the conflicts in Sind. On learning of the Hasan Qarluk's success in Multan at the expense of Kushlu Khan, Shir Khan

459 *TN*, vol. II, p. 788

460 Jackson (2003), pp. 112–13

461 *TN*, vol. II, pp. 790–01. See also Jackson (2003), p. 96. For discussion on whether specific offices automatically qualified the recipient for particular *iqtas*.

drove out the Qarluk forces and installed one of his own *maliks,* Ikhtiyar al-Din Kurez. As we have seen, it did not take long for him to start fighting with his rival *malik* Balaban Kushlu Khan. The result of this conflict was to leave him as the dominant power in Sind. The response from Delhi was swift and he was driven out by the sultan's forces and forced to seek refuge at the Mongol court of the Great Khan Mongke. After some time, he returned to Lahore in 651/1253 where he expelled *malik* Jalal al-Din Mas'ud, one of iltutmish's sons who had established a rebel regime there under Mongol auspices. The Shamsid prince's entourage fell into the hands Shir Khan.[462] That *mamluk* then promptly set about reacquiring his old fief at Tabarindh, currently allocated to Arslan Khan. Shir Khan invaded Tabarindh territory and was promptly pushed back by Arslan Khan. Ultimately, the government in Delhi intervened. Shir Khan was awarded his old fief and its dependencies and presumably Lahore, which he struggled to hold and seems to have given up trying.[463] Arslan Khan received the *iqta* of Awadh. However, Shir Khan continued his old disputes with Kushlu Khan to the extent that he was recalled to Delhi. The sultan intervened and Tabarindh was awarded to Nusrat Khan as a means of averting serious intra *ghulam* warfare on the sensitive northwest frontier of the sultanate. Shir Khan, whose military abilities were not in question, received Kol, Bhayana, Balaram, Jalesar, Mahir, Maha'un and the fortress of Gwalior in return. Presumably, this posting was a reaction to the rising power of the Hindu princes and their encroachment on this frontier of the sultanate. He was still in post there at the time of Juzjani's writing. Subsequently in 688/1269–70, while holding the *iqtas* of Lahore, Sunnam and Deopalpur, he was poisoned by his cousin, Sultan Ghiyath al-Din Balaban, formerly Ulugh Khan. Shir Khan had been all too aware of his relative's ambitions and had refused to come to court during the reigns of Nasir al-Din or that of his cousin – a number of Shamsi *maliks* having already suffered the same fate at the hands of the ruthlessly ambitious Balaban.[464]

Sayf al-Din Aybak Kishli Khan titled *malik al-Hajib* – head chamberlain – was the younger brother of Balaban Ulugh Khan and, as such, another member of the Olberli clan who were forced to flee during the tumult in the steppes caused by the westward expansion of the Mongols. Apparently, he was captured as a young boy having fallen into a marsh from a wagon during his tribe's flight from the Mongols. His elder brother returned for him only to be taken prisoner as well. They were sold into slavery by their Mongol captors. Kishli Khan was

462 Ibid., p. 793

463 P. Jackson (2003), p. 89

464 Ibid., p. 77

acquired, probably in Baghdad, by the emissary Ikhtiyar al-Mulk Rashid al-Din Abu Bakir. He was part of an embassy sent to Cairo and Baghdad by Iltutmish at the time when the Delhi sultan was seeking approval from the caliph as ruler of Muslim lands in India.[465] Kishli Khan was subsequently bought by the sultan and served in his household. Under Radiyya, he became *sar-i-jandar-* – deputy commander of the sultan's guard – and was promoted to head of that body under Sultan Bahram Shah. During the reign of Nasir 'Ala' al-Din, he became *amir-i-akhur* – head of the stables and under Sultan Nasir al-Din he was made *amir-i-hajib* or military chamberlain. When Kushlu Khan was driven out of Nagawr by Kishli Khan's brother Ulugh Khan and the sultan, that fief was entrusted to the *amir-i-hajib.* In this capacity Juzjani informs us that Kishli Khan made great efforts to accommodate Turkish, Tajik and Khalaj *maliks* of all levels. However, when Ulugh Khan fell from favour in 651/1253 following a power struggle among senior Shamsi *ghulams* and was dismissed from court, he was forced into exile to estates at Nagawr. He was originally sent to Hansi but had to relinquish that fief to one of the sultan's young sons. Kishli Khan, Shir Khan and his other supporters lost out in the process as did Juzjani who was removed from his position as *qadi.*[466] Kishli Khan was later given the district of Kara and when his brother was reinstated in the sultan's favour, Kishli Khan returned to Delhi and was reinstated in his old position of *amir-i-hajib.*[467] Ulugh khan's return was not bloodless and the Ghurid *amir* Qutb al-Din Hasan, the *na'ib* who had attempted to arbitrate in the earlier power struggle, was arrested and executed. Apparently, he had made a comment not to the sultan's liking.[468] Following these events Kishli Khan was given the *iqta* of Meerut and the territory extending to the foothills of the Kumaon Mountains from where he proceeded to extort tribute from and conquer independent Hindu rulers. He died of illness there in 657/1259.

The final biograpy of Juzani's list is that of Baha al-Din Ulugh Khan who following his capture by the Mongols had been sold into slavery, along with his younger brother, ultimately reaching Baghdad via Bukhara. He was descended from a Khan of one of the ruling clans of the Olberli.[469] From there he was brought by the *khwajah* Jamal al-Din of Basra who seeing some potential took

465 *TN*, vol. II, tr. Raverty, p. 796 note 8

466 P. Jackson (2003), p. 72

467 *TN*, vol. II, tr. Raverty, p. 798

468 Jackson (2003), p. 74

469 *TN*, vol. II, p. 789. Juzjani says that his knowledge of their origins he learnt *verbatim* from *malik* Kuret Khan.

him into his household and educated him. In 630/1233 the *khwajah* took him together with other potential *mamluks* to Delhi where Iltutmish bought the lot. Balaban, sometimes known as Balaban the lesser, was given a place among the falconers as *khasadar* by the sultan. Later, under Sultan Radiyya he was promoted to *amir-i shakir* – intendant of the hunt – and subsequently Bahram Shah promoted him to the position of *amir-i-akhur* – supervisor of the stable. He was rewarded with the fief of Hansi by Sultan 'Ala' al-Din for his actions during the siege of Delhi and the overthrow of Bahram Shah. He had previously received the *iqta* of Rewari thanks to the influence of Badr al-Din Sonqur Nusrat Khan who had subsequently lost his position of *amir-i-hajib.* As we have seen, he was killed on the orders of Bahram Shah, and this may have inspired Balaban to join in the revolt to avenge his former patron. Later, Balaban almost certainly engineered the death of Sultan 'Ala' al-Din who had attempted to reduce the power of the Turkish *ghulams* by employing *Habashi* slaves.[470] By 647/1249, Balaban had become *na'ib* – viceroy – and had received the title of Ulugh Khan. At around the same time the sultan Nasir al-Din married Ulugh Khan's daughter, thus further cementing the viceroy's position. As *na'ib* he was able to promote his allies among the Shamsid nobility together with his own slaves to positions of authority.[471] However, as has been mentioned, his rise did not pass unchallenged by some of the Shamsid *ghulams,* Kushlu Khan and Qutlugh Khan among them. In 651/1253 the rivals managed to have Ulugh Khan banished to Hansi and then Nagawr.

However, Ulugh Khan and his supporters regained power by allying with the sultan's rebel brother Jalal al-din Mas'ud who had created his own state around Lahore with Mongol support. Jalal al-Din was subsequently reconciled with the sultan and took no further part in proceedings, accepting Lahore as an *iqta*. Ulugh Khan and the sultan having reached a rapprochement arrived at Delhi in 652/January 1255. This episode is puzzling. In one instance, Balaban is removed from power, apparently with the sultan's connivance, and then reinstated in the sultan's favour after about a year. The circumstances surrounding the events at Nasir al-Din's court give rise to the impression that the highly religious and ascetic sultan was disconnected and somewhat aloof from the power struggles and intrigues among his chief *ghulams*.[472] He seems to have been unable or unwilling to impose his will on the warring factions and to have preferred to leave them to their own devices. His marriage to the daughter of a slave is unlikely to have improved

470 Jackson (2003), p. 68

471 Ibid., p. 78

472 Ibid., p. 48

his standing among other *mamluks* and officials. On his return to favour future sultan Ghiyath al-Din Balaban was able to reimpose his authority at court. He and his supporters managed to prevent his rivals from obtaining positions of power at the heart of the government in Delhi. However, the two opposing parties were in some respects broadly equal in their military resources, each having sought the support of rival Mongol rulers. As we have seen the situation could have devolved into an all encompassing civil war.[473] Ultimately, Ulugh Khan and his adherents prevailed. As viceroy he put himself, over the following decade or so, into an unassailable position, eliminating powerful rivals on the way. From here he would usurp the throne. The former *mamluk* of Iltutmish had taken the throne of the dynasty established by his master. Juzjani is silent on the fate of Nasir al-Din and it is not clear if foul play by Sultan Ghiyath al-Din Balaban, as Ulugh Khan became, was the reason.[474] It is also unclear whether Balaban had been manumitted prior to his accession.

Of these twenty-four biographies of *mamluks,* the majority of whom were recruited by Iltutmish, and of Kuret Khan the one non-slave, the largest by far is devoted to Juzjani's patron sultan Ghiyath al-Din Balaban. In these profiles, the author of the *Tabakat-i-Nasiri* provides us with an insight into the Ghurid Empire in India, how it developed and the part these individuals played in that evolution. While the narrative is at times repetitive, it does provide detail and illustration of the succession struggles among Iltutmish's heirs and the activities of the various *mamluk* factions involved. The vast territory conquered in the Indian subcontinent by the Ghurid *mamluk* armies had been ultimately consolidated under the rule of Sultan Iltutmish. Within these largely slave armies, there had evolved a cadre of leading *mamluks* who are unlikely to have exceeded more than a couple of hundred individuals at the very most. Within this grouping would have been an elite corpus of possibly thirty to forty.[475] These individuals would have had *ghulams* of their own and the ability to field significant armies. This Turkish *ghulam* aristocracy hailed from specific tribal groupings, the majority originating from the Qipchak steppe. These Turks dominated other categories, such as free Turks, Afghans, Indians and *Habashis* – black African slaves – and immigrants from Ma'wara, Khwarazm and Khurasan. They were ruthlessly successful and had been recruited from nomadic societies where they, as Andre Wink says, '...

473 Ibid., p. 75

474 *TN*, vol. I, tr. Raverty, p. 716. See also Jackson (2003), p. 52.

475 A. Wink (2020), p. 79. Juzjani provides details of twenty-four. Another ten to fifteen or so senior *mamluks* some serving as deputies to the most powerful would seem reasonable, viz Iltutmish's role as Aybak's lieutenant.

enjoyed significant military advantages over sedentary townspeople and peasants: mobility and virtually unrestricted access to horses, a near-universal male participation in organised violence, and the unparalled stamina and toughness engendered by life in a wild and inhospitable environment …'[476] It was their social grouping that mattered to them not where they came from. This provided the cohesion. However, the Ghurid armies were not nomadic armies despite the ethnicities of the recruits and nor was the Ghurid state in India a nomadic one. The Ghurid sultans and their *mamluk* armies engineered a military revolution in the Indian subcontinent, whereby the combination of heavy cavalry and mounted archers armed with the compound bow gradually marginalised the war elephant as the foremost offensive arm of Indian warfare. The Hindu dynasties unable to breed horses with such ease, due to the climate and its effects on pastoral viability and topography, had failed to develop a tradition of mounted archery.[477] As we have seen on Iltutmish's death, the lack of authority among his successors and the power of the group of elite *mamluks* led to constant infighting over *iqta's,* and positions at court. These disputes among the warring factions undermined the sultan's ability to rule effectively and the security of the Muslim territories in India. The situation was further compounded by the activities of the more junior *ghulams* striving for positions of power within the administration. *Mamluk* loyalty seems to have functioned well under the initial purchaser sultan Mu'izz al-din and this allegiance could be transferred successfully to his *ghulam* Aybak and later to Iltutmish. However, both had at times to fight significant rival claimants from among their peers. In the main, both rulers commanded respect, and were able to impose their authority while also being in a position to offer incentives and rewards for outstanding service. Loyalty to a successor could transcend the next generation but, to be successful, it required a strong ruler. Iltutmish's *mamluks* were prepared to and did support the dynasty he established. Any weakness in the central government led to anarchy, which could only be compounded by outside pressures such as incursions by the Khwarazmshah and the Mongols. Control of Bengal from Delhi was always an issue. Iltutmish campaigned and ultimately conquered the area. His successors had ongoing problems of sedition

476 Ibid., p. 59

477 Ibid., p. 90. Professor Wink states that the Hoysala dynasty who ruled most of what is now Karnataka had been recruiting Turkish and Mongol archers from the 1140s. Athough how they reached Hoysala territory in any numbers is unclear. Presumably, by taking advantage of the extensive coastal shipping routes available along the Indian litoral. There is a frieze at the sun temple of Konark depicting the eastern Ganga ruler Narashima I, mounted on a war elephant, being presented with a giraffe by Arab merchants. Further evidence of the diverse and thriving trade across the Indian Ocean to the subcontinent.

with various appointees to that fief. The *iqta* of Lakhnawti and its dependent territories provided the holder with great wealth and resources, potentially equal to the other holdings of the Delhi Sultanate. The region had been conquered independently from the Ghurid *mamluk* campaigns and, as such, had evolved outside the Ghurid central government in Delhi, despite acknowledging the authority of the Ghurid sultans and later Aybak. If the fiefholder in Bengal began to operate unilaterally and cast off allegiance to Delhi it was a major undertaking to rein them in and required the cooperation of other senior *mamluks*. In many cases the new appointee was just as likely to run amok, leading to further ruthless fighting among the *ghulam* grandees. Other great fiefs at Uch, Multan, Lahore and Awadh at times all produced similar problems for the sultan and administration in Delhi. The Ghurid conquest of the Indian subcontinent is inconceivable without the *mamluk* armies. However, the death of Iltutmish saw the elevation of some of his senior slaves to the position of sultan-makers, with their own armies, pursuing their own agendas and who by their actions almost broke the nascent Muslim power in India. The situation was further compounded by weak institutions of government and a series of fraught successions. Having conquered and reinstated, in some cases powerful local Hindu dynasties, the Ghurids and their *mamluk* successors had failed to adequately integrate them within the new polity. This, in turn, made the emerging Islamic state vulnerable to attack from these entities, who were admittedly not averse to fighting each other, particularly when the Delhi Sultanate itself was riven by internal upheaval.

However, Ibn al-Athir makes it clear that when Mu'izz al-Din's army met and defeated Jaychandra, the king of the Ghadavalas in 590/1193–4, the army of the Hindu ruler contained 'several Muslim amirs, who had been in those lands following their fathers and grandfathers since the days of Sultan Mahmud ibn Sabutakin upholding the Shariah of Islam and observing their prayers and good deeds'.[478] This episode further illustrates that conquest not religion was the Ghurid motivator and, to the indigenous dynasties, the Ghurids were just another invader from the Punjab like the Ghaznavids before them. While Juzjani is the perfect example of a contemporary author extolling the virtues of an Islamic society practising *Jihad* and the raiding and plundering that accompanied it, conversion of the populace was not an aim. Juzjani talks about *jihad* and *ghazis* but, in reality, there is little evidence that this was the case. He was writing sixty years and more after the initial campaigns, which were against Isma'ilis in Multan and the Ghaznavids in Lahore. His views may have been coloured by the Mongol onslaught and the ensuing flood of refugees seeking refuge in the secure Muslim

478 *al-Kamil fi'l -Ta'rikh*, part 3, tr. Richards, p. 13

territory of the Delhi Sultanate created by the conquests of Mu'izz al-Din who was only subsequently construed as a holy warrior.[479] Mosque construction over the ruins of Hindu temples was a gradual process. In actual fact, despite the endless ravaging of religious centres and the vast wealth this yielded, together with the financial burdens in the form of tribute imposed on local rulers by the conquerors, agrarian destruction and disruption of society as a whole was not an issue. Islam was gradually imposed and the ruling model developed along the lines of an absolute Persian monarchy. The Ghurid rulers and their servants were able to utilise the huge monetary yields of their conquered territory in a more efficient way than their Hindu predecessors. The arrival of non-military fugitives encouraged by Iltutmish, men of the pen and other notables fleeing the Mongol invasions, gradually gave what had been a frontier territory a more settled nature. The status within the Islamic world of the lands beyond the Indus was further formalised by the recognition of Iltutmish as ruler of all the territories he had conquered by the caliph in Baghdad.

The reign of Iltutmish and his *ghulams* coincided with the rise of Sufism in India. Sufism was the mystical side of Islam.The Sufis believed in the universal love of God and aspired to a mystical union with Him through pious living. They emphasised the need for compassion towards all faiths and people of all races and promoted the idea of the equality of mankind. The most important Sufi order to enter India were the Chishtis who traced their origin to Chisht situated on the Hari Rud 150 kilometres east of Herat. Chisht includes the remains of a substantial madrasa/mosque complex embellished under the patronage of Ghiyath al-Din. Mu'in al-Din Chishti, the most famous saint from that order, came to India in the late twelfth century or early thirteenth around the time that Mu'izz al-Din took Lahore.[480] He spent most of his time in Ajmer and died there in (633/1236). His white marble shrine is a place of pilgrimage for all faiths even to this day. His disciple and spiritual successor Qutb al-Din Bakhtiar Kaki d.632/1235)moved to Delhi where Iltutmish was a great devotee and was influenced by the mystic's views on religious tolerance. The Chishti Sufi order had an enormous impact on Indian culture. Even today innumerable Sufi shrines are dotted across the landscape of India, from Delhi to Kerala, where the destitute are fed without religious and racial distinction.

479 R.M. Eaton (2019), p. 41

480 A. Patel, *Iran to India: The Shansabanis of Afghanistan, c.1145–1190 CE* (Edinburgh, 2022), p. 217

CHAPTER FOUR

The Ghurids and Their World

This work is primarily concerned with the political events surrounding the rise of the Ghurid Empire, its subsequent decline and the establishment by the Ghurid *ghulams* of the Delhi Sultanate. It would be easy to dismiss the Ghurids as uncouth and barbaric mountaineers. They were more than tribal chieftains ruling a semi-nomadic society, from a remote and inaccessible province in the mountains of an extension of the Hindu Kush, between Herat and Kabul. They belonged very much to a Persianate cultural world surrounded by two great Persianate dynasties, the Ghaznavids and Seljuks, and could not fail to have been influenced by them. They, in turn, inherited this culture, which had evolved and flourished originally under the auspices of the Samanid dynasty 214–395/818–999, who considered themselves heirs to the traditions of pre-Islamic Iran. The Samanids at their height ruled much of Iran and Central Asia and their territories straddled the major trade routes emanating from China and India. They promoted New Persian as the lingua franca to replace earlier regional Iranian languages and dialects. This accelerated a fusion of the cultures of Arab Islam and the largely concealed civilisation of pre-Islamic Iran. This melded culture had been adopted by the Ghaznavids and Seljuks. The collapse of the Ghurid's powerful neighbours not only left a vacuum but created an opportunity for the Ghurids, thrusting them into the mainstream of this vibrant cultural milleu.

The Ghurids had been peripheral up until that time, but they would have been aware and exposed to the cultural world beyond Ghur and its contiguous territories. The Ghaznavid capital of Ghazna, with its historical and cultural significance, and the great emporium of Herat bordering the Ghurid heartland combined with the proximity of trade routes from India and those of Central Asia were the conduits through which cosmopolitan influences came to be experienced and perceived. In due course, the Ghurids were to control the Persianate oasis cities of Merv, Tus and Nishapur as part of a multicultural empire. Herat, the cosmopolitan, manufacturing and trading city became the Ghurid capital in the west. Ghiyath al-Din realised that while Firuzkuh provided security, it could not fulfil the role of the capital city of an empire. The requirement to be able to satisfy Ghurid aspirations and illustrate the power of his dynasty was paramount. The city was embellished accordingly. His younger brother had established himself at Ghazna under his brother's auspices where he ruled for more than thirty years. While Lahore became a second capital, under the governance of Aybak, serving Mu'izz al-Din as a springboard for campaigns in India. Under the later Ghaznavids, Lahore and the surrounding areas as part of the much-reduced Ghaznavid Empire had also been exposed to Persianate culture and particularly that way of government as part of a centralised and bureaucratic state. This consisted of a salaried bureaucracy and military slave institutions tied to the *iqta* land revenue system. It was this infrastructure the Ghurids were to adopt throughout their conquered territories. Ghiyath al-Din abandoned the *karramiyya* school, choosing the more mainstream *shafi'i* tenet as a way of broadening the Ghurid's appeal to their newly acquired urbanised subjects in the cities of Khurasan. In India, Mu'izz al-Din, by reinstating Indian rulers following their defeats at the hands of his armies, sought to incorporate these conquered Indian potentates and princes into the new Ghurid imperial order.[481] As professor Eaton points out, 'Members of the former Indian ruling classes would thereby have been folded into a larger imperial order that adhered to Persianate ideologies and institutions.'[482] However, a lack of central control following the death of Iltutmish exposed the fragilities of the system. The establishment of the *iqta* structure, primarily to reward Turkish *mamluks* in India, is further evidence of the use of Persian bureaucratic systems within the Ghurid's conquered territories. The senior *mamluks,* Aybak, Toghril, Qubacha, Yildiz and later Iltutmish, were able to establish their own states following the death of Mu'izz al-Din. They continued the Ghurid traditions despite fierce competition among themselves. Over time, they had been able to acquire dependent client kings and *mamluks* of their own. Their courts, Qubacha's at Uch, Yildiz at Lahore and Iltutmish in Delhi, flourished. Qubacha ruled a substantial and cosmopolitan empire, which included much of Sind and the Indus valley. From his port city of Mansura, then on the middle Indus, and now ruined, he was able to connect with Thatta at the apex of the Indus Delta and from there, the maritime cities of Gujerat including Diu and Cambay and the Arabian ports of Muscat and Aden. To the north, he could access via Lahore and Afghanistan the trade routes of Central Asia and beyond.[483] The overarching rule of the Ghurid Empire had integrated northern India, Afghanistan and Khurasan under a single polity for the first time since the Kushans in the first centuries AD. This enabled trade on every level from the subcontinent to expand dramatically into the markets of the Persianate and Islamic worlds. In common with his competing *mamluk* rulers, Qubacha sought to attract leading intellectuals, *sufis* and skilled craftsmen from a variety of trades to his court. These arrivals at the various courts served to increase the prestige of their patrons. The historian 'Ali Kufi was one of these luminaries. He completed the *Chachnama* in 622/1226. This Persian chronicle has been viewed as an attempt to legitimise Turkish rule in India and specifically the independent sultanate and empire of Qubacha.[484] Another example of the cultural richness of

481 *al-kamil fi'l-Ta'rikh*, part 3, tr. Richards, pp. 59–60. See Aybak's restoration of the Chaulukya/Solanki ruler to Nahrawala/Anahilapataka modern Patan.

482 R.M. Eaton (2019), p. 43

483 R.M. Eaton (2019), p. 45

484 Ibid. and p. 407 note 48

his court was the publication of the first major anthology of Persian poetry in Uch, rather than the Persian cultural centres in Khurasan, in 618/1220. This work was the *Lubab al-albab* compiled by Sadid al-Din Muhammad 'Aufi.[485]

It was not, however, just literary prowess that illustrates the cultural breadth of the Ghurids and their *ghulam* protégées. The plastic arts thrived. Herat, the emerging western capital of the Ghurid polity, which could reasonably be described as comprising of three distinct regions, Afghanistan and the traditional Ghurid heartlands, the lands acquired to the north and west in Sistan and Khurasan and the conquests in India, was suitably embellished. The city was an important entrepot and major metal working centre and became one of the main recipients of Ghurid patronage. It had been fought over by the Seljuks, Ghurids and Khwarazmshahs as well as the Ghuzz and the Qara-Khitai for much of the second half of the twelfth century. Despite this instability, the city continued to thrive. Significant building projects in the city and the surrounding areas took place. The major work carried out by Ghurid sultans was the restoration of the congregational mosque. The building had been built on the site of an earlier mosque destroyed in an earthquake in 495/1102 and had subsequently suffered a fire at some stage during early Ghurid rule. In the 1190s, Ghiyath al-Din, despite his adherence to the *shafi'i* school, in his refurbishment maintained the building's western orientation in keeping with the practice of the building's original *hanafi* congregation. Ghiyath al-Din's work was extensive. The building has noteworthy calligraphic detail, a significant feature of Ghurid architectural projects, including two inscriptions bearing the name of Ghiyath al-Din, one dated 597/1200–01. The Ghurid sultan was buried there in early 599/1203 and his tomb, subsequently destroyed and rebuilt in the 1940s, was completed by his son Sultan Mahmud.[486] The corpus of Ghurid architectural survival is relatively small given the extent of their empire. The propensity to use baked brick and stucco rather than stone probably has something to do with this, combined with the remoteness of many of the sites. The most significant Ghurid structures in stone are in India itself. Arguably, the most important survival being the red sandstone Qutb Minar, seventy-two and a half metres in height and built on the orders of Aybak to commemorate the Ghurid victory in the second battle of Tara'in and begun 595/*c.* 1199. The *ghulam* commander built the first level, which includes an inscription praising his master sultan Mu'izz al-Din. The structure was completed in 617/ *c.* 1220 by Iltutmish who added a further three stories. The caligraphy is still sharp and is embelished with floral and vegetal motifs, and with these *naksh* inscriptions the minaret remains a stunning monument to Ghurid

485 Ibid., p. 61 and p. 410 note 75

486 S. Blair (2019), p. 74

endeavour. Originally, the Ghurids had little need nor the requisite skills to embark on major architectural projects. Once the Ghurid/Shansabanid dynasty evolved from their more nomadic transhumant existence to formal sedentarism for the ruling elite at least, the requirement changed. Their emergence as a regional power in the later twelfth century required patronage.[487]

At Firuzkuh, the summer capital of the senior Shansabani branch of the Ghurid dynasty stands the remarkable brick minaret of Jam. It survives precariously on the banks of the Hari Rud. It was built 570/1174–5, along with a mosque, to commemorate the Ghurid conquest of Ghazna the previous year and possibly the elevation of Mu'izz al-Din to that sultanate by his brother. The minaret is an impressive sixty-five metres high and a band of cursive script circling the lowest section of the shaft gives the name of the builder as 'Ali ibn Ibrahim al Nishapuri from Nishapur in Khurasan.[488] This is evidence that by the mid-twelfth century, the Ghurids had access to skilled labour and with it mainstream Persianate trends as espoused by the Seljuks and Ghaznavids. This, in turn, meant that the new dynasty was in a position to commission a variety of buildings, including mosques, *minars, madrasas* and *'idaghs* – open spaces where prayers are performed, taking advantage of their increased revenue streams to fund these endeavours.[489] However, the *minar* at Jam is also noteworthy for the use of the complete Surat Maryam chapter XIX in the Qu'ran, depicted in the intricate calligraphical bands decorating the minaret. This is an unusual choice of text and was probably selected with the Ghurid populace's adherence to the *karramiyya* sect in mind. By the end of the century, the rulers were beginning to favour the *shafi'i* school as their imperial ambitions demanded.[490] The tower also proclaims in glistening tiles of turquoise bricks the titles of its patron, the sultan Ghiyath al-Din, and his recognition of the Abbasid caliph in Baghdad. There are a number Ghurid sites with significant epigraphic decoration. Two buildings on Hari River at Chisht between Jam and Herat are part of an impressive complex, which mentions Shansabanid rule in three of the inscriptions and Ghiyath al-Din is noted as having restored the better preserved and larger of the two structures in 562/1167.[491] The remains of the *madrasa* at Shah-i Mashad on Murghab River in Gharchistan provide an insight into what must have once been a magnificent series of buildings. These were probably commissioned by

487 A. Patel (2022), pp. 21–2

488 S. Blair (2019), p. 70

489 Patel (2022), pp. 143–4

490 Ibid., p. 146

491 Ibid., p. 194

the wife of Sultan Ghiyath al-Din, Juahar *malikah*, and may have contained the tomb of the assassinated Saif al-Din d.558/1163, son of 'Ala' al-Din *jahan suz*. The patroness was the sister of Saif al-Din.[492] Mu'izz al-Din, after he had conquered Ghazna, set about restoring some significant buildings, particularly the palace complexes in both Ghazna and at Bust Lashkari Bazaar. One of the only buildings that we know to have been commissioned in the Ghazna territories, rather than renovated by the Ghurid rulers, is the arch at Bust. This edifice served as a triumphal monument to Ghurid success. It may have been built contemporaneously with the minaret in Jam, celebrating the final extinction of the Ghaznavids and the Ghuzz and the establishment of Mu'izz al-Din as a sultan and perhaps constructed by him in anticipation of his own imperial ambitions in northern India.[493] The Bamiyan branch for their part seem to have concentrated on re-using existing structures and complexes, particularly the fortresses at Shah-i-Zuhak and Shah-I Golgola. However, there is evidence of a possible palace construction at Sarkusak under these rulers, pointing to a more sedentary court life and accompanying ceremonial.[494] This evolution would be commensurate with the environment of the fertile Bamiyan valley and wealth available to this branch from the trade routes traversing it. Their cousins in Firuzkuh seem to have preferred to maintain the more traditional semi-nomadic existence, using Firuzkuh as a tented summer encampment, no doubt with pavilions and furnishings fit for a sultan. There is no archaeological evidence of a palace complex as such but there is evidence of significant fortifications to protect the itinerant court and any trading community, some of whom were Jewish, who lived permanently within. The summer complement would have included the Ghurid elite, administrative and religious officials, as well as the sultan's bodyguard and perhaps senior *mamluks*. The bulk of his retinue, his army and particularly the cavalry, would have needed adequate pasturage not available in the narrow confines of this part of the upper Hari Rud. The probable location for this encampment is on the plain at Ahangaran at a crossing of the river east of Firuzkuh.[495] Mu'izz al-Din's works and refurbishments in Ghazna and elsewhere also point towards a move to a more settled court culture like his cousins in Bamiyan. He was also to use Lahore, the capital of the last Ghaznavid sultans, as an alternative centre of his own, following in their imperial traditions and as a way point for his campaigns into northern India. It is likely that Lahore also received Ghurid embellishments to important buildings, but none survive. To see the full magnificence of Ghurid

492 Ibid., pp. 194–5

493 Patel (2022), pp. 253–4

494 Ibid., p. 192

495 Ibid., p. 87

architectural survivals, it is in India that that they are to be found. There are three mosques in Rajastan, Arhai Din-ka Jhonpra in Ajmer, the Shahi Masjid in Khatu and the Chaurasi Khamba in Kaman. The latter was built by the *mamluk* Baha al-Din Toghril who was governor of Bayana *c.* 591–606/1195–*c.* 1210?. Toghril had declared himself sultan following the death of Mu'izz al-Din in (602/1206) and an inscription around the doorway of the mosque refers to him as '*padishah wa al-sultan jahan pahlwan*'.[496] This would seem to imply that it was built during the short period post 1206 when Toghril continued as an independent ruler before Iltutmish unified the Muslim territories in India. It is unclear how long Toghril continued to rule his fief following the death of Mu'izz al-Din. Presumably, he existed in an uneasy truce with Aybak, as neither former *ghulam* was sufficiently powerful to dominate the other. Juzjani tells us that Toghril died shortly after losing out at the capture of Gwalior, but he may have lived for up to four years after the death of Mu'izz al-Din. The most impressive Ghurid building in India is the Qutb Minar and the Quwwat ul-Islam – the might of Islam – mosque complex, which also contains Iltutmish's marble mausoleum now bereft of its dome, in Delhi. The decorative carving of the tomb chamber includes Hindu motifs as well as Islamic inscriptions. The structures exhibit both *kufic* and *naksh* script, much of it in high relief and still legible. The buildings at these locations are almost entirely constructed of red sandstone built often on Hindu and Jain temple sites while reusing architectural elements from them in their construction.

It was not only architecture that carried the Ghurid imperial message. Coinage was another medium through which this was disseminated. From Ghazna westwards, the Ghurid mints produced coins that conformed to the standards of the Islamic world bearing the title of Sultan Mu'izz al-Din in Arabic calligraphy. Those issued in India conformed to the exising practice and in particular closely resembled the coinage of the defeated Chauhan dynasty bearing the Nandi bull on the obverse and a spear-carrying horseman on the reverse. Some of the coins portrayed the goddess Lakshmi on one side and on the reverse the Ghurid sultan Mu'izz al-Din's name in Devanagari script. These adaptations if nothing else served to project the image of imperial continuity to the conquered peoples of northern India and their dynastic rulers.[497]

496 S. and M. Shokoohy, 'The architecture of Baha al-Din Tughril in the region of Bayana, Rajastan'. In: *Muqurna IV: An Annual on Islamic Art and Architecture* (Ed. Oleg Grahar) (Leiden, 1987), pp. 114–15

497 R.M. Eaton (2019), pp. 43–4

Conclusion

The political success of the Ghurid Empire is to all intents and purposes the history of two great men: Sultan Ghiyath al-Din, 'the Ghurid', as he was sometimes referred to by contemporaries, and his younger brother Sultan Mu'izz al-Din. They oversaw the emergence of Ghurid power. Ghiyath al-Din was able to impose his authority on the various Shansabanid factions, particularly his cousins in Bamiyan who were arguably the richer and more established branch at the time of his accession. He and his younger brother Mu'izz al-Din shared a rare sibling understanding and were able to pursue a common endeavour. Mu'izz al-Din's ability to work with his brother and to effectively command and deploy the significant Ghurid *mamluk* armies was crucial to their success. This arrangement drove the Ghurid conquest in northern India. Mu'izz al-Din's willingness to put these forces at the disposal of his elder brother for campaigns in the west gave the dynasty the ability to impose Ghurid hegemony wherever necessary. Even so, the requirement to move the Indian armies westwards for major campaigns must have created logistical pressures and could also be viewed as a strategic weakness. The wealth the dynasty acquired from plunder in India, combined with an enhanced access to the Central Asian trade routes via conquest of the great emporia in Khurasan, enabled the Ghurids to take advantage of the political vacuum created by the collapse of the Ghaznavid and Seljuk Empires. Following the death of Ghiyath al-Din, Mu'izz al-Din was able to continue strong and dynamic Ghurid rule despite his advancing years and the major setback at Ankhud. But his assassination found the dynasty unprepared. The typical concerns manifested themselves with the succession of a minor or inexperienced ruler lacking the support or ability to convince or impose their will on potential rivals. The Ghurid/Shansabanid confederation, which seemed to have enjoyed a *modus vivendi* with the various branches accepting the primacy of Firuzkuh and subsequently that of Mu'izz al-Din as heir to his elder brother, came to an abrupt end. The Ghurid territories descended into anarchy following the deaths, first of Mu'izz al-Din and then, within a matter of weeks, of Sultan Baha al-Din, the powerful, respected and wealthy ruler of the Bamiyan branch. The heirs of Baha al-Din tried to annexe Ghazna and laid claim to the Ghurid conquests in India. In the meantime, Ghiyath al-Din's son, Ghiyath al-Din Mahmud, sought to regain his inheritance as sultan in Firuzkuh, a position denied to him by Mu'izz al-Din. This led to intra-Shansabanid disputes and conflict with powerful *mamluk* factions, which hastened the collapse of the Ghurid polity. The situation was exacerbated by recent military failures in the west, following the defeat of

Andhkud at the hands of the Khwarazmshahs and the Qara-Khitai, together with the subsequent appearance of the Mongols. The Ghurid successors lacked vision, ability and individual resources to maintain their state. Arguably, there is a third individual who should be considered a Ghurid heir, certainly at least to Mu'izz al-Din. If anyone could lay claim to being one of his 'sons', it was Iltutmish, a *ghulam* of Aybak, Mu'izz al-Din's viceroy, manumitted by the Ghurid sultan before his master. Iltutmish's momentous reign established Delhi as the most significant Islamic city in the east. He consolidated Muslim dominion east of the Indus and created a significant empire in northern India that reached as far as the Bay of Bengal and the borders of Assam and Orissa. He ruled for twenty-six years and established a dynasty of his own after much fighting, having managed to defeat his *mamluk* rivals and avoid being drawn into conflict with the Khwarazmshahs and the Mongols. The Ghurid imperium was admittedly shortlived but their achievements, given where they came from and the extent of their territories at the height of their power and influence, are remarkable. They established Islam as the dominant force in the northern subcontinent and integrated the area politically into the mainstream of the Iranian world for the first time in a millennium.

Appendix I

MAMLUKS, THEIR OWNERS, *IQTA* AND ORIGINS

Name	Owner	*Iqta*	Origin
Sanjar-i-Gajz-Lak Khan	Sultan Iltutmish	Wanj-rut of Multan, Kuhram, Tabarhindh, Uch and dependencies (d.629/1231)	Unknown
Kabir Khan-i-Ayaz	Sultan Mu'izz al-Din, *Malik* Nasir al-Din Husain, Sultan Iltutmish, Sultan Firuz Khan, Sultan Radiyya, Sultan Bahram Shah	Multan, Palawal in Haryana n of Delhi, Sunam N. Punjab, Lahore, Multan. Succeeded in Multan by his son Taj al-Din Abu Bakr b. Ayaz (d.639/1241)	'Rumi' Turk
Nasir al-Din Aytemur al-Baha –i. Ayatim	(Sultan) Nasir al-Din Toghril, Sultan Iltutmish	Siwalik country centred on modern Aravali range. Huge territory; see text.	Unknown
Saif al-Din Aybak *muqta* of Uch	Sultan Iltutmish	Narnul, Baran, Sunam, Uch	
Saif al-Din Aybak *Yaghanutut*	Sultan Iltutmish	Sursuti, Bihar, Lakhnawti (d.631/1233)	Qara-Khitan
Nusrat al-Din Tayasai	Sultan Mu'izz al-Din, Sultan Iltutmish, Sultan Firuz Shah, Sultan Radiyya	Jind, Barwalah, Hansi, Bhiyana, Sultankot, fortress of Gwalior and territory, Awadh	Turk
'Izz al-Din Toghril – Toghan Khan	Sultan Iltutmish, Sultan Radiyya, Sultan Bahram Shah	Buda'un, Bihar, Lakhnawti-Lakhnahor	Qara-Khitan

Qamar al-Din Qiran-Temur Khan	Sultan Iltutmish, Sultan Radiyya	Qinnawj, Kara, Awadh and dependencies	Qipchak
Hindu Khan	Sultan Iltutmish, Sultan Radiyya, Sultan Bahram Shah	Uch, Jalandhar	Hindu convert
Qaraqush Khan-Ikhtiyar al-Din Aytegin	Sultan Iltutmish, Sultan Radiyya, Sultan Bahram Shah, Sultan 'Ala' al-Din Mas'Ud Shah	Barihun, Darangawan, Tabarindh, Multan, Lahore, Bhayana	Qara-Khitan
Ikhtiyar al-Din, Altunapa	Sultan Iltutmish, Sultan Radiyya	Baran, Tabarhindh	Unknown
Ikhtiyar al-Din, Aytegin	Sultan Iltutmish, Sultan Radiyya, Sultan Bahram Shah	Mansurpur, Kujah, Nandanah, Buda'un	Qara-Khitan
Badr al-Din Sonqur –i-Rumi	Sultan Iltutmish, Sultan Radiyya, Sultan Bahram Shah	Buda'un (d.639/1241)	Rumi
Taj al-Din Sanjar-i-Qabaqulak	Sultan Itutmish, Sultan Radiyya, Sultan Bahram Shah, Sultan 'Ala' al-Din Mas'Ud Shah	Baran, Sursuti, Buda'un	Qipchaq
Taj al-Din Sanjar-i-Kuret Khan, not a *mamluk*	Sultan Iltutmish, Sultan Radiyya, Sultan Bahram Shah	Buda'un, Awadh (d.640/1242)	Qipchaq
Saif al-Din Bat Khan-i-Aybak	Sultan Iltutmish, Sultan Radiyya, Sultan Bahram Shah, Sultan 'Ala' al-Din Mas'Ud Shah, Sultan Nasir al-Din Mahmud Shah	Kuhram and Samanah, Baran	Khitan

Taj al-Din Teniz Khan	Sultan Iltutmish, Sultan Radiyya, Sultan Bahram Shah, Sultan 'Ala' al-Din Mas'Ud Shah, Sultan Nasir al-Din Mahmud Shah	Jhinjhanah, Kasmandi and Mandiyana, Buda'un, Awadh	Turk from Transoxiana
Ikhtiyar al-Din Yuzbeg Toghril Khan	Sultan Iltutmish, Sultan Radiyya, Sultan Bahram Shah, Sultan 'Ala' al-Din Mas'Ud Shah	Tabarindh, Lahore, Qinnawj, Awadh, Lakhnawti	Qipchaq
Taj al-Din Arsalan Khan	Sultan Iltutmish, Sultan Radiyya, Sultan Bahram Shah, Sultan 'Ala'al-Din Mas'Ud Shah, Sultan Nasir al-Din Mahmud Shah	Balaram in Awadh, Bhayana, Tabarindh, Awadh, Kara	Khwarazmian Turkic origin
Izz al-Din Balaban Kushlu Khan	Sultan Iltutmish, Sultan Radiyya, Sultan Bahram Shah, Sultan 'Ala'al Din Mas'Ud Shah,	Barhamun, Baran, Nagawr and Siwalik, Multan, Uch, Buda'Un, Multan and Uch again	Qipchaq
Nusrat Khan, Badr al-Din Sonqur	Sultan Iltutmish, Sultan Radiyya, Sultan Bahram Shah, Sultan 'Ala' al-Din Mas'Ud Shah, Sultan Nasir al-Din Mahmud Shah	Kol, Bhayana, Tabarindh, Sunnam, Jhajar and Lakwal as far as River Beas	Rumi
Sayf al-Din Aybak Shamsi-yi Ajani	Sultan Iltutmish, Sultan Radiyya, Sultan Bahram Shah, Sultan 'Ala' al-Din Mas'Ud Shah, Sultan Nasir al-Din Mahmud Shah	Palwal and Kama, Baran	Qipchaq

Nusrat al-Din Shir Khan	Sultan Iltutmish, Sultan Radiyya, Sultan Bahram Shah, Sultan 'Ala' al-Din Mas'Ud Shah, Sultan Nasir al-Din Mahmud Shah	Tabarindh and dependencies, Kol, Bhayana, Balaram, Jalesar, Baltarah, Mihir, Mahawan and the fortress of Gwalior	Olberli
Sayf al-Din Aybak Kishli Khan	Sultan Iltutmish, Sultan Radiyya, Sultan Bahram Shah, Sultan 'Ala' al-Din Mas'Ud Shah, Sultan Nasir al-Din Mahmud Shah	Nagawr, Kara, Meerut	Olberli
Baha al-Din Balaban Ulugh Khan – later Sultan Ghiyath al-Din Balaban	Sultan Iltutmish, Sultan Radiyya, Sultan Bahram Shah, Sultan 'Ala' al-Din Mas'Ud Shah, Sultan Nasir al-Din Mahmud Shah	Rewari, Hansi, Nagawr	Olberli

APPENDIX II

MILITARY LOGISTICS UNDER THE GHURIDS AND EARLY DELHI SULTANATE

The following observations are taken from Simon Digby, *War-horse and Elephant in the Delhi Sultanate: A Study in Military Supplies* (Orient Monographs: Oxford, 1971).

In the thirteenth century, the Indian subcontinent imported horses from as far away as the Russian steppes and elephants from southern Burma. The adequate availability of both were considered essential to the armies of the nascent Ghurid polity and those of their *mamluk* successors. Initially, it was more about securing supply rather than denying access to any particular resource to their opponents.

The question arises as to why the Ghurids and their slave armies were so successful. If we study the silver *tankas* of Aybak and Iltutmish, the horsemen depicted on these coins reflect 'Turkish ideals in warfare'. This was not unique, however, as the coinage of the preceding Indian dynasties depict the Nandi bull of Shiva and a horseman, thereby reflecting pre-existing equestrian values. At the same time, Indian skills in horse management and husbandry enjoyed an appreciable standing among Muslim rulers and their entourages.[498] The idea that specific equipment gave one side a particular advantage over the other is unlikely and probably had more to do with the user than the animal or weapon involved. The Muslims had the horseshoe and the stirrup; while the latter was available in India before the Ghurid invasions, the horseshoe may not have been so widely used in the subcontinent.[499] As far as weapons were concerned, the quality of Indian steel enjoyed a high reputation in the Islamic world and Indian swords had been exported to Ummayad Spain and Seljuk Anatolia.[500] While Ghur was renowned for the manufacture of high-quality weaponry, technological superiority does not seem to have been the issue. The bows of the Ghurid cavalry may have been superior but not decisively – although access to mail coats in quantity from the significant iron deposits in Ghur cannot be entirely discounted. This equipment could have provided the advantage to Mu'izz al-Din's *mamluks*.

498 S. Digby, S., *War-Horse and Elephant in the Delhi Sultanate: A Study of Military Supplies* (Orient Monographs: Oxford, 1971), p. 12 note 5

499 Ibid., p. 13

500 Ibid., pp. 17–18

The decisive factor would seem to be the *mamluks* themselves. Mu'izz al-Din's reaction after his defeat in the first battle was to recruit large numbers of heavy cavalry from Transoxiana to make good any failings in the Ghurid cavalry arm. The Indian armies did not possess a force of similar ruthlessness, skill and adaptability in their ranks. To be effective, however, on the long and arduous campaigns in northern India, the *ghulams* required adequate supplies of horses and particularly remounts. It was the Ghurid *mamluk* cavalry that gave the Muslims the advantage through their ability to access quality war-horses initially from Central Asia. The inference seems to be not that the Indians were worse horsemen but that they had less access to quality war-horses, due to the recruiting activities of Mu'izz al-Din and the loss of the horse-breeding areas of the North West Frontier. The arrival of the Mongols created similar problems for Aybak and Iltutmish. But despite these incursions, these rulers still controlled the Punjab, Sivalik and other northern areas, which produced adequate numbers of quality horses.[501] In time, the emerging Ghurid state in India and their *mamluk* successors served to degrade the Indian armies, opposing them by depriving them of access to war-horses, which not only compromised fighting ability but also their capacity to dominate their territories and collect revenue from them.[502]

Unlike elephants, war-horses were not considered an exclusively royal possession. The Delhi Sultanate, as in other Indian kingdoms, tried to maintain control over horse traders. In time, the Muslim rulers sought control of the trade in horses and *mamluks* by financing traders and ordering them not to sell slaves in Khurasan or horses to Hindu rulers.[503] Eventually, ships equipped by the Delhi Sultanate sailed from Gujerat to the Persian Gulf to purchase the animals.[504] The best breeding grounds for war-horses in the subcontinent were in the Punjab and the northwest. Although areas imperfectly subjected by Delhi on the periphery such as that of the Khokhars could provide horses, they were considered of lesser quality than those imported from the Persian Gulf and the Hadramhaut in southern Arabia. With the arrival of the Mongols, this seaborne trade increased in importance. Indian rulers had been importing horses from overseas since at least the sixth century. The monk and hermit Cosmas Indicopleustes who had earlier been a merchant mentions horses being shipped from the Persian Gulf

501 Ibid., p. 21

502 Ibid., p. 22

503 Ibid., p. 26

504 Ibid., p. 25

to Sri Lanka.[505] Following the end of the Monsoon, horse transports left from the straits of Hormuz. The more southerly the Indian kingdoms the more they relied on importing horses from Iran and Bahrain, another equine entrepot for animals from Iraq and Syria, on the Arabian side of the Gulf. On the south coast of Arabia from Aden eastwards, any port of significance was involved in the export of horses from the hinterland.[506] The overland trade was more prone to disruption. While theoretically the areas of the Punjab, Salt Range and the North West Frontier could produce superior war-horses, breeders there required enough suitable foodstuffs to maintain these animals. This issue prevented a consistent volume of horses for export to Delhi.[507]

The survival of the early Delhi Sultanate, considering its reliance on horses from Central Asia, is remarkable, particularly in the face of the Mongol onslaught. It is likely that, when political conditions allowed, caravans of horses came down the Khyber and other passes leading from Afghanistan into the subcontinent. These horse drovers brought animals from as far away as the areas north of the Caspian Sea, the Qipchak steppe and Transoxiana. Others took a more southerly route, bringing their caravans to the ports on the Persian Gulf.[508] Horses seem to have been available from the northeast beyond the boundaries of Bengal despite the difficulties of access. This trade must have been one of the attractions for Muhamad b. Bakhtiyar in his ill-fated expedition through Assam and probably Bhutan. Whether he actually reached Tibet is a moot point. Presumably, he hoped to ensure a supply of horses without having to rely on animals brought across northern India.

The increasing strength of the Delhi Sultanate under Iltutmish would have compromised the surviving northern Indian rulers' ability to acquire war-horses. Rulers of dynasties further south such as the Hoysalas and Pandyas were significant buyers of horses from Iran and Arabia.[509]

The other animal that had a significant place in the military inventory of the subcontinent was the elephant. It has a long history as a weapon of war in the armies of Indian rulers. Alexander the Great was confronted with them in the army of Porus at the battle of the Hydaspes. Seleucus, one of Alexander's successors, bargained away the trans-Indus territories of his empire to the

505 Ibid.

506 Ibid., p. 31

507 Ibid., p. 37

508 Ibid., p. 36

509 Ibid., p. 48

Mauryan ruler Chandragupta in return for 500 elephants. Ibn al-Athir mentions that the Ghaznavids maintained a considerable elephant force. We learn that Mahmud of Ghazna inspected 1,300 of the animals in 419–20/1023–4 and his son Mas'ud more than 1,600 in 427/1031. These are considerable numbers and larger than the figures mentioned by Juzjani during the Ghurid period. It is possible that the proximity and demands of the Ghaznavid Empire had reduced supplies of the elephant from northwest India. However, under the Ghurids and Shamsids, a force of between 750 to 1,000 animals would seem possible. Elephants were expensive to keep, requiring butter, hay, rice and barley for food and skilled and costly attendants to manage them.[510] Despite these drawbacks, they were considered significant animals. Throughout the writings of Juzjani and Ibn al-Athir on the campaigns in northern India, elephants and the numbers taken in combat or tribute are rigorously recorded. While supplies of wild elephants in northwest India may have been depleted, we know that elephants were trapped locally in Bengal and Orissa. The numbers available to Iltutmish and his successors from these regions would have been considerable. There are grounds to believe that elephants were imported across the Bay of Bengal from the kingdom of Pegu near Yangon in the Irrawaddy Delta.[511]

Despite the expense and complications of elephant husbandry, the Ghaznavids, Ghurids and Shamsids put their faith in the elephant as a machine of war. But it was not only for the animal's martial qualities but also the prestige of owning elephants as a symbol of royalty and independent power that made them important.

510 Ibid., p. 59

511 Ibid., p. 75

Appendix III

GENEALOGICAL LISTS AND REGNAL DATES

The Ghurids:

The main branch of the Shansabanid Dynasty of Firuzkuh/Jam

Qutb al-Din Muhammad r. 540–1/1145–6 founded fortress city of Firuzkuh

Izz al-Din Hussain r. 493–540/1100–46

Saif al-Din Suri r. 540–44/1146–49

Baha al-Din Sam r. 544/1149

'Ala' al-Din Hussain *jahan-suz* r. 544–56/1149–61

Saif al-Din Muhammad r. 556–8/1161–3

Ghiyath al-Din b.543–5/1140r.558–99/1163–1203

Mu'izz al-Din/Shihab al-Din r. 599–602/1203–06 sultan in Ghazna from 547/1152–3

Ghiyath al-Din Mahmud r. 602–07/1206–10 deposed d.616–17/1220

'Ala' al-Din Astiz – vassal of Khwarazmshah son of *Jahan suz* r. 607–10/1210–14

'Ala' al-Din Muhammad – vassal of Khwarazmshah r. 610–12/1214–15 deposed. Nephew of Mu'zz al-Din, previously appointed to rule in Firuzkuh 599–602/1203–06 by his uncle

Shansabanid rulers of Bamiyan

Fakhr al-Din Mas'ud r. 540–58/1145–63

Shams al-Din Muhammad r. 558–88/1163–92

Baha al-Din Sam r. 588–602/1192–1206

Jalal al-Din r. 602–12/1206–15

See Thomas (2018), Tables 3:1 and 3:2, pp. 72–3 for further details

Ghaznavids

Bahram Shah r. 511–52/1117–57

Khusrau Shah r. 552–5/1157–60

Khusrau Malik r. 555–82/1160–86

The Great Seljuks

Sanjar (sultan 511–52/1118–57) ruled Khurasan as *malik* from 490/1097

Mahmud Khan r. 552–7/1157–82.

Sanjar's nephew who ruled in Khurasan was not universally accepted as the legitimate Seljuk ruler and was ultimately murdered. See Peacock (2015), p. 323.

Khwarazmshahs

Ilarslan b. Asiz r. 551–67/1156–72

'Ala' al-Din Tekish r. 567–96/1172–1200

Mahmud Sultan Shah r. as rival 567–88 /1172–93

'Ala' al-Din Muhammad r. 596–617/1200–20

Jalal al-Din r. western Iran 623–30/1224–31

Abbasid caliphs

Al-Muqtafi r. 530–55/1136–60

Al-Mustanjid r. 555–75/1160–70

Al-Mustadi r. 566–75/1170–80

Al-Nasir r. 575–622/1180–1225

Al-Zahir r. 622–3/1225–6

Al Mustansir r. 623–39/1226–42

Qara-Khitai

Yelu Yilie r. 545–58/1151–63

Yelu Pusuwan r. 558–72/1164–77

Yelu Zhilgu r. 573–607/1177–1211

Kuchlug, Naiman prince r. as usurper, 608–14/1211–18

See C. Baumer, The History of Central Asia Volume Three: The Age of Islam and the Mongols *(London and New York, 2016), p. 317.*

Shamsid Dynasty

Shams al-Din Iltutmish r. 607–33/1210–36

Rukn al-Din Firuz-Shah r. 633–4/1236

Radiyya bint Iltutmish r. 634–7/1236–40

Mu'izz al-Din Bahram Shah r. 637–9/1240–2

'Ala' al-Din Mas'Ud Shah r. 639–44/1242–6, Iltutmish's grandson and son of Rukn al-Din Firuz-Shah.

Nasir al-Din Mahmud Shah r. 644–64/1246–66

Khalaj rulers of Bengal

Muhammad b.Bakhtiar *c.* 601–03/1204/5–06

?? 603–04/1206–08

? First reign Husam al-Din 'Iwad 604–07/1208–10

'Ali-yi Mardin later Sultan 'Ala' al-Din (r.607–*c.* 609/1210–13)

Husam al-Din 'Iwad later Sultan Ghiyath al-Din r. 609–24/1212–27

Mu'izz al-Din 'Ali-yi 'Iwad, probably son of above co-ruler 616–24/ 1219–27

Indian dynasties:

Chaulukyas (Solankis) of Anhilwara – Patan-

Mularaja II r. 571–3/*c.* 1176–8

Bhimadeva II r. 573–636/1178–1241

Tribhuvanapala r. *c.* 636–80/1240–44

Chauhan/Chahamana dynasties

Rulers of Ajmer and Shakambari

Prthviraja III – Rai Pittora – r. 572–87/1177–92

Govindaraja IV r. 587/1192

Hariraja r. 588–9/1193–4 dethroned his nephew Govindaraja IV.

See Ray (2017), vol. II, pp. 1,136–41 for various Chauhan branches ruling in Punjab, Rajputana and Gujerat.

Ghadavala Dynasty of Varanasi and Kannauj/Qinawwj

Jayachandra – Jaichand – r. *c.* 589–613/1170–94

Harishchandra r. *c.* 613–37/1194–7

Chandellas of Jejakabhukti – Bundelkhand

Yashovarman II r. 559–60/1164–5

Paramardideva r. 560–99/1165–1203

Trailokyavarman r. 599–641/1203–45

Viravarman r. 641–81/1245–85

Sena Dynasty of Bengal

Lakshmanasena r. 574–602/1179–1206

Vishvarupasena r. 602–21/1206–25

Keshavasena r. 621–6/1225–30

The Eastern Ganga Dynasty of Orissa/Kalinga

Rajaraja II r. *c.* 565–85/1170–90

Ananghabima II r. *c.* 585–93/1190–98

Rajaraja III r. *c.* 593–608/1198–1211

Anangbhima III r. *c.* 608–35/1211–38

Narashima I r. *c.* 635–61/1238–64

BIBLIOGRAPHY

PRIMARY SOURCES

Arabic

The Chronicle of Ibn al-Athir for the Crusading Period from al-Kamil fi'l Ta'rikh, Part 2, *The Years 541–589/1146–1193: The Age of Nur al-Din and Saladin* (Trans. D.S. Richards) (London and New York, 2016).

The Chronicle of Ibn al-Athir for the Crusading Period from al-Kamil fi'l Ta'rikh, Part 3, *The Years 589–629/1193–1231: The Ayyubids after Saladin and the Mongol Menace* (Trans. D.S. Richards) (London and New York, 2016).

Persian

Hasan ibn 'Ali of Tus, Nizam al-Mulk, *Siyasat-Nama* (Trans. H. Darke) (London and New York, 2006).

Juzjani, Maulana, Minhaj-ud-Din, and Abu -'Umar 'Usman, *Tabakat-i-Nasiri: A General History of the Muhammadan Dynasties of Asia, including Hindustan from A.H.194 (810 A.D.) to A.H. 658 (1260 A.D.)* (Trans. Major H.G. Raverty), 2 vols, 3rd reprint, The Asiatic Society (Kolkata, 2010).

ABBREVIATIONS

CHI Cambridge History of Iran

EIr Encyclopedia Iranica online. www.iranicaonline.org

TN Tabakat-I-Nasiri

SECONDARY SOURCES

Amitai-Preiss R., *Mongols and Mamluks: The Mamluk–Īlkhānid War, 1260–1281* (Cambridge, 1995).

Baumer, Christoph, *The History of Central Asia, Volume 3. The Age of Islam and the Mongols* (London and New York, 2016).

Bausani, A., 'Religion in the Saljuk period'. In: *The Cambridge History of Iran, Volume 5: The Saljuk and Mongol Periods* (Ed. J.A. Boyle) (Cambridge, 1968).

Behrendt, Kurt A., *The Art of Ghandhara in the Metropolitan Museum of Art* (New York, 2007).

Bivar, A.D.H., 'The history of Eastern Iran'. In: *The Cambridge History of Iran, Volume 3(I): The Seleucid, Parthian and Sassanian Periods* (Ed. E. Yarshater) (Cambridge, 1993).

Blair, Sheila S., *Text and Image in Medieval Persian Art. Edinburgh Studies in Islamic Art* (Series editor R. Hillenbrand) (Edinburgh, 2019).

Bosworth, C.E., 'The political and dynastic history of the Iranian world (A.D. 1000–1217)'. In: *The Cambridge History of Iran, Volume 5: The Saljuk and Mongol Periods* (Ed. J.A. Boyle) (Cambridge, 1968).

Bosworth, C.E., *The Later Ghaznavids: Splendour and Decay – The Dynasty in Afghanistan and Northern India 1040–1186* (Edinburgh, 1977).

Bosworth, C.E., 'The early Ghaznavids'. In: *The Cambridge History of Iran, Volume 4: From the Arab Invasion to the Saljuks* (Ed. R.N. Frye) (Cambridge, 1999).

Busse, H. 'Iran under the Buyids'. In: *The Cambridge History of Iran, Volume 4: From the Arab Invasion to the Saljuks* (Ed. R.N. Frye) (Cambridge, 1999).

Cahen, C., 'The Turkish invasions and the Selchukids'. In: *A History of the Crusades. Vol. I: The First Hundred Years* (Eds K.M. Setton and M.W. Baldwin) (Philadelphia, 1969).

Clauson, Sir Gerard, *An etymological dictionary of pre-thirteenth-century Turkish* (Oxford, 1972*)*

Cohn, N. (Trans.), *Gold Khan and Other Siberian Legends* (London, 1946).

Desai, D., *Khajuraho* (New Delhi, 2010).

Digby, S., *War-Horse and Elephant in the Delhi Sultanate: A Study of Military Supplies* (Orient Monographs: Oxford, 1971).

Donaldson, T., *Konark* (New Delhi, 2010).

Eaton, Richard, M., *India in the Persianate Age: 1000–1765* (London, 2019).

Ertug, A. (Ed.), *The Seljuks: A Journey through Anatolian Architecture* (Istanbul, 1991).

Ferdowsi, A., *Shanameh* (Trans. D. Davis) (New York, 2006).

Herrman, G., *The Monuments of Merv: Traditional Buildings of the Karakum* (London, 1999).

Hillenbrand, C., *The Crusades: Islamic Perspectives* (Edinburgh, 1999).

Hodgson, G.S., 'The Isma'ili state'. In: *The Cambridge History of Iran, Volume 5: The Saljuk and Mongol Periods* (Ed. J.A. Boyle) (Cambridge, 1968).

Holt, P.M., *The Age of the Crusades: The Near East from the Eleventh Century to 1517* (London and New York, 1992).

Humphreys, R. Stephen, *Islamic History: A Framework for Inquiry* (London and New York, 1991).

Jackson, P., *The Delhi Sultanate: A Political and Military History* (Cambridge, 2003).

Jackson, P., *The Mongols and the Islamic World: From Conquest to Conversion* (New Haven and London, 2017).

Kennedy, H., *The Great Arab Conquests: How the Spread of Islam Changed the World We Live In* (London, 2007).

Knauer, E.R., *The Camel's Load in Life and Death* (Zurich, 1998).

Lambton, A.K.S.,'The internal structure of the Saljuk Empire'. In: *The Cambridge History of Iran Volume 5: The Saljuk and Mongol Periods* (Ed. J.A. Boyle) (Cambridge, 1998).

Lane-Fox, R., *Alexander the Great* (London, 1973).

McEvedy, C., *The New Penguin Atlas of Medieval History* (London, 1992).

Patel, A., *Iran to India: The Shansabanis of Afghanistan, c.1145–90 CE* (Edinburgh, 2022).

Peacock, A.C.S., *The Great Seljuk Empire* (Edinburgh, 2015).

Pourshariati, P., *Decline and Fall of the Sasanian Empire: The Sasanian-Parthian Confederacy and the Arab Conquest of Iran* (London and New York, 2009).

Ray, H.C., *The Dynastic History of Northern India: Early Medieval Period,* 2 vols (New Delhi, 2017).

Rezakhani, K., *ReOrientating the Sasanians: East Iran in Late Antiquity* (Edinburgh, 2017).

Robinson, F., *The Mughal Emperors and the Islamic Dynasties of India, Iran and Central Asia* (London, 2007).

Shokoohy, S. and M., 'The architecture of Baha al-DinTughril in the region of Bahayana, Rajastan'. In: *Muqurna IV: An Annual on Islamic Art and Architecture* (Ed. Oleg Grahar) (Leiden, 1987).

Skelton, R., 'Bengal; The historical background'. In: *The Arts of Bengal: The Heritage of Bangladesh and Eastern India* (Eds Robert Skelton and Mark Francis) (London, 1979).

Slugett p. with Currie A., *Atlas of Islamic History* (Oxford and New York, 2014).

Smail R.C., *Crusading Warfare, 1097–1193* (Cambridge, 1976).

Thomas, David C., *The Ebb and Flow of the Ghurid Empire* (Sydney, 2018).

Tillotson, G.H.R., *Mughal India* (London, 1990).

Vassiere, E. de La, *Sogdian Traders: A History* (Trans. J. Ward) (Leiden and Boston, 2005).

Vassiere, E. de La, *Asie Centrale 300–850: Des routes et des royaumes* (Paris, 2024).

Wink, A., *The Making of the Indo-Islamic World: c.700–1800 CE* (Cambridge, 2020).

Zeimal, E.V., 'Iranian settlement east of the Pamirs'. In: *The Cambridge History of Iran: Volume 3(I): The Seleucid, Parthian and Sasanian Periods* (Ed. E. Yarshater) (Cambridge, 1993).

Index

'Abbas (uncle of Jalal Din) 77–78
Abu 'Ali ibn Sulayman ibn Sis 76
Abu-l-Abbas, assassination of 23
'Ala' al-Din al Ghuri 47–48
'Ala al-Din Husain of Wajiristan 11, 13–21
'Ala al-Din Muhammad, Khwarazmshah *see* Khwarazmshah Muhammad
'Ala' al-Din Muhammad (nephew of Mu'izz al Din) 60, 67, 71, 102
'Ala' al-Din Muhammad (son of Baha al-Din Sam, sultan of Bamiyan) 71–77
al-Haji 'Ala' al-Din Muhammad 56
al-Husayn al-Marghani 57
al-Husayn ibn Muhammad al-Marghani 49
'Ali b. Muhammad 5
Ali Chatri 19
'Ali ibn Abi 'Ali 78–79
Ali Karmakh 30
'Ali Kufi 143–144
'Ali Shah 43–44, 94–96
Ali-yi Mardan 70, 92, 98, 107
Alp Ghazi 49, 55, 56
Altunapa, Ikhtiyar al-Din Altuniya 122–123
Andkhud (Andkhoy) 58–59
Aram Shah 98
architecture, Ghurid 144–147
armies, Indian and Ghurid 89–90
Arslan, Malik (Arslan Shah) 7, 8
Arslan Khan, Taj al-Din 128–130
Asi (Asni) 42
Astiz, 'Ala' al-Din 96, 101
Ayatim, Nasir al Din Aytemur al-Baha-i - 116–117
Aybak, Qutb al-Din
  origins 91
  campaigns 42–43, 45–47, 61–62
  conflict with Yildiz 86, 91–92
  and Ghiyath al-Din 86
  purchase of Iltutmish 99–100
  reputation and status 82–84, 92–93
  death and aftermath 92–93, 97
Aybak Bak 60
Aytegin al-Tatar 76, 84–86

Badr al-Din Sonqur 123
Baha al-Din Balaban *see* Ulugh Khan Balaban, Baha al-Din
Baha al-Din Sam (father of Ghiyath al-Din) 11
Baha al-Din Sam (son of Ghiyath al-Din Mahmud) 95, 96–97
Baha al-Din Sam, sultan of Bimiyan 34, 62, 66, 70–72
Bahram Shah 7–15, 19
Balaban *see* Ulugh Khan Balaban, Baha al-Din
Balaban i-yuzbegi, 'Izz al-Din 129–130
Balkh 34, 79
Bamiyan brothers 75–78 *see also* 'Ala' al-Din Muhammad (son of Baha al-Din Sam, sultan of Bamiyan); Jalal al-Din
Bamiyan rulers and Qara-khitai 34
Benares (Varanasi) 42
Bhimadeva II 43, 45
Bihar 53
Buddhism 4, 53

cavalry 38, 89, 154–156
Chakradeva 30
Chandawar (Chandawal), battle 42
Chandella dynasty 38, 118–119
Chauhan kingdom 37–38, 39–41
Chaulukya (Solanki) territory and dynasty 37–38, 45–47

Chingiz Khan 104
Chishti 140
coinage 147
court of Ghiyath al Din 50–51
court of Qubacha 143–144

Daulat Shah 15
Delhi
and Aybak 42, 93
and Iltutmish 98, 100
place of asylum 110–111, 114
Diya al-Din Muhammad 44

elephants
armies and use of 89–90, 156–157
incidents with 14–15, 39, 41, 54
embankments, built by Sultan Ghiyath al-Din 107

Fakhr al-Din 23–24, 26
Ferdowsi 7, 44
fighting technique *see* armies, Indian and Ghurid; cavalry; elephants; infantry, Ghurid
Firuz Shah 116
Firuzkuh 55, 145, 146
flooding, as military tactic 19, 50, 57–58

Gajz-Lak Khan, Sanjar-i 115, 117
Gandhara 3–4
geographical knowledge of Ghurids 2–3
Ghazna
and Seljuk army 7–8
and Bahram Shah 11
and 'Ala al-Din 13–17
and Ghiyath al-Din 25
and Mu'izz al Din 47
following death of Mu'izz al Din 70–77
and Aybak 85
and Yildiz 103
Ghaznavid court 7
Ghiyath al Din
early life 18
campaigns 22–26, 37, 43–44, 49
disagreement with Mu'izz al Din 44–45
religion 32
Sultan Shah and Tekish 32–33, 35–36
death 50
character and achievements 28, 43–44, 47, 50–51, 144, 145–146
Ghiyath al Din Balaban *see* Ulugh Khan Balaban, Baha al-Din
Ghiyath al-Din Mahmud
and Mu'izz al Din 52, 55–56
as successor to Mu'izz al-Din 66, 71–73
rule of 78–86
assassination of 94, 96
Ghiyath al-Din, Sultan (Husam al-Din Iwad) 107–109
ghulams see mamluks
Ghurids
ascendancy of 6
culture 142–147
ethnicity and language 5
pre-Islam 3–4
rule in India 138
Sunni orthodoxy 21, 28–29, 32
Ghuzz 20, 24–25
government, Persianate system 142–143
Govindaraja 39, 41
Gwalior, sieges 46–47, 112–113

hanafi School 64, 144
Hasan Qarluq, Sayf al-Din 106, 107, 111, 113, 117, 131–132
Hazar-Asp (Hazorasp), engagement at 58
Herat
building work 144
and Khwarazmshah Muhammad 49–50, 55–56, 93–94
population 9
Hindu Khan 36–37, 43, 77, 121–122
horses 154–156

Husain ibn Kharmil *see* Izz ud-Din Husain ibn Kharmil

Ibn Kharmil *see* Izz ud-Din Husain ibn Kharmil
Ikhtiyar al-Din Aytegin 122–123
Iltutmish, Shams al-Din
- early life 97–100
- and Yildiz 103
- and Jalal al-Din 105–106
- campaigns 108–110, 112–113
- success 111–112
- Shamsi *ghulams* 115
- death and evaluation of 113–114

Indian administrators 121–122
Indian territories and *mamluk* power 137–139
Indus, River 104–105, 110
infantry, Ghurid 14–15
iqta system 38
Islam
- in Ghur 4
- in India 41, 67, 139–140
- Mongol threat to 110–111
- Mu'izz al Din 45, 59, 63

Isma'ilis 28, 44–45, 63–64
'Iwad, Mu'izz al-Din 'Ali-yi 108–109
Izz ud-Din Husain ibn Kharmil 30, 35, 48, 49, 56, 58, 59, 67, 78–79, 93

Jalal al-Din (son of Khwarazmshah Muhammad) 103, 104–106
Jalal al-Din (son of Sultan Baha al-Din) 72, 74, 77–78, 84–85, 101
Jaldik ibn Tughril, 'Iz al-Din 93
Jam, minaret of 145
Jaqar 36–37
Juzjani
- appointments in Gwalior 113
- changes sides 111
- helped by *mamluks* 123–124

Jayachandra 42

Kabir Khan-i-Ayaz 115–116
Kalinjar 47, 118
Kamrup, Rae of 68–69
karramiyya School 32, 64, 143, 145
karwah (hide defences) 14–15
Khalaj, nomadic people 39
Kharmil-i-Sam Banji 14
Kharmil-i-Sam Husain 14
Khokhars 30, 60–62
Khusrau Malik 21, 29, 30–31
Khusrau Shah 19, 21
Khwaja al-Sahib 93, 94
Khwarazmshah Muhammad
- and Ghiyath al-Din 47–50
- and Mu'izz al Din 50, 55–57, 60
- following death of Mu'izz al Din 78–80
- and Ghiyath al-Din Mahmud 93–94
- and Ghurid heartlands 96–97
- and Herat 78
- success in Bamiyan and Ghazna 101–103

Kishli Khan (Sayf al-Din Aybak) 126, 128, 134–135
Kuret Khan, Taj al-Din Sanjar-i 124–125
Kushlu Khan, 'Izz al-Din, Balaban 130–132

Lahore 30
Lakhnawti 67, 107–109, 119–121
Lakshmana Sena 54
looting 43–44
loyalty, *mamluk* 138

Majd al-Din Musawi 12–13
Makran 2
mamluks
- Iltutmish's 115–137
- meritocracy 82
- nurture of 99–100
- origins and character of 88–89
- power in Indian territories 137–139

recruitment of 9
and successor to Mu'izz al-Din 72–73, 81–82
manumissions 81–84
Merv 20
military logistics 138, 154–157
Mongols 104–105, 106
mosques and minarets 144, 145, 147
Mount Abu 37, 43
Mu'ayyad al-Mulk 65, 72–73, 75, 76, 102
Muhamad ibn Kharnak 37
Muhammad b. Bakhtiar 52–55, 67–70
Muhammad b. Tekish 36–37
Muhammad ibn Abi 'Al 60–61
Muhammad ibn 'Ali ibn Bashir 79
Muhammad ibn Kharnak 35, 37, 48–49, 55
Muhammad Shams al-Din 19
Mu'izz al Din
early life 18, 23
in northern Indian subcontinent 28–30, 34, 38–41, 60–62
Chandawar, battle 42
in Khurasan and Quhistan 44–46
disagreement with Ghiyath al Din 44–45
supreme Ghurid sultan 51–52
in Khwarazm 55–59
and Qara-Khitai 60–62
death 63–67
character and achievements 64–65
mamluks 47–48, 89, 90–91

Nab, battle 19
Nahrawala (Anahilapataka) 45–46
Nasir al-Din Husain 101
Nasir al-Din Mahmuḍ 108–109, 112
Nasir al-Din, Sultan 136–137
Nishapur 43, 48
Nudiya (Nabawip), sacking of 54
Nusrat Khan, Badr al-Din Sonqur 133

Pala dynasty 53
Paramiradideva 47
parasols 83
peace plan between Ghiyath-al-Din Mahmud and the Khwarazmshah 83–84
Prthviraja III (ruler of Chauhan) 37, 39–41

Qara-Khitan Empire (Western Liao dynasty)
establishment 9–10
and Tekish 32
campaigns against 34–36
and Mu'izz al Din 57–60
Qarasu, battle at 57–58
Qilich Khan 129–130
Qubacha, Nasir al-Din 97, 98, 103–107, 109–111, 143–144
Quhistan 44–45, 60
Qumach 23–24
Qutb al-Din Hasan b. 'Ali 122, 135
Qutb al-Din Muhammad b.Hussein 10–11, 16–17
Qutb Minar 144
Qutlugh Khan 129–130
Qutlugh Takin 102

Radiyya, Sultan 116, 122–123
Ragh-i-Zar, battle at 23–24
religious beliefs
conquest and 90, 139–140
Ghiyath al Din 50–51
Ghurids 21, 28–29, 32
Mu'izz al Din 64–65
River Jaxartes/Syr Darya 2
River Oxus/Amu Darya 2
'Rumi' 115

Saif al- Din Muhammad 21–22
Saif al-Din Aybak 117
Saif al-Din Aybak-i- Yaghantut 117–118
Saif al-Din Bat Khan-i-Aybak 125

Saif al-Din Suri (Sultan Suri) 11–13, 16–19
Samanid culture 142
Sanjar (Seljuk sultan) 6, 7, 10, 20
Sanjar-i -Qabaqulak, Taj al-Din 123–124
Sarakhs, siege 48
Savinj 65, 80
Sayf al-Din Aybak (Kishli Khan) 126, 128, 134–135
Sayf al-Din Aybak Shamsi-yi Ajami 133
Seljuks 6–8, 18–19, 20, 34
Sena dynasty 38, 54
shafi'i school 32, 64
Shah, Sultan 32–33
Shah Muhammad *see* Khwarazmshah Muhammad
Shahnameh (Ferdowsi) 44
Shams al-Din, Muhammad 19, 24, 26, 33–34
Shamsi *ghulams* 115
Shansabani dynasty 5–6
Shi'i missionaries 21
shipping 124–125
Shir Khan, Nusrat al-Din Sanjar 126, 128, 132, 133–134
Sialkot 30
slavery, *mamluks*, *ghulams* and 88–89
spoils of war 42, 43, 62
Sufism 140
Sunni orthodoxy 21, 28–29, 32

Tabarindh 38, 39
Talaqan, fighting at 35–36
Tara'in (Taraori), battles 39–41
tax collection 48
Tayasai, Nusrat al-Din 118–119
Tekish 32–36
Temur Khan 119, 120–121
Teniz Khan, Taj al-Din 125
Tibet, conquest in 68–70
Tiginabad 14–15
Toghan Khan, Toghril-i- 119–120
Toghril, Baha-al Din 46, 147
Toghril Khan, Ikhtiyar-al-Din Yuzbeg 125–128
Trahi tribal grouping 62–63
Trailokyavarman 118–119
treasury of Mu'izz al Din 65, 73
troops
  ethnicity 19
  numbers 19, 45, 49, 155
Tughril, Baha al-Din 23–24, 33

Uch, siege of 110
Ulugh Khan Balaban, Baha al-Din 126, 128–129, 134, 135–137
Uthman, Sultan 58, 59, 74

War-Mesh 22

Yelu Dashi/ Emperor Dezong 10
Yildiz (governor of Herat) 23–24
Yildiz, Taj al-Din
  and Aybak 84–86, 91–92
  and Bamiyan brothers 73–79
  and Ghiyath al-Din Mahmud 80–84, 86
  and Jalal al-Din 73–78, 84–85
  and Khwarazmshah Muhammad 100–104
  and Mu'izz al Din 63, 66
  origins 90–91
  struggle for succession 73–75